A VILLAGE AT WAR

To Nina
with love.

John Calvert

Newdigate Roll of Honour

George Ackland	8.2.1919. Age 29.	*Newdigate (St. Peter) Churchyard. North of church spire.*
William Beadle	16.8.1916. Age 28.	*Thiepval Memorial, France.*
Wilfred S. Bird	9.5.1915. Age 31.	*Le Touret Memorial, France.*
Gerald T. Bray	9.8.1915. Age 30.	*Helles Memorial.Gallipoli, Turkey.*
Sidney J. Burberry	21.11.1914. Age 19.	*Ploegsteert Memorial, Belgium.*
Benj. Burrows	23.10.1918. Age 34.	*Englefontaine British Cemetery, France.*
William C. Chatfield	29.7.1916. Age 21.	*Dernancourt Communal Cemetery,France.*
Walter W. Cottle	31.7.1916. Age 22.	*Ypres (Menin Gate), Belgium.*
Frederick W. Goldberg	3.10.1916. Age 34.	*Struma Military Cemetery, Greece.*
Herbert W. Goldberg	31.7.1915. Age 35.	*St. Sever Cemetery, Rouen, France.*
Roy F. Goldsack	30.6.1918. Age 20.	*Dernancourt Communal Cemetery Extension, France*
Stephen C. Harber	14.7.1916. Age 29.	*Thiepval Memorial, France.*
Cyril D. Herron	13.5.1915. Age 19.	*Potijze Chateau Grounds Cemetery, Belgium*
Kenneth C. Herron	24.4.1918. Age 37.	*Vignacourt British Cemetery, France.*
Walter F. Herron	3.4.1916. Age 44.	*Etaples Military Hospital, France.*
Cecil T. Hills	3.11.1917. Age 25.	*Beersheba War Cemetery, Israel.*
George C. Howson	12.10.1918. Age 21.	*Vis-en-Artois Memorial, France.*
Aubery Hudson	28.7.1916. Age 15.	*Thiepval Memorial, France.*
John A. Innis (Croix de Guerre)	9.9.1918. Age 37.	*Terlincthun British Cemetery, Wimille, France.*
Wesley Johns	20.1.1916. Age 18.	*Newdigate (St. Peter's) Churchyard. North of church.*
John Kempshall	13.7.1916. Age 21.	*Thiepval Memorial, France.*
Arthur H. Monk	30.9.1916. Age 24.	*Contay British Cemetery, France.*
Benjamin Taylor	14.4.1918. Age 18.	*Canadian Cemetery No. 2, Neuville-St. Vaast, France.*
Alfred H. Tyler	11.11.1914. Age 44.	*Ypres (Menin Gate), Belgium.*
Albert Tyler	12.11.1914. Age 21.	*Ypres (Menin Gate), Belgium.*
John C. Tyler	18.4.1915. Age 21.	*Ypres (Menin Gate), Belgium.*
Ernest Weller	4.11.1918. Age 42.	*Le Rejet-de-Beaulieu Communal Cemetery, France.*
George Weller	7.6.1917. Age 32.	*Ypres (Menin Gate), Belgium.*
Percy F. Weller	22.7.1917. Age 34.	*Baghdad (North Gate), Iraq.*
Bernard Whitehouse	7.6.1917. Age 20.	*Lone Tree Cemetery, Spanbrockmolen, Belgium.*
Alfred V. Wooltorton	14.7.1918. Age 19.	*Edinburgh (Seafield) Cemetery, Scotland.*
William Wyatt	14.7.1916. Age 49.	*Basra War Cemetery, Iraq*

Names as recorded on the Newdigate War Memorial. Note incorrect spellings: Gerald T. Bray should be Gerard, Aubery Hudson should be Aubrey, John A. Innis should be Innes and Wesley Johns should be Westley.

In addition are included the dates of death, ages at time of death and memorial/burial sites.

A VILLAGE AT WAR

BY JOHN CALLCUT

The story of Newdigate, a small Wealden village, on the Surrey-Sussex
borders during the period of World War One
1914-1918

Reveille
PRESS

Reveille Press is an imprint of
Tommies Guides Military Booksellers & Publishers
Gemini House
136-140 Old Shoreham Road
Brighton
BN3 7BD
www.tommiesguides.co.uk

First published in Great Britain by
Reveille Press 2011
For more information please visit
www.reveillepress.com

© 2011 John Callcut

ISBN 978-1-908336-27-9

Cover design by Reveille Press

Typeset by Graham Hales

Printed and bound by
CPI Group (UK) Ltd, Croydon, CR0 4YY

Contents

Acknowledgements

R.Verner-Jeffreys – grandson of Gerard T. Bray
The late Mary Cra'ster – descendant of Barbara Craster
Jim Elliott – descendant of James Frederick Elliott
Pat Bird – descendant of Rev H.G.Bird
Robina Arbuthnot – grand-daughter of Thomas Edmund Harrison
Anthea Bryan – descendant of Harrison family
Jo Winfield – descendant of George Ackland
Ian Pasley Tyler – descendant of Alfred Herbert Tyler
Eileen Funnell whose mother worked for Mrs. Janson
Harold Hopkins – son of William Henry Robert Hopkins
The late Kenneth Vernon Chester Herron – son of Kenneth Chester Herron
Captain Dan Shorland Ball – descendant of Francis Shorland Ball
Bill Johns – descendant of Purdey Johns
Sylvia McPhee – grand-daughter of Percy Weller
David Schenck – researcher of Sanders family
The late Sir Geoffrey Chandler – son of Dr Frederick George Chandler MD., FRCP
Neale Box – great grandson of Alice Hills, sister of Cecil T. Hills
Andy Thompson of Eye Witness Tours for military advice
Jane Lilley for local advice and proof reading
Tina Callcut for proof reading
National Newspaper Archives – Colindale
The National Archives
The Newdigate Local History Society
The Dorking Advertiser
The Trustees of the Imperial War Museum
The Recorder – Charterhouse School
The Malvernian
Dr Dawn Crouch – Curator, Westgate-on-Sea Museum
Douglas McCarthy – Picture Library Manager at The National Maritime Museum
The Curator – Marylebone Cricket Club
The Commonwealth War Graves Commission
Hillingdon Local Heritage Service
K.Pearce – Uxbridge Local History & Archives Group
Jacki Harrington – Artwork

Foreword

A book on the Great War that avoids the regular themes of the leaders, the men, the battles and the poetry. *Newdigate – A Village at War* is refreshingly different in that it details the impact of the war on a small village in Surrey – although Newdigate could be any rural community in early 20th Century Britain. The writer skilfully takes us on a superbly researched journey from the comfort and certainty of pre-war England to the challenging and changing post-war period. The increasing tempo of the war in Europe is mirrored by the traditional rhythms of the tranquil Surrey countryside.

Like most villages the landed gentry dominate the social structure with the village Rector, the Rev. H.G.Bird, leading his flock in a paternal and benevolent role whilst the matriarchal Mrs Janson worries about the village boys not having enough to fill their spare time. This changes in August 1914 as Newdigate sends a succession of its young men to war and 32 are destined not to return. Through his regular newsletters the Rev Bird urges all to do their duty and continues to do so until his own son is killed in 1915. Thereafter his thoughts, like so many across the land, change appreciably. At least one of the village's 'brave boys' has to be force-marched back to his train when returning to his unit and, once at the station, foretells of his death to his 'escorts'. All too sadly this becomes a reality when he is killed weeks later.

The writer, a local historian, spent over 25 years meticulously researching the material for the book and travelled the length and breadth of the country following the leads that make the human stories in the book so accurate and moving. The story of each dead or wounded man confirms the human impact felt by so many families as the war wore on. The book also contains many original and unpublished photographs (including some taken at Gallipoli by an officer the morning he was killed – the images being found in his camera many years after his death). The writer covers much ground – the impact of the war in the village (surely women can never plough the land?) and the stories of the individual men away at the front are woven together by a commentary of the major events happening in the theatres of war. Thus the book adds much to our knowledge of the Great War as we contrast the urgent need for sandbags and bandages with the suffering of those fighting for King and country and the community they left behind.

Andrew Thompson

Introduction

In the years prior to the Great War the people of Newdigate led a predictable, well ordered but class structured life. Situated deep in the Weald of Southern England amidst the leafy oaks, with a population of about six hundred people, the villagers pursued their lives in much the same way as generations had done before them. The village was remote and insular, two miles from the nearest main road, but things changed from the 1870s with the coming of the railway to nearby Holmwood, when wealthy people started seeking estates in the country. These people took a prominent place in village welfare, joining and often chairing positions within the school and church and organising bazaars and cultural events. Many of these people play an important part in the narrative that follows.

The Rector, the Rev. H.G. Bird, M.A. (1847 – 1925), was inducted in 1913 just a year after his wife, Henrietta, had died at their previous parish in Hillingdon. Immediately he busied himself in settling into the rectory and getting to know his parishioners. His daughters, Ethel and Muriel, helped with the Sunday schools and his son was a teacher at Ludgrove School and a cricketer of some renown.

Mrs. Ellen Charlotte Janson of Newdigate Place, together with her daughter, Miss Lillian Herron, sat in their regular places in church on Sundays. Sometimes they would be accompanied by her sons, when they were down in the country for the weekend. Mrs. Janson devoted much time and energy to the village and – with the assistance of the Headmaster, Henry Hackwood – she provided the workshop (with electric light) and instructed and organised a wood-carving class. Young men from the village would walk, on Monday nights, down the lanes to Newdigate Place, where they would sign a register and spend the evening carving. Many examples of their skills can still be seen in the church today.

Mrs. Farnell-Watson of Henfold House had the Village Hall (or Institute, as it was then called) erected in memory of her husband, William, in 1901. It provided welcome relaxation for the men of the village, with billiards, cards, miniature rifle shooting and concerts. Only tea, coffee and cordials were served as Mrs. Farnell-Watson disapproved of alcohol being provided in the hall, although the family fortune emanated from the Isleworth Brewery.

The Goldberg family lived at The Red House. The head of the family was a widower, Leopold Goldberg, a prominent London solicitor of Prussian origin. His two youngest sons had become barristers and they both excelled not only in sports but also in music and the classics. Two of his daughters, Maud and Lizzy, supported many local activities such as the Nursing Association and the Girls' Friendly Society and they arranged fund raising concerts and parties for the married women of the village. Most years they organised a New Year Day's party for the children, complete with a bran tub and Christmas trees.

The Tyler family lived at Linden House in Highgate and owned High Trees Farm in Newdigate which they used for visits to the country. The organ in the church is dedicated to the memory of Sir Henry Whatley Tyler who died in 1908. He had twelve children and one of his daughters, Margaret Lucy Tyler, wrote poetry and a novel. She became a leading doctor at the London Homoeopathic Hospital and wrote a book entitled 'Homoeopathic Drug Pictures'.

The largest estate in the parish, Lyne, was the home of the Broadwood family, the well known piano and furniture manufacturers.

The highlight of the summer for the children was the choir outing to the seaside. One year, thanks to the offices of Capt. Alfred William Gibbs, of Hillview, the party went from Holmwood by train to Portsmouth, where they boarded a submarine and were allowed to view HMS Dreadnought.

Henry Hackwood had been the Headmaster of the school since it was first built in 1873. Complete with greying beard and quill pen he attended to the children's educational needs until they left at the age of fourteen, probably to join their fathers in the fields or their mothers in service at one of the large estates. He was continually frustrated by pupils being absent from school at harvest time or for acorn-collecting.

Nothing disturbed the general order – the choir was singing in the Leith Hill Musical Festival and the bell ringers practised at St. Peter's. Billiards was played at the Institute; Alfred Dean supplied the groceries; the Six Bells and the Surrey Oaks served liquid refreshments and the cricket team strove for greater achievements. The men worked in the fields or at their trade and the women worked in the big houses or laundered and sewed.

On the 5th August 1914 Tom Boult, the village policeman, could be seen leaving his home at Hillside in the very early morning and striding towards the centre of the village. He could smell baking bread in the warm air as he approached Dean's Stores. He turned and knocked at the door where Walter Carpenter was busy removing loaves from the oven. 'We are at war with Germany'. Grabbing his peel, the baker tapped on Alfred Dean's window and the three men sat up the rest of the night, reminiscing and predicting the future.

Next morning, on the field called the Glebe, now occupied by the school, a meeting was held for the purpose of recruiting eager young men into the army. There was no shortage of volunteers and no lack of advice and encouragement from the older folk. Here was a chance for travel, glory, excitement and for widening horizons.

When one sees pictures of hundreds of smiling and happy young men queuing outside army recruitment offices, it is interesting to reflect upon their motives. Was it a desire to join the army and get away from the humdrum of daily life? Was it to avenge 'poor little Belgium'? Was it a general hatred of Germany? Was it that so many simply became engulfed within the frenetic mood of the time, thinking that it would soon be over and that it would be an adventure – or was it simply too hard to say no? Neither the parish magazine nor the local newspaper, in the weeks leading up to the outbreak of the war, give any indication of an impending crisis. Apart from the educated members of the community who would be better informed, the war must have come as a surprise for the majority of villagers.

So let us now transport you back to those terrible times through the writings and observations of the people who lived in Newdigate during those dark days.

John Callcut
Newdigate 2011

This book was born in the summer of 1984 when the Rector of Newdigate, the late Rev. Dennis Parker, gave the Newdigate Local History Society a set of parish magazines for safekeeping. At that time my youngest son was seriously ill in Great Ormond Street Hospital, so – to while away the interminable hours sitting next to his bed – I gradually read the magazines one by one. I soon realised that here was an important and informative store of information about the village covering the First World War period. My written notes turned into a play-reading which was performed not only in Newdigate but also at Dorking Halls and the University of Surrey. The script and my notes turned into this book. My son made a complete recovery.

In most cases
An *italic* font is used for text from newspapers and magazines.
A **bold** font is used for text for local comments.
A ***bold italic*** font is used for text for national comments.

The Widow

Nellie the widow of Percy Weller with her children

Newdigate in the days leading up to the Great War

Coombers Farm

The Cross Ways

Cudworth Manor

Parkgate Road looking north

Dean's Corner looking north

Village Street with Dean's Stores looking south

Gaterounds Farm

Grove Cottage at Cudworth

Old Brewery Cottage and High Trees Farm

Rabbit Hunt outside the Surrey Oaks at Parkgate

The Brocus looking south towards the church

Kingsland

St. Peter's Church, Newdigate

Parkgate

School Pond

The Six Bells

Six Bells Cottages

Village Street

Sturtwood – A Ghost Story from an old Newdigate Farm House

Queer are the ways of old houses. Sometimes there is an inexplicable strangeness that is never fully understood, but is believed nevertheless, – believed because it happens to the folk who are one's friends, and we know that they are telling us the truth.

In our village, on the Newdigate – Rusper Road there stands an old white farmhouse called 'Sturtwood'. There are new tenants living there now; but the previous family (our friends of many years standing) experienced something very 'queer' indeed. This is their tale as they told it to me:

On one particular day in late Autumn, year after year, when the mists crept across the distant fields and the woods glowed russet and bronze against the pale sky, there came to their ears the <u>tolling of a bell.</u> Deep and resonant, with an eerie, hollow sound, it seemed to come from the deep well at the back of the house. Yet as they tried to shut out the sound, it met them wherever they went – upstairs or down.

They could all hear it; it was not confined to anyone in particular, although Mrs—— had had several other psychic experiences and premonitions not vouchsafed to the rest of the family.

The sound of its tolling came and went, sometimes faint and faraway, at other times very close. They could not ignore it, – especially on one occasion.

It was late evening, – no wind abroad, – only intense darkness outside, the droppings of the cinders on to the hearth in the wide old fireplace, and the gentle ticking of the clock. They talked, sewed and read. A pipe – knocking ash on the log-basket, – the quick 'snips' of the scissors; the crackle of the newspaper; the shifting of a log and the starting up of a tiny tongue of flame; the yawn of the spaniel as he rolled over. Suddenly he bristled,...... growled. The flame died.

Sturtwood Farm

Then up the middle pathway there came the muffled sound of tramping <u>feet.</u> They could not be mistaken – marching men were coming – coming right into the house. They waited for the expected knock. It did not come. Somehow Mrs.——— knew it would not come. The sound of the tramping; – measured, slow, <u>came into the house...</u>

Someone ran to open the door – only to look out into an EMPTY passage.

And the bell tolled.

The day was November 11th.

Anonymous Author from the archives of the Newdigate Womens Institute.

The Clergy's Agony

In 1913 following the death of his wife, the 67 year old Rev. Henry G. Bird M.A. left his busy church in Hillingdon and looked forward to spending his twilight years in a quiet country parish. His parishioners hired an omnibus and came to see their former, popular priest at his new home in Newdigate. At the outbreak of the war he encouraged the young men to join the colours, but by 1917 war fatigue had set in. His son's grave had been obliterated and his body was lost to the mud of the battlefield, his daughters were fully engaged in voluntary work in London and the National Mission of Repentance and Hope had not been the success that he had hoped for. As he sat alone in his rambling and draughty rectory there seemed little hope. His letters – to his parishioners whom he referred to as 'My Dear Friends' – had stopped, as he had run out of words of encouragement. As the Parish Magazine ceased in 1918, we will never know the thoughts of this kindly and sincere man upon the ending of hostilities. He had seen so much sadness and had comforted many broken families in spite of his own personal grief. Did he think the war was justified? Would the world be a better place?

From 1869 to 1899, in quieter and calmer days, the rector of Newdigate was the Rev. Lancelot Studdert Kennedy (1832- 1899). An Irishman, he supervised the church renovations and enlargement in the mid 1870s. His nephew was the famous World War One chaplain named Geoffrey Anketell Studdert Kennedy (1883-1929) who became known to the troops as 'Woodbine Willie'. He mixed with all men regardless of rank and exposed himself to many dangers whilst helping and succouring wounded soldiers. He always carried cigarettes in his haversack for the men and his advice to other chaplains was to carry fags and much love. He was not above joining in with the men and telling saucy jokes. He was incredibly brave and was awarded the Military Cross in 1917 for running across no-man's land at Messines Ridge to help the wounded. He was also a much loved poet, writing with poignancy and empathy for the soldiers as he understood their humour. In 1914 he urged his parishioners in Worcester to join the forces, but as the war progressed and he saw so much hurt and sorrow, he understood the soldiers' thoughts and desires.

WASTE
Waste of Muscle, waste of Brain
Waste of Patience, waste of Pain
Waste of Manhood, waste of Health
Waste of Beauty, waste of Wealth

Waste of Blood, and waste of Tears
Waste of Youth's most precious years
Waste of ways the Saints have trod,
Waste of Glory, waste of God,—
War!

Rev. Geoffrey Anketell Studdert Kennedy

In 1927 many of his poems were published under the title of The Unutterable Beauty.

Another chaplain, Padre Phil. J. Fisher CF, published a book in 1917 entitled Khaki Vignettes. In it he describes setting up an altar for communion made of biscuit boxes but covered with a snowy cloth. The area was full of shell holes and the altar stood out startlingly amidst the surrounding chaos. He recognised that many of 'his lads' were about to take part in one of the biggest battles in history, and he commented upon the words of the communion service.

"And now the Bread – 'This is My Body which is broken for you' (but which of these young bodies must be broken also ere this holy rite be celebrated again?). And the Wine – 'This is the new testament in My blood' (and who shall seal his testimony with his life's blood in to-morrow's dawn?) A few moments later there is no sign of our sanctuary, unless it be a rough cross, rudely inscribed, which sticks up out of a neighbouring shell-hole".

1914

The dark clouds of war had been rolling through the palaces and houses of government of Europe throughout the warm, idyllic summer of 1914.

The Archduke Franz Ferdinand, the heir to the Austro-Hungarian Empire, and his wife the Duchess of Hohenburg were murdered at Sarajevo on June 28th by the Bosnian patriot Gavrilo Princip. Further troubles in the Balkans may have caused ripples in the Foreign Office but, for the man in the street, problems in that far off land were not cause for concern.

The crisis that the murder provoked began on the 23rd July when Austria, assured of support from Germany, issued an ultimatum to Serbia. This contained a number of requests to gain compensation for the murder, and to ensure that such an outrage could never happen again. A reply was requested within forty eight hours. Serbia confided with Russia, and accepted most of the demands, excepting those which would violate her constitution. At

Archduke Franz Ferdinand and his Family. (Ref. Q 81810). Reproduced by kind permission of the Imperial War Museum

ten o'clock on the evening of Saturday, 25th July, the Austrian Minister in Belgrade stated that the Serbian reply was unacceptable. Three days later a formal declaration of war was issued.

In Britain the last public holiday of the year was approaching, the weather was good and foremost in people's minds was to spend a few precious hours by the sea or in the countryside. Besides, storm clouds had gathered before and been dispersed. So Britain went on with her pleasure-making but, as the days of July wore on, a sense of urgency spread through the country as it became evident that more than a local war was possible. Life in Newdigate, however, seemed to be unaffected.

On the 22nd July 1914 a Grand Bazaar and Fête, in aid of St. Peter's Church Restoration Fund and for providing heating apparatus for the church, was held at Ockley Lodge. It was opened by Lady Adeline Rose Goodrich, a friend of Mrs Janson, who had married Vice Admiral James Edward Clifford Goodrich at St George's, Hanover Square in London in 1887. The Parish Magazine reported the event.

Parish Magazine – October 1914

Rev. Bird at the opening of the fête

Ockley Lodge

The morning broke cloudless and our spirits rose at the hope of a glorious day for the long talked of Bazaar.

Overnight the large marquee and several of the smaller side show tents had been erected and when we arrived at 10 a.m. things seemed in great swing.

In the marquee eight of the daintiest looking stalls had been set up by various helpers. These were prettily draped with green gauze and festoons of that most lovely rambler 'Dorothy Perkins' hung from the top and down the sides. Soon the various Stall-holders began to arrive – laden indeed with all sorts of tempting articles, from juicy looking ducks to hats that looked as though they came from Madame Louise, Regent Street. All that morning these kind people worked like Trojans. Another stall was furnished with the most lovely hot-house plants – carnations and sweet peas of every hue, and luscious fruits, including enormous bunches of grapes, peaches, nectarines etc. Then we saw Madame Louise side by side with Peter Yapp (this latter department caused much amusement during the afternoon, as many Cinderella Sisters vainly tried to squeeze their dainty trilbies in the daintiest of shoes!). The suddenly we became transported to the Continent to behold vivid coloured beads and foreign novelties of every description – together with the most fascinating toys and dolls to make the mouths of all youthful beholders water. Then the bon-bons! How tempting they looked in their little multifarious coloured baskets.

A few yards removed from the tent were two quite small ones; in one some boxes of Turkish cigars, De Reske cigarettes, Player's Navy Cut – in fact smoking requisites of all kinds, whilst in the other samples of everything imaginable were to be found – fragrant perfumes, hair dyes, insect killers, &c.

Whilst the Stall-holders were thus busily engaged decorating their stalls on the lawn in the front of the house, those in charge of the tea and refreshments were laying little tables for tea and cutting up delicious bread and butter and preparing plates of the most lovely bits of cake.

Alas! When at length at 2.30 Lady Goodrich arrived, she was accompanied by rain.

At 2 p.m. the gates opened and the people began to hustle in to be ready for the opening. At 2.30 Lady Goodrich drove up in the Rector's car accompanied by the Rector and Miss Bird. Lady Goodrich was met by the Boy Scouts who escorted her to the tent entrance, and there she declared the Bazaar open.

The Rector said it was a great honour and pleasure for them to have Lady Goodrich to come and open the Bazaar. Perhaps some might say he was a newcomer in the neighbourhood and some older inhabitants ought to have the honour of introducing but since he had been in Newdigate he had had so many opportunities of experiencing her kindness in many ways, and he felt there could be no one better fitted to open the Bazaar for them. Lady Goodrich replied by declaring the Bazaar open. She went on to say it was a great pleasure to her to come to Newdigate. She admired Newdigate so much and thought it such a sporting little village. She made special mention of the Choral Society and the unexpected way in which Newdigate had distinguished itself.

Captain Gibbs seconded a vote of thanks to Lady Goodrich. Mrs Innes's two charming little girls then presented a bouquet to Lady Goodrich and at once business began.

Unfortunately, with the opening of the Bazaar the rain came and continued till 4.30. During the afternoon several kind ladies and gentlemen from the neighbourhood came and bought *nobly, but since we have heard many intending buyers were prevented from coming by the uncontrollable elements. Tea on the lawn was impossible, but in the various rooms of Ockley Lodge delicious teas were served by charming looking waitresses in muslin caps and aprons.*

Rain ceased about 4.30 and gradually more and more people began to arrive. During all this time various side shows were in full swing. A splendid representation from some scenes in 'Alice through the Looking Glass' was given by some members of the Band of Hope, under the direction of Miss Elliot. A delightful Japanese dance and song was arranged by Mrs Winfield. Later in the evening the illuminations were lit from 8.30 till 10.30 – great revelling took place. There was a dancing green where stately waltzes, two-steps and lancers were enjoyed, and for the more frivolous that ceaseless joy, 'The Merry-Go-Round'. It is extraordinary what a joy it is to sit on a horse and go round and round and up and down to the accompaniment of jingling music!

It was a very happy day for many and especially perhaps for those who for weeks, nay months, had been working to get together and exhibit a splendid collection of goods on the various stalls.

The Rector, the Rev. H.G. Bird M.A., passed a vote of thanks to Miss Ferard and Miss Wilson for allowing the Bazaar to take place at Ockley Lodge and informed parishioners that the net proceeds would realise about £100.

The senior members of the choir had expressed a wish to go to Boulogne for their summer treat following visits to South Coast resorts in previous years. 'Fancy going to France for our outing!'

During the holidays the school was to be thoroughly renovated giving a very different appearance after the cleaning and painting.

Following Austria's declaration of war on Serbia, Russia backed Serbia and Germany backed Austria. A sequence of declarations followed. Diplomatic threats became real war as the large conscripted armies were mobilised. For Germany to attack Russia, she had also swiftly to attack France (who had an alliance with Russia) which involved a huge army movement through Belgium to Paris. Belgium's neutrality was guaranteed by France's ally – Britain.

In the last week of July anxiety spread across the City as the bank rate rose from 4% to 8%. On August 1st the rate rose to 10% and the Bank of England took steps to protect gold.

In its editorial of the 1st August 1914, the Dorking Advertiser speaks about the crisis for the first time under the heading 'A Tragic Week'.

This is a tragic week, great in its happening, more terrible in its surmises. The latter, after the mere vapourings of fools, may be the vivid pictures of imagination drawn by the prescience of seers. May the future not fulfil Dryden's couplet 'It wafted nearer yet, and then she knew that what she had surmised was but true'.

On Monday we were startled with the tragic news from Dublin. News that we not only deplore, but which politicians of all shades will agree makes an already complex question enormously more difficult to solve. Then quietly, but full of big issues to our great historic church, is that solemn and secret conclave of Bishops, who are to make unities out of the differences of

Mombasa and Zanzibar. But to-day, our party politics, our ecclesiastical enigmas, even our plans of social reform, all seem to lose their hold, as we see the whole horizon filled with awful luminous clouds that are fast fashioning themselves in that one dread, enthralling word – war. There is no need to be an alarmist. Really facts are so stupendous as to leave no room for exaggeration. Already war is declared. The rest is in the lap of the gods. That the conflict may be kept within the bounds is the hope of all, but it is no use denying that an Armageddon, such as the exile of Palmer never dreamed, is within the range of practical politics. Apparently the current situation then came like a bolt from the blue, and the idea that the murder of a prince by a fanatic, however deplorable, should send Europe in flames seems too absurd to be true. But true it is. Only ignorance attempts to find in the first a sufferance cause for the second. Great racial enmities have long troubled Austro-Hungary and her near neighbours, and the fact that Servia (sic) has played some sinister part in the recent outrage has furnished excuse for hostilities. It is not the moment for pious platitudes, but it is the moment for the church to ask itself the serious question. What has Christianity been doing that in spite of all its creeds, its systems, the moment bad passions are roused in a nation it becomes the brute savage, even its peaceful people seem to revel in the war dogs being loose? In the uncertainties of the moment there is one comfort. The arbiter of the moment, the Emperor of Germany is a strong man, though he is peaceful. He can afford to be. He knows the horrors as well as the costliness of war. He knows, even in sight of his legions, that he who puts on the harness cannot boast as he who takes it off, so that so far as diplomacy can do anything it is no doubt at the moment being powerfully used. But the course of events may be too strong even for him; hence the dread uncertainty over-all. For England to be drawn into it must of course mean sacrifice to the masses of people, and in a larger measure perhaps than ever known, but we children of Norman and of Norsemen, while praying 'give peace in our time, O Lord' and now more devoutly than ever, will not fail when the call comes, if come it must, to meet it with serenity and to give all our country may demand. There is one thing those of us who remember the Boer War know, that war wields us into an unity, as peace never does, and if ever there was a time when we needed Empire to mean more, and petty interest less, it is surely today. If for nothing else the war cloud that rises charged with ghastly horrors may after all prove to be a hand of benediction.

This editorial occupied the same amount of space as an advertisement announcing the arrival of 'Bronco Bill's Great Wild West Exhibition and Mammoth Two-Ring Circus' on the Dean at Dorking – there were to be cowboys and cowgirls, indians, prairie mustangs, lassoo throwers etc. etc. The editorial occupied far less space than the cricket reports, but this was soon to change as sports clubs announced that all fixtures were to be cancelled. The war was becoming a reality.

Sunday, 2nd August was a day of intense excitement – weekday papers appeared on Sunday and Belgium refused to allow German troops free passage through her territory. Over the weekend the British Fleet prepared to go to sea and on the 3rd August the British Regular Army was mobilised. Soldiers and sailors could be seen mingling with holiday makers at the main London stations on that hot afternoon. German troops crossed the border and approached

Liège, and on the next day Germany declared war on Belgium. Following this insurgence Britain issued an ultimatum to Germany to withdraw her troops. It expired on midnight on the 4th August (11 p.m. British time) and Great Britain declared war on Germany.

By 8th August the whole tone of the Dorking Advertiser had altered as the war filled the columns. Under an editorial entitled 'War of Nations', the newspaper laid out the basic facts for its readers. Its opinion of Germany and the Kaiser suffered a complete reversal within one week and at the same time sympathy for Belgium, the underdog, was stirring. War frenzy grew.

At last all doubts are removed and we know that practically the whole of Europe is in the grip of war.

The doubts which had been entertained in some quarters as to the attitude of Great Britain were largely dispelled by the very impressive speech delivered by Sir Edward Grey on Monday afternoon to a crowded House of Commons. He announced that the King of Belgium had addressed to King George a supreme appeal to protect the integrity of Belgium.

With a callous disregard of Treaty obligations, of the rights of nations, of common humanity not equalled since the Kaiser's ancestor Frederick the Great stole Silesia from the widowed Empress, Maria Theresa, Germany has defied Great Britain and set at nought the warning to respect the neutrality of Belgium. Her troops have invaded the little kingdom which under the Treaty of 1839, she pledged herself to protect from outside aggression. She has reiterated her insolent demand for free passage of her army in its campaign against France. And when the Belgian government once more refused the request, Germany sent her a declaration of war. Great Britain has now answered this international outrage by the dispatch of an ultimatum to Germany, calling on her to fulfil her signed and sealed Treaty promise. This ultimatum expired at midnight on Tuesday, and now we also are in a state of war with Germany.

Sir Edward Grey, the Foreign Secretary, surveyed the joyous scenes through his office window and declared ominously, 'The lamps are going out all over Europe, we shall not see them lit again in our life time'.

Nothing, however, seemed to be changing in Newdigate.
Cricket Results:
August 1st – Newdigate v. Beare Green at Beare Green – lost by 70 runs.
August 3rd – Newdigate v Broome Hall at Newdigate – won by an innings and 97 runs.

Holy Baptism:
August 2nd – Maudeline Caroline, the daughter of Walter and Mary Beedle was baptised.

On 6th August Lord Kitchener, the War Minister, appealed for half a million recruits, with 100,000 to be raised immediately. On the 15th August the Dorking Advertiser gave the following advice:

The first and most imperative duty of every man and woman in the country is to keep still. It is only by placing implicit confidence in the Government and the leaders at the front that we can maintain that spirit of calmness which is so important at a time of national crisis.

The Parish Council under the chairmanship of Henry Hackwood (former Headmaster) met on the 10th August at the school. Other committee members were F.G. Rose (of Myrtle Villa), J. Horley (wood dealer of Rose Cottage, Broad Lane), A. Dean (shopkeeper at Dean Brothers), G.J. Butcher (landlord of the Surrey Oaks), W. Greenfield (saddler and harness-maker at Foresters Villas) and H.G. Winfield (smallholder and dairyman of Brooks Farm, Cudworth Lane). The main items of business were:

1. *Clerk was absent due to a broken leg – sympathies sent.*
2. *The Lord Lieutenant's circular to the Council was read and discussed*

    Re: 1. Recruits

    2. Distress

    3. Collection of funds for Prince of Wales' Fund, Soldiers' and Sailors' Families and British Red Cross Society (Surrey)
3. *It was decided that a public meeting should be held in the school to appoint a committee to carry out the necessary arrangements.*

Members of the Royal West Surrey Regiment at Dorking. (Ref. Q53594) Reproduced by kind permission of the Imperial War Museum

Group of officers and NCO's of the Royal West Surrey Regiment

4. *The footbridge at Halesbridge was reported by the sub committee. It was decided that it should be repaired, to have new posts and hand rail. Mr. J. Horley was authorized to give the order and see that the work was properly carried out.*

5. *Hedge at Shop Corner. The sub committee met Mr. White, the agent, by arrangement and it was agreed that the hedge could be cut as suggested.*

On the 17th August the British Expeditionary Force had arrived in France and by the Saturday two army corps were in position around Mons. On Sunday, the 23rd, fighting began. Immediately the French and British forces had to retire as the British alone lost 16,000 men in the first full scale engagement of the war. The British standing army at that time consisted of about a quarter of a million highly trained soldiers and a similar number of Territorials. This 'contemptible little army' compared with the millions of German and French conscripted armies.

A very well-attended meeting was held on Monday, 24th August with Mr. Henry Hackwood in the Chair. The chairman stated that it was 'desired to form an Emergency committee to take measures for recruiting and for the prevention and relief of distress during the war'. The committee consisted of 'members of the Parish Council, the Clergy and Ministers of all denominations and three representatives from each of the Rifle Club and Village Guard, Newdigate Useful Service Brigade, Mrs. Janson's Working Class, Miss Bird's Working Class, The Ambulance Class, The Nursing Association, Soldiers and Sailors Families' Association and the Red Cross Society'. The treasurer was the Rev. H.G. Bird and the secretary, John Steeds (headmaster). The enthusiastic meeting closed with a hearty vote of thanks to the Chairman, cheers for the King and the singing of the National Anthem.

The Schoolhouse

HENRY FERDINAND HACKWOOD (1845-1915)

Henry Hackwood was born in Wolverhampton in 1845 and was the third child of Josiah Ferdinand and Elizabeth Hackwood (née Brooks). His father was a blacksmith whose work took the family to Bishopwearmouth near Sunderland but his religious beliefs lead him into becoming a 'scripture reader' at the Radcliffe Mission in London where he died in relatively poor circumstances. Henry had a teaching post in Albury where he met his future wife, Helen Chart (1841-1889), who was working there. In 1873 he married Helen in London and in the same year took the post of headmaster at Newdigate. They had three children, John Henry F. (b.1874), Percy William (b.1878) and Mabel Kate (1876-1973) and lived at the school house. He later moved to Loompits (now Oakfield House) which had been the Chart family home. He retired in July 1910 and lived at The Cottage in New Barn Lane. He was a parish councillor and helped Mrs. Janson run the carving class. He possessed a splendid resonant baritone voice and sung such songs as 'Nancy Lee' and 'Jack's come home'. He was a 'true and staunch Conservative and an Imperialist to his backbone' and 'his personality and impartiality gained for him the deep respect of all classes of society'. He died at his home in Newdigate in 1915 and two years later his daughter, Mabel, married Alfred William Gibbs in Lancaster.

John Steeds was 34 in 1914 and came from Somerset. He married Isabel Stewardson in 1910 at Hambledon in Surrey, and after Henry Hackwood retired he became headmaster of Newdigate School until he had to join the forces. He was a good player in the cricket team and two months before the outbreak of war he scored 102 in a partnership with R. Rowland who scored 122 not out. John Steeds was also a church warden.

The Rectory

The Rectory, Newdigate
August 26th, 1914

My dear Friends,
Never in our time has England been called upon to face such a terrible trial as she has at this moment. As we fortunately live on an island it is difficult for us to realize the magnitude of the war which is now raging in Europe. The loss already has been very great, and what will be the total loss when the war is ended no one can venture to guess. Some of you think it will soon be over – I hope you are right, but such is not the opinion of experts. Germany will not easily give in; she has so much at stake. Neither must England, for we are fighting for a just cause and not for gain. Poor little Belgium has been most brave, but how sad for her to have lost so very many men and to see her towns and villages destroyed! Those of us who have visited Belgium will realise this more, and if we are spared to see it again how different it will appear!

The question for each one of us to ask himself is what am I doing and what can I do to help my country. How different England is from other nations. How different her position would be now if she had listened to the sound words given by Lord Roberts years ago and so frequently repeated, that every young man, whatever his position or rank may be, should be trained so as to be able to take an active and intelligent part in the defence of his country. The business of warfare has to be learnt. If the Germans consider it necessary for every man to spend three years in learning it, we cannot expect to make ourselves efficient in a few weeks! May God guide us all to do what is right and best.

There are various ways in which we can help. The young men should enlist in the Regular Army or join Lord Kitchener's Force. One could have wished that all the young men in the Parish had regarded it as their duty and privilege to offer themselves in this time of great trouble. We shall undoubtedly be obliged to send more men to the Front before the war is over and if not voluntarily, I suppose the Government will be forced to take other steps.

Those over 30 and from 16 to 18 should join our Rifle Club (the entrance fee has been reduced from half-a-crown to a shilling), and so do their best to make themselves efficient in the defence of their country should such an emergency arise. We can trust our Navy, but that Germany will endeavour to land some troops in England at some time or other is quite evident. Ostend, where some of her troops are at the moment, is not far from England. As Germany has made use of Belgium, so she will not scruple if she considers it will advance her cause, to make use of Holland for her Navy. We must hope for the best but must prepare for the worst. My word to the men is to train themselves – to become efficient. 'Be sober, be vigilant!' 'Fear God, honour the King!'

We must look well after the families of those who have gone or are preparing to go to the front from this Parish. The number is small at present but it may become larger by and by. At any rate let us be determined to do our very best for the families of those gone from us. A Committee is being formed for doing this and will commence work as soon as possible. All funds should be sent to the Central Committee, the members of which will see that they are administered with the greatest care and efficiency.

Mrs. Janson has enrolled a number and if they prepare themselves thoroughly for any emergency it will be a most helpful thing. Preparing means the practice of much self-denial.

The public meeting held on Monday was well attended. I trust it will be productive of much good. We must be prepared to make sacrifices for the cause in money and comforts. We will, God helping us, do our best.

The Day of Intercession was fairly well attended. I wish I could have said there was not a man or woman in Newdigate who did not attend one of the services on that day. 'More things are wrought by prayer than this world dreams of' and we cannot expect to win unless we are earnest in our supplications before the Throne of God. Will everyone in the Parish say the following prayers every day so long as the war lasts? Let Newdigate's motto be 'Work and Pray'

With every best wish, I am, Your sincere friend, H. G. Bird

A General Intercession

O merciful Father, we come into thy presence, beseeching thee at this time to look down in mercy upon our country. Guide and protect the King and all his counsellors. Give wisdom and courage to those who bear command in our Navy and in our Army. Grant to us and our Allies, if it be thy will, victory and success. Preserve our own land from bloodshed, and remove the horrors of war from other lands. Stay, we beseech thee, the pain and the misery, the sorrow and the want, the fierceness and the cruelty, which now desolate the earth. Look down in compassion upon those who are our enemies in this war, especially upon their sick and wounded. And speedily, if it be thy will, send forth upon the nations of the world thy blessing of peace; through Jesus Christ our Lord. Amen.

Lord Roberts of Kandahar (known to his men as Bobs) was the Commander-in-Chief of the British Army from 1901-1904. He was among the highest-ranking and most respected officers of the British Army. Lord Horatio Herbert Kitchener of Khartoum was Secretary of State for War. Lord Kitchener died in 1916 on board HMS Hampshire which struck a mine, west of the Orkney Islands, whilst en route to Russia.

ELLEN CHARLOTTE JANSON 1848 – 1941

Ellen Charlotte was the eldest daughter of Frederick James Chester of Poyle Park, near Guildford and was descended from Edward III. In 1869 she married a widower, George Oliver Mellick Herron who was a wealthy wool merchant living at 14 De Vere Gardens, Kensington. He had two sons by his first wife, Herbert and Robert, and by his second marriage produced four sons and three daughters.

In 1887 Mr. Herron purchased Newdigate Place (now Home Farm) and the accompanying estate, consisting of 1,400 acres, and built a large mansion. His wife personally supervised the architectural portion of the building under J. Hatchard Smith the architect. George Herron died in 1902 and two years later she married John William Janson, but she was soon a widow again as he died in 1906.

Mrs Janson took a great interest in wood-carving and in 1902 she started classes at Newdigate Place for the young people of the village. She loved the work, which continued for 27 years, and had a maternal interest in the members of her class. Many results of their handicraft can still be seen.

The First World War exacted a high toll at Newdigate Place. Mrs. Janson lost two sons, Walter Fitzroy Herron and Kenneth Chester Herron. Her step-nephew, Cyril Douglas Herron and another nephew Douglas Fenton de Wend were also killed and to add to her misery ten of her wood-carving students also lost their lives. A small hand-carved plaque to their memory can be seen in the vestry.

Mrs. Janson was interested in all matters concerning the welfare of the village, being involved in the management of the village school and club and the local nursing association. She also continued running the estate and house with the attendant estate workers and servants. She died in 1941 and the local paper reported:

> *'She was 93 and yet, until a few weeks ago, how beautiful was her talk, her mind alert, her interests so keen, her spirit untouched. She had the art of growing old beautifully, and she had been taken in the autumn when things are most beautiful. She had made all round her beautiful.'*

She died in the midst of another war. Her house had been taken over by the Canadian Army and its condition after the end of the war was so poor that it was totally demolished and the materials sold or used elsewhere.

Newdigate Place

The Great Hall

A rear view

Harvest-time

The Lake

Mrs Ellen Charlotte Janson

REV. HENRY GEORGE BIRD M.A (1846-1925)

Henry George Bird was the son of John and Sally Bird and was born in North Molton in Devon in 1846, the youngest of five children. His father was a cordwainer and Parish Clerk for twenty five years. Henry studied theology at Wells and qualified at Trinity College in Dublin where he took a 'steamboat' degree, which meant that he did not reside in halls but went over to take the examinations. By his mid thirties he was assistant Diocesan Inspector of London and a curate at Christ Church in St. Pancras in London. In 1881 he became the vicar of St. Matthew in Yiewsley, and a year later he married Henrietta Maria Greenham (1850-1912) at Holy Trinity in Halstead, Essex where her brother, Frederick John Greenham was rector. Henrietta had grown up in some comfort at Hendford Manor near Yeovil where her father, Frederick, was a magistrate and landowner.

They had four children, Wilfred Stanley (1884-1915), Muriel Henrietta (1885-1964), Charles Henry G. Bird (1887-1919),who was committed to a private mental institution when he was about twenty years of age) and Ethel Mary Bird (1890-1962).

In 1891 he became the second rector of St. Andrews at Hillingdon near Uxbridge and was described as a 'High Churchman'. He set out to beautify the sanctuary and chancel. About £500, which was a large sum in those days, was spent on mural paintings by Hemmings. He was a member of the Ancient Order of Foresters at Old Treaty House.

On the 19th May 1912, his wife Henrietta died. In March 1913, Henry and his daughters moved to Newdigate in an exchange with the Rev. F.O. Sutton. The Rev. Bird was 68 years of age, and a quiet rural parish probably seemed appealing. He also had a local connection, inasmuch as he had been the accompanist and a committee member of the Leith Hill Musical Festival since 1905, whereby he would have come into close contact with Lucy Broadwood of Lyne and the composer, Ralph Vaughan Williams.

The First World War was a heart-rending period for the Rev. Bird as he ministered to his parishioners and offered sympathy to the bereaved whilst having to cope with his own sorrow. He immersed himself in village activities and became vice president (whilst one of his daughters was secretary) of the District Nursing Association. He also encouraged the choir and he had a love of bell-ringing.

In 1921 he retired to the 'quietude of the old-world town of Wotton-under-Edge, which nestles under the shelter of the Cotswold Hills'. He died on the 27th February 1925 and the Middlesex Advertiser and Gazette carried a full report of his burial which took place at St. Andrews, Hillingdon. The village was represented by the Misses Goldberg and floral tributes were sent by the rector, choir and his Newdigate friends, Maud Elizabeth Goldberg and Francis and Ada Ethel Shorland-Ball.

The greater part of his life was lived in St. Andrew's parish, where his 'devoted ministrations to his people were deeply valued and his great work for the church highly appreciated' – no doubt the parishioners of Newdigate would have echoed similar sentiments.

Rev. H.G. Bird welcoming his old parishioners from Uxbridge to Newdigate in May 1913

Rev. Henry G. Bird M.A.

The Dorking Advertiser reported on a largely attended meeting of the Newdigate and Charlwood Useful Service Brigade which was held in Newdigate School on the evening of Saturday, 5th September to explain the duties required in case of emergency, and to induce unmarried men to enlist.

The Rector, the Rev. H.G.Bird who presided, at the outset read telegrams from Mr. H.C. Lee-Steere, JP **(H.C. Lee-Steere lived at Jayes Park in Ockley and was a major land-owner within Newdigate. His son, Lt. John Henry Gordon Lee-Steere, was in the Grenadier Guards and was killed on the 17th November 1914, aged 19 years. He was buried at Zillebeke Churchyard Cemetery in Belgium which later became known as the Aristocrats' Cemetery. The village hall at Ockley is dedicated to his memory.)** *and others expressing their regret at being unable to attend, and wishing the meeting all success. Proceeding, the Chairman said the first thing they would all wish to do was to thank Mrs. Janson for arranging*

Lieut. John Henry Gordon Lee-Steere of Jayes Park, Ockley

the meeting. They knew her heart was in the right place, and they trusted her endeavours would meet with great success. Never in their lives, or in the lives of generations past, had England passed through such a critical period. What they wanted to do was to face it like men, but it was a great pity they did not listen ten years ago to the wise words of Lord Roberts. The Rector then called upon Dr. Hugh T. W. Blakeney, **(Dr. Hugh T.W. Blakeney (1855-1916) was a much loved and admired doctor living in Dorking. His nephew, Lt. H. E. H. Blakeney served with the Sussex Regiment and survived the war.)** *who first of all complimented Mrs. Janson on the work she has so nobly taken up and was so ably fulfilling. In other words she was getting together a portion of the British public in the little village of Newdigate, showing how absolutely important it was in these serious times that they should, in their own localities, stick together, shoulder to shoulder (hear, hear), that they should have a pivot upon which they knew they could work, to which centre they might come from the circumference, and get their information, their decision, and their training. Now he took it that that was Mrs. Janson's meaning in starting the useful brigade – and he thought that the words themselves spoke for its motive – then all those who rallied under the flag should be ready to do their part in their particular sphere of life to which it had pleased God to put them. They would take their order, and apply their abilities to the very best, looking to their Colonel-in-Chief – because he was quite sure in Mrs. Janson they would have a Colonel-in-Chief who had a remarkable love for her country – to keep them on the right lines (applause). After contrasting the peaceful life of their own countryside with the devastated lanes of France and Belgium, Dr. Blakeney said there was not a single man or women amongst them who was not thinking of those brave fellows of ours, the soldiers and sailors, fighting for them at the present moment. Did they all realise, did they all think of them, because they were peaceful and quiet in Newdigate? Perhaps they had not yet realised what a terrible time our country had to look forward to, and what a critical crisis we were going through. There seemed to him as he wandered from village to village, as he had done with his good colleague, the Recruiting Officer, Colour Sergeant J. F. O'Byrne, such a want of knowledge of what was going on, a kind of apathy. It was not their fault, he felt sure; he believed it was because things had not been put clearly before them in the matter of that terrible and awful war which was now waging. Let them picture to themselves for one moment that it was a European war, a war of nations against nations, and what did it mean? It meant the hoarding together of millions of men who were fighting for their lives.*

Mrs. Janson, then briefly explained the objects of the Brigade, which were to enrol men willing to help serve their country when emergency occurs, to encourage recruiting and for helpers who (in case of invasion) could be sent according to their occupation, where required. The Brigade has the approval of the Social Service and the National Service League. Mrs. Janson mentioned that they had already enrolled 139 members. Mrs. Janson expressed her thanks to Mr. F. A. Clark, who had given his valuable time. **(Frank Albert Clark was a builder and decorator and agent for the Ocean Accident & Insurance Corporation Ltd. He was also a sidesman at the church and was secretary of the Choral Society. In the parish magazine of March 1915 the rector simply wrote that 'Mr. Clark, who has been in the choir for some years, is also greatly missed'. There was no explanation as to why he had left.)** *During the evening patriotic songs were rendered and Mr. Bird proposed a hearty vote of thanks to all the speakers.*

On the 17th September Lieutenant Evelyn H. T. Broadwood of the 1st Norfolk Regiment wrote two letters to his sister and brother-in-law, Audrey and John Innes. It took nine days for the letter to arrive at their home at The Greenings in Charlwood. (Audrey Julia Innes (née Broadwood) was the daughter of James Henry Tschudi and Margaret Broadwood and was born in 1887. She married John Alfred Innes at St. John the Baptist Church in Capel on the 18th November 1908. Her brother Evelyn Broadwood gave her away. At the celebrations a bonfire was lit for the estate workers and there were fireworks, showing the initials J.A.I., after which the workers had their supper. John and Audrey later had three children.) At the outbreak of war Lt. Broadwood was in barracks in Ireland, in fact he had evidently been there for some time as in September 1913 he had ordered a spare axle for his Gregoire car and the manufacturers had to explain that they could not ship it beyond Liverpool owing to a strike in Ireland. He was amongst the first to see action, on the 23rd August, in what later was to be called the Battle of Mons. Clearly, at this time, the censoring

Capt. Evelyn Henry Tschudi Broadwood

of letters to sanitise the situation was not fully effective. A myth arose at Mons on the German side that the British had far more machine guns than in fact they really had. This was due to the rapid rifle fire by the highly trained regulars.

Dearest A

Your letter of Aug 22nd has reached me today! Thanks so much for it.

I am all right, I'm glad to say and hope that most of us will come out of it. I have had a slight touch of dysentery which fortunately I took in time so am as well now as I have been for ages. The war can scarcely last long at this pace. I understand that things are looking a lot brighter for us now than formerly, which is satisfactory. Many of the German prisoners we have taken are very hungry and tired of the war but they are only the stragglers it is true.

I grew a beard while I was poorly which was about four days and looked like a Boer prisoner, but it is not unusual to see both officers and men with beards. Personally I did not care for it as it felt prickly, so it has been shaved off. It is quite difficult to recognise acquaintances. I should <u>so</u> <u>much</u> like a pair of rather thin socks – also a little plain chocolate. If you could send them all in one small package there is more chance of my getting them and they will no doubt reach me in October sometime. People here give the war another month or so to last and the sooner it is over the better in many ways. Many of the villages are utterly deserted – like places of the dead with only cocks and hens running about and occasional signs of a shell. The lyddite explosives blow great holes in the ground and you pass great pits in ploughed fields and orchards where the shell has burst. Those villagers who have stuck to their houses have been much better off whereas when the Germans enter an empty village they turn houses upside down and inside out and even the French and English who arrived at a place that is shut up and have to find billets for the night, break open the doors or windows of houses sometimes to get in. We have slept in all kinds of places, mostly alas a bit 'whiffy' and one often really finds clean straw the most pleasant. The houses of the poorer people in France have no accommodation for washing! I have never once found a jug, a basin or washstand and seldom a decent towel beyond a greasy rag which is a great nuisance if one has not ones own to hand. We have our kit in our valises which follow after us on a wagon, so one often does not get it at night. – 35lbs is our full allowance. Don't forget <u>not to</u> leave the house empty in case the enemy lands, which I hope won't happen.

Dear John,

I have been doing some splendid bullet dodging. One went through my haversack (which I wear on my left thigh) without touching me, and another day a bullet passed between my nose and that of a corporal to whom I was speaking. The shells are very alarming at first, especially the shrapnel, but the worst wounds so far have been caused by the lyddite. I believe our own guns are a little inferior to German cannons. The situation up to date is satisfactory I understand.

    Ever yours E.H.T.B.

By now there was much activity in Newdigate and the Rector wrote about stirring deeds at the front.

The Rectory

St. Michael's and All Angels' Day, 1914

My dear Friends,

We are passing through most anxious times and we who are at home can best help the cause by earnest prayer that God may bless our Forces and those of our Allies. Everyone should be doing some definite work to further the cause. What stories some will be able to tell their children and grand children fifty years hence of what they have witnessed abroad! It is the greatest war that has ever been waged, not only from the fact that more men are taking part in it than have ever before been brought together, but is the greatest especially from the fact that the issues that will follow from it will have far more important results than anything that has happened from any war before. May God grant that it may be for the advance of his Kingdom on Earth and for the good of all mankind. "To be or not to be". Such were the words written by von Bernardi, three years ago respecting the German Empire, and they certainly can well be applied to England today. (**General Friedrich von Bernardi was born in Petrograd in 1849 and lived on his estates in Silesia. He was described as 'tall, spare, very erect, his beard streaked with grey, his head straight in the back, a typical heel-clicking Prussian Officer, very aggressive in his manner.'**) It is true that we were bound in the first place to undertake this

The road at Kingsland heading towards the Wyatt family home

war to save our honour – but it is now equally true that we must go on with it to the bitter end in order to save our very existence. If we were conquered, which of course is out of the question, then England and the Empire would cease to exist. So let us one and all do our very best in the way open to us to obtain the result as speedily as possible. It is now the eighteenth day of this huge battle, and although the Germans have during the last few days made some fierce and stubborn attacks on us and our Allies all along the line they have all been ably resisted by the French and our soldiers. May God bless and guide our forces. Especially dear to us must be those who have gone from our midst. We have heard of many escapes. Only yesterday I was told that a bullet

The interior of Newdigate Church

had passed through Lieutenant Broadwood's cap and another through his leggings without touching him. You know the story of Captain Nicholson, who was saved after being nearly three hours in the water. Another neighbour, Captain Harrison, whose sister conducted the Ockley Choral Society last winter, perished at the same time. William George Wyatt saw most of the men in his Battalion cut down whilst he and a very few others escaped. **(William George Wyatt (1888-1954) was the eldest of the fourteen children of William (1867-1916) and Ann Selina Wyatt (1869-1975) and lived at Kingsland. Although over age, his father joined up and was killed in 1916 leaving his wife to bring up the family. In spite of this she lived to the magnificent age of 106!)** Let us not relinquish our prayers for those. James Frederick Elliott was in church on Sunday evening and hopes to go to France in about a fortnight's time. **(James Elliott came from a family which had resided and worked on the land in Newdigate for generations. At this time he was living at Brook Cottages on the Parkgate Road.)**

Mrs. Janson's three sons are all taking part in the great struggle. We wish them every best wish. George belongs to the Automobile Service Corps, **(George Frederick Herron (1870-1949) married Edith Dubois and for a short while became chairman of the family firm of wool merchants.)** Walter has joined the Royal Reserve Regiment of the Cavalry and Kenneth, who is waiting for a commission in the Essex Yeomanry, is drilling some Scouts.

We thank very heartily those who have already given to the Emergency Fund. We think there are many others who would wish to give and shall be very glad to receive any amount that may be sent. It is especially our duty to look after the Wives and Families of those who have gone to the front, and although there is not much distress in the Parish at present, we are sure to have some as the winter advances.

We are not certain whether we shall be able to continue the Choral Society this winter in consequence of the scarcity of young men who are willing to join. Newdigate did extremely well last year as it was the first occasion of competing. We shall be sorry if we are not able to go on. It was a source of pleasure to many and this winter especially, it would be a valuable thing to have something to take our thoughts away from the war...

We have lost one of our Bell-ringers, Albert Monk, who is training to go to the front. We would be glad to welcome one or two young men who would be keen to learn the method which, though difficult, gives very much pleasure.

I was not able to join the Choir at their outing, but am very glad to hear the day was most enjoyable. Brighton was selected for their destination and proved most attractive in every way.

Please remember the following in your prayers.
  Broadwood, Evelyn Henry Tschudi, Lieut. Norfolk Regt. In France.
  Wyatt, William George, L/Cpl., 17th Field Co of the Royal Engineers. In France.
  Horley, Alfred Henry, Pioneer 17th Field Co. R.E. 5th Div II Army. In France.
  Rowland, Frederick, L/8214, Drill Sergeant, RWS. At Dover.
  Johns, Walter, Stoker, HMS Staghound. Was at Malta in June.
  Monk, George, on HMS Queen. Was at Portsmouth.

HMS Renown (reproduced by kind permission of the National Maritime Museum)

Purdey Johns

Purdey Johns on board HMS Renown in 1916

Wooltorton, George, Flying Squadron. Gone to the front

Batchelor, George, Able Seaman. Was at Portsmouth in August.

Potter, Anthony William, Royal Engineers

Still, Arthur **(son of John and Frances Charlotte Still who ran The Surrey Oaks. John died in 1898 and Frances married John Harknett in 1900 and continued running the pub),** *HMS Lynx, 4th Destroyer Flotilla*

Johns, Purdey (SS7032), training ship **(later served on HMS Renown)**

Potter, Frank Raymond **(brother of Anthony),** *Training 5th Battalion Royal West Surrey at Dover*

Taylor, Charles, *Training 5th Battalion Royal West Surrey at Dover*

Monk, Arthur Henry, *Training 5th Battalion Royal West Surrey at Dover*

Burberry, Sidney John, *Training 5th Battalion Royal West Surrey at Dover*

Bourne, Ernest William Henry, *Training at 5th Battalion Royal West Surrey at Dover*

West, Walter Henry, *Training at 5th Battalion Royal West Surrey at Dover*

Elliott, James Frederick, *Training at 5th Battalion Royal West Surrey at Dover*

Hudson, George **(b. 1899 at Ifield and the son of George and Rosa Hudson who farmed at Home Farm)**, *Training at 5th Battalion Royal West Surrey at Dover*

Harewood, Charlie, *Training on Salisbury Plain*

Dean, William Luther, **(son of Michael Dean who ran the Post Office)**, *4th Royal West Kent at Sandwich*

"England expects that every man will do his duty"

With my very wish,

I am your sincere friend, H. G. Bird.

The Monk family outside the Old Brewery

It must have been very strange for the young men of Newdigate who may never have been abroad – possibly had never been on a boat – before. The transports were generally crowded with soldiers, horses, mules and equipment. All lights had to be turned off as they left the harbour and, apart from the searchlight from the destroyer or torpedo-boat escorts, nothing could be seen. Upon reaching France, after a journey which may have taken many hours, they would have stepped upon French soil and heard a different language, probably have seen the enemy for the first time in the guise of sneering prisoners of war, and experienced sights and smells strange and new. After a brief period at base camp, there would be the interminable train journey and then a long march to the front, where they would see the devastation and all that war truly meant. For the new recruits there would have been a feeling of excitement, but for the returning soldiers just one of dread. Their thoughts, no doubt, would have been passed on to the young and impressionable youngsters. So there was a whole mixture of emotions passing through every soldier's mind as they marched over the strange cobbles with their comrades.

The incident relating to Captains Nicholson and Harrison, to which the Rector referred, took place in the North Sea. On the morning of the 22nd September three elderly cruisers, the Aboukir, Cressy and Hogue were patrolling off the Dutch coast when at 6.25 a.m. the Aboukir was struck by a torpedo and rolled over and sunk in thirty minutes. Lifeboats were sent to the aid of her people but before they could get away the Hogue was struck on the starboard side amidships, under the 9.2 magazine. There was a very heavy explosion and she immediately began to heel to starboard. The Cressy was manoeuvred so as to render assistance when a torpedo, fired at a range of 500 to 600 yards, was spotted and it struck her on the starboard side just before the after-bridge. The ship listed about ten degrees but remained steady until another torpedo struck her and she began to heel rapidly and finally turned keel up, remaining so for about twenty minutes before she finally sunk, at 7.55 a.m. In all 837 men were rescued by Dutch and British fishing vessels, including Lieut. Commander Bertram W.L. Nicholson of the Cressy but 1459 men died, amongst whom was Lieut. Commander Thomas Edmund Harrison of the Aboukir. The commander of the submarine, Otto Weddigen, returned home to a hero's welcome and a medal was struck in his honour but he later died whilst commanding U29 when it was rammed and sunk by HMS Dreadnought.

Lieut. Commander Thomas Edmund Harrison (1879-1914) was the son of Comdr. Matthew James Harrison (1846?-1926) and Lucy (née Wedgwood, 1846-1919) who were friends of the Broadwoods and attended the wedding of Audrey Broadwood and John Innes in 1908. They were an interesting family and well known in the area. Lucy's uncle was Charles Darwin and her father was Josiah Wedgwood (3rd) and her sister was the mother of the composer, Ralph Vaughan Williams. One of Matthew's first expeditions whilst serving in the navy was to the Easter Islands and his collections from this voyage were donated to the British Museum. He later had shore leave from Vancouver where he crossed the Kootenay Lake and fell in love with the area. He built a retirement home and in 1911 was joined by his wife and two daughters. He built a church called the Harrison Memorial Church which was dedicated to his three dead sons and Lucy. A younger son, Geoffrey, died aged 6 from scarlet fever and another son Lieut. Commander George Basil Harrison was killed in 1915 when HMS Natal blew up in Cromarty Firth in mysterious circumstances. Thomas Edmund Harrison had married Maud Winifred Godman at Horsham in 1907 and lived at Wey Lodge in Liphook with their three children. His name appears on the Chatham Naval Memorial, the Waterlooville War Memorial and also the memorial at Cowfold (along with his brother, George Basil Harrison). There is a small statue to both brothers at Coldharbour.

The Dorking Advertiser published a similar list along with the names of Henry Harber, son of Charles and Ada Harber of Myrtle Cottage and christened Harry, Private Stephen C. Harber and Corporal Sydney R. Bourne, L/8402, Royal West

Surrey Regiment, in a section where all the 'heroes', of all the local villages were listed. In a similar vein they also published the following under the title 'A Fine Record':

Commander Bertram Lothian Nicholson of the ill fated 'Cressy' which was torpedoed and sunk at the same time as the 'Aboukir' and 'Hogue' has been visiting his mother, Lady Nicholson, at Parkland Cottage, Oakwood, on short leave. He has now returned to his naval duties. Lady Nicholson's family are nobly serving the country. Col. Cecil Lothian Nicholson is with the East Lancashire Regiment, Commodore Douglas Lothian Nicholson is with the Agincourt, Captain Octavius Lothian Nicholson is with the Yorkshire Regiment and Captain Francis Lothian Nicholson is with the Indian Army.

THE HON. LADY MARY NICHOLSON (1842-1922) AND HER SONS

Lady Nicholson was the daughter of John Romilly who was a knight and Master of the Rolls. She married Sir Lothian Nicholson who was Lt. Governor of Jersey from 1878 – 1883 and Lt. General of Gibraltar where he died from malaria in 1893 at the age of 66. They married at Kensington in 1864 and had ten children. She was a friend of the Broadwoods and attended the wedding of John Innes and Audrey Broadwood in 1908.

Capt. Bertram William Lothian 'Nick' Nicholson (1878- 1958) was born in Jersey. On his naval service record it was stated that he 'moves in the best society'. His grandfather's (George Thomas Nicholson) estate was Waverley Abbey House near Farnham where his sister-in-law, Florence Nightingale, was a frequent visitor and Sir Walter Scott used the name for his 'Waverley Novels'. During the war the house was used as a military hospital and over five thousand officers were cared for, but today it is used as a training and conference centre.

Maj. Gen. Cecil Lothian Nicholson (1865-1933) was the eldest son of Lothian and Mary. His only son, 2nd Lt. Geoffrey Douglas Lothian Nicholson, was killed in France in 1917 aged 19. He lived at Camberley in Surrey.

Admiral Sir Douglas Lothian Nicholson was born in Gibraltar in 1867 and married Edith Mary Sybil in 1907.

HMS Agincourt (27,500 tons) was originally built for the Brazilian Navy by Vickers Armstrong. The Brazilian Government cancelled the order due to financial restraints and it was sold to Turkey prior to completion and then appropriated by the Navy in August 1914, much to the disgust of the Turkish people who had raised the money for the purchase by public subscription. She took part at the Battle of Jutland but was scrapped in 1924 due to restrictions imposed by the Naval Limitations Treaty of 1923.

The other sons were Maj. Gen. Octavius Henry Lothian Nicholson (1877-1938) and Maj. Gen. Francis Lothian Nicholson (1884-1953)

The home of the Broadwood family

Lyne House

The interior of Lyne House

Stirring tales were being published by the paper, sent from the front by local soldiers, and one entitled 'Eulogy of British Bravery' was sent by Lieut. Broadwood on the 29th September to his uncle Canon Shearme (1842-1925) Rector of St. John the Baptist at Oakwood Hill who had married Mary Stewart Broadwood in 1881.

Capt. Evelyn Henry Tschudi Broadwood

I have been awaiting a chance to write to you for a long time. It seems to all of us six months at least since we left Ireland, and it is only six weeks as a fact. But what a lot has happened! We were in the engagements near Mons and at Le Cateau, and again in the subsequent advance we were engaged at the battle on the Marne and on the Aisne. It has been one long battle the whole time. Only one day were we out of the sound of cannon or shells bursting. So really the so-called battles are incidents in this long fight, where we fight a little harder than usual. It was satisfactory when we ceased the retreat and began to advance again. I think that all told now, we have done slightly better than the Germans. The present situation is a kind of stale-mate, just at the crucial point where we are now. We are pushing on slowly, however, in other parts of the line, and I heard yesterday from a Divisional Staff Officer, that the situation is favourable and slightly improving.

I do not know what people at home think of the war, whether they have got the right idea or not. One does not want to be too gloomy writing, but as far as what both sides have been going through this last six weeks it is more horrible than anything that can have previously been imagined. I think, too, that the Germans are having a worse time of it even than the French and ourselves. Of course, just lately, they have been simply massacred by us, and the French, and letters have been found on dead and wounded saying what a 'hellish' time they have been having, and hoping for the end of the war. Their infantry cannot stand up to ours. It has been proved again and again; but their strong point is their artillery. They seem to pick up their targets quickly, and they seem to outnumber our guns nearly everywhere. Curiously enough, a letter written by a German officer says the same about our guns and says that we are superior in artillery. So what we think may be imagination, but it always seems to us that our artillery is weaker.

Wherever we can we dig ourselves right into the earth, and cave right underneath; this protects us from bullets and most shrapnel, but it is practically impossible to be safe from the bigger and high explosive shells. They have an uncanny way of finding out where one is and are especially fond of shelling brigade headquarters if they can find them. This also may be imagination, or evidence of a good system of espionage, or else chance, for certainly our Brigadier (to whom we are attached, not our own) had to move three times in three successive days because of the annoyance of shells. Some of the staff took refuge in the cellar, when a shell burst inconveniently close, the second shell knocked at the cellar door with one fragment – so runs the tale! The lyddite high explosive shells make the most fuss, but are, I am told, very weak in effect, though I have not tried! They say, too, that they stun people sometimes only for the time, and, apropos of this, a Duke of Cornwall Light Infantry Officer, Lt. B (his father is a Unionist MP) told me the other day that at the Marne one of his Cornwall companies had a hot time with lyddite, and were knocked down all over the place. However, next day, they rejoined. They said that they had 'gone to sleep' without knowing it about 5 p.m. the previous afternoon. This, my friend told me corresponded with the time the German attack took place. The men woke up in the middle of the night about one or two am and found themselves lying among the dead. They saw Germans moving about all around them in the wood, and so they feigned death. When the Germans had retired they rejoined their regiment, apparently none the worse.

We have come across dreadful sights, men blown to pieces literally by shells, and dead Germans lying about with dead horses all along the road in some places. That was during their retreat; the road was strewn with their knapsacks and equipment of various kinds. Our ambulances as they come along bury the dead, and burying parties go and search woods and so on for the dead. They are reverently buried (by a chaplain, if possible) and where possible a little wooden cross is put over the end of the grave with the man's name on, and his regiment and the date he died, and perhaps R.I.P. or 'Buried by his affectionate comrades of the ...... Regiment'. One comes across these sad little tokens everywhere, sometimes in the middle of a village square or in a field or orchard, and one hopes that their friends at home may get to hear, but there must be thousands who have no such luck as to be buried or are recognisable. We have been very well fed all this time, and I think this reflects great credit on our Army Service Corps and the Ordnance departments. As a result of this we have really had very little sickness. Just a touch or two of light dysentery here and there among the men caused by the wet chiefly – but we have been very lucky with the weather too. So we have a great deal to be thankful for among all our groanings.

On the same day Lieut. Broadwood also found time to write to his sister, Audrey Innes.

Sept. 19th, 1914

Dear A,

We were as you have heard, in the thick of it at the Battle of Mons. Our regiment and the Cheshires with a battery of Artillery were sent off to the left of our position in front of a village called Elevge. This was the part which was most heavily attacked. The shell fire from the German artillery was indescribable and our baptism of fire was worse than anything that was known in all the South African war.

We found later that our force was outnumbered by 3½ to one on the most conservative estimate.

We deployed into line about 11.30 a.m. on the Monday, after waiting to see from which direction the German attack was coming. My platoon (50 men) was in the second line of D company and some 200 yards behind the firing line to start with. I was soon ordered to bring them up, which was not a too comfortable job, as shells were bursting by now just in front of us. However, I shouted to the men telling them to go on and saying they would be safer up the hill. Then the battery doing most of the firing on us stopped for a moment to reload and resight and I got the men on a hundred yards, and then – the shells began bursting like hail just where we had come from! Then they kept altering their range and you could sometimes hear the shot and shell come down only a few yards off, and of course you could always hear the shell singing through the air and sometimes felt the breath of them!

There was such a pandemonium that one could only know in the firing line what was going on just around one ...... so I will only write now of what I saw and did myself, so forgive the constant repetition of the word 'I'.

Around me the men behaved splendidly (the whole regiment has been congratulated on all having done well). We lay there in the potato crop like partridges. I think we were all too petrified to move. We lay just below the crest of a ridge waiting to crawl up to see if any German infantry came along. As a fact before any came we had an order to retire, so that just where my platoon was we did not fire at all. This made it almost more trying, not being able to hit back.

We lay under that shell fire for three hours and I think that none of us will ever forget the feeling of thinking that the next moment we might be dead – perhaps blown to atoms. I kept wondering what it was going to feel like to be dead and all sorts of little things that I had done and places I had been to years ago and had quite forgotten kept passing through my mind. I have often heard this happening to a drowning man but have never experienced it before and don't want to again! I think you get so strung up that your nerves get into an abnormal condition. My brain seemed extraordinarily cool and collected which I was proud of, but I looked at my hands and saw them moving and twisting in an extraordinary way, as if they didn't belong to me, and when I tried to use my field glasses to spy at the Germans, it was as much as I could do with the greatest effort to get them up to my eyes and then I could scarcely see.

When the order came to retire our company got it late, our unfortunate adjutant who was going on a message was killed by a shell. His name was Captain Cresswell, and he was such a nice chap too. I told my platoon – those who were left – to double back and assemble behind a house in a sunken road behind us. From there they got back by dodging around some coal refuse stacks as we had a colliery just behind us, and so back to the road along which the battalion was retiring. I stopped behind to collect stragglers and to carry in a couple of wounded into the house where the doctor was seeing to them and I believe that I was the last to leave.

By this time the bullets had begun to sing around us and the German infantry were getting close, so it was high time to clear out. But the shelling was ceasing lest they should hit their own men.

I could not get some of the men along. They were too dead beat, as it was a broiling day and all the time the sun had been beating on us, but I and a last party of five, all Norfolk except one

Retreat from Mons – British Cavalry retiring, August/September 1914. Photograph by Paul Maze (Ref. Q60702)
Reproduced by kind permission of the Imperial War Museum

cavalry man, climbed up a pear tree and over a garden wall, and so creeping along with bullets now flying all around we got over another wall and so up a path exposed for a short way. We ran along this and I remember – as an instance of the stupid things one does in moments of excitement – my little hair brush jumped out suddenly from my haversack and I ran back five or six yards to pick it up, and risked a life for a hair brush! I found subsequently two holes in my haversack where a bullet had passed through just grazing my clothes, and it may have been then that it went through.

We ran into a cutting where there was a railway line for shunting coal and ran along this. I went over an embankment to my right front and dropping down the sheltered side I turned round to fire at the enemy to cover the rest if I could. The rest of our small party went along the cutting under the bridge. I never saw any of them again, and none have been seen since, so I almost wish they had waited for me. I fired 20 rounds and dropped two Germans. Then I turned sharp left and ran along below the embankment to put them off the scent. I came to a bridge under the railway and there underneath lay an officer on a stretcher, all laid out properly with a handkerchief over his face. I reverently lifted the handkerchief and there was the dead face of poor Cresswell. I had not heard of course and was prepared for anyone. It has always given one worse shocks to see people one knows well in the regiment or has just talked to, lying dead or wounded or blown about, but I am getting more used to seeing dead and wounded who are complete strangers. It does not seem quite so bad (and the German dead and wounded I don't so much mind incidentally). Don't think this dreadfully morbid. Perhaps it is better not written, but you can tear it up, and it gives you an idea of what we have had to think of these last weeks.

I think my running has scarcely ever come in more useful than that day. After a bit of dodging about I got to the village where I caught up with some of the fragments of the regiment in twos and threes, and I routed out some who had taken wounded men into houses and collected about 15 or 20 men. In this varied crowd was our regimental pet, 'the wardof' — and also the headquarter flag which we carry instead of our colours. It was lucky we were together. As we got out of the village five German Hussars hove in sight and approached us. We fired at them and I think — one of the men told me we had for certain — wounded one man and we certainly disabled two horses because they all fled behind cover close by and only three reappeared. They circled round at a most respectful distance and made for their own lines again. The map showed me the direction of the French frontier, so we took the road and a couple of miles further on we came on some infantry in the distance. We signalled to these on chance, hoping it was not more German Hussars and we were glad enough to find they were our own divisional cyclist company — though all ready to receive us with shot in case we were frauds, as the Germans are up to all sorts of tricks. I recognised Capt. Burnett (of David Fairbarn's regiment) whom I know and they told us they were the last part of the British rearguard and there was no one behind us. We got back to the regiment in two or three hours and found it sadly diminished. In the end I think we lost four hundred men wounded, missing and killed and 8 officers, Major Orr, Capt. Cresswell, Lieut. Briard, Openshaw, Oakes, Paget, Reeves and Lieut Jephson wounded. He was hit in the leg and most pluckily walked till he got back to a British ambulance. We are hoping that some of the others are wounded only or captured. Now goodbye until I write again ..... It is not likely that we shall meet yet for a bit, but I look forward to seeing you all in the flesh again. Very best love to all of you and to the aunts and Uncles and all the relations, whose eye this gloomy epistle may catch. Send me a few packets of chocolate if you are writing. There is nothing to be bought anywhere here. All groceries even sold out, but we are being fed all right by the government.

Your ever loving brother E.H.T.B.

Of the names mentioned above, Major John Boyd Orr (age 43) from Camberley, Captain (not Lieutenant) Ernest Felix Victor Briard (25) a Jerseyman from St Aubin and Captain Cresswell were killed on the 24th August. Lieut. Harold Michael Openshaw from Winchester died four days later.

Captain Francis Joseph Cresswell was born in King's Lynn in 1883. He was the son of Col George Francis A. Cresswell (5th Bn. Norfolk Regiment) and his wife Harriett Eva L (née Gurney). He married Barbara Flolkes at Ferrybridge, Lynn in 1907. In 1918 she remarried to Edward P. Strickland. Francis is buried at the Aubershicourt British Cemetery and his name is also recorded on the war memorial at Hunstanton.

At 3.45 p.m. on the 24th October John Innes sent a telegram to his brother-in-law, Gerard T. Bray, in New Westminster, British Columbia stating "Evelyn slightly wounded thigh doing well". He had travelled across to France with his car to assist the Red Cross and he wrote to his mother on the same day, in a hurried manner, from the Hotel Moderne, Rue Faidherbe, Boulogne-Sur-Mer, France.

My dear mother,

I hope that you will excuse pencil as I have no ink up here. As you will have heard from Audrey they left me waiting for a day or two at Folkestone before I could get over here and when I got here there was nothing to do at first but during the last few days we have all been very busy taking wounded from two hospital trains to various hotels here which have been fitted out as hospitals. I think that they have three trains fitted up for wounded which run backwards and forwards. They have kitchens and everything on board and the wounded get moved very comfortably there being nurses and orderlies. The medical staff have been working like slaves they receive wounded at all times between 7.00 a.m. and 12.00 midnight, seem very shorthanded, I am sure I do not know when they sleep.

I was very surprised to meet Evelyn so soon. From his relatives point of view it seems the best thing that could have happened to him. I think that he is bound to go home and it will be sometime before he comes out again. He appears much as usual though lying in bed and is very well looked after. Temperature quite normal today, I do not think that there will be any after effects.

Though a long way from the front we see some of the effects of the war here with all these wounded coming in, some of them seriously. I am afraid that there will be a lot of cripples in England after this and hope that they will be properly provided for. I am thankful to say that the wounds are all dressed before they reach us. The slightly wounded are full of hope and very anxious to tell all and sundry their experiences but many of them think that they are really the sole survivors of certain actions and this does not turn out to be the case.

I see more than ever now that too much attention must not be read into correspondents who write of news from here and neighbouring places. New information is all second hand and coloured afterwards. I am having quite a good time here and expect in a few days to go with an ambulance convoy near the front, though not right up to it, which should be very interesting. As the organisation of the Red + here gets more efficient your car should be very useful and crew and me will have plenty of chauffeurs absolutely destitute of French to consort with. They are for the most part a very decent lot. The English seem to have taken entire possession of the town, the French seem absolutely out of place. The children insist on saying good night and shaking one's hand. Their hands are not often washed.

I am afraid that it is possible that you will only hear from me at long intervals as when I do go off I shall have very little time for writing and posts will be very uncertain.

Your loving son, John Innes

The Dorking Advertiser advised its readers on the 24th October that a shortage of radishes had been reported as the bulk of the usual supply came from Germany. They also reported that a wealthy young Englishman, before going to the front, insured his life for £200,000, the risk being split between offices. The first premium was £10,000.

Evelyn Broadwood's name appeared on the casualty list in the Advertiser of the 31st October. His luck had seemingly run out when a bullet hit him in the thigh. In hindsight this probably saved his life. On Tuesday, 27th October he wrote letters to

his sisters Audrey and Joan from the Allied Forces Base Hospital in Boulogne. They were addressed to Audrey with a request to forward the other letter on to her sister.

Dearest A,

I was wounded on Tuesday afternoon by a bullet in the thigh. I've been through a bad time with it, but I hope I shall pull through all right now with all the care and kindness lavished on us here, though they are quite full up just now. I am fit to write a letter to you today. You don't know how my mind was relieved by knowing that you had heard the news of me, as I couldn't write.

It was a surprise seeing John! He walked into this very room ten minutes after getting your wire. It seemed such a strange situation seeing him in uniform talking to me – a kind of wreck lying on a bed. I've not been allowed to move my right leg an inch since I was hit, as the shot hit me just on or close to an artery. So don't expect to see me in England for sometime.

Who do you think else is here but Barbara Craster! It was such a surprise to see her too and she is actually taking a turn of night work in this very hospital tonight on the floor above. This is a hotel converted. Give my love to Uncle John and Aunt Mary and to all and let Aunt Bertha and others hear that I am doing all right so far. Barbara and John have been most good in coming to see me. I said goodbye to John this morning. He left with his ambulance. He tells me you wired to Joan.

Barbara Craster

Dearest J,

Audrey first got news of my being hit and she was very good and sent you a wire. I got a bullet through the thigh last Tuesday but this is the first day I've been fit to write – just a week – so I'm sending a letter to both of you, but it has been a relief to know that you heard.

It will be a long job I'm afraid and I have to lie very still, as it is either through or near an artery but I'll pull through now I'm sure. I've actually had both John Innes and Barbara Craster to visit me. John appeared the very next day I was brought here having had a wire from Audrey letting him know I was hit just ten minutes previous to him seeing me. I was in the first hospital he called at. He went off this morning with his ambulance car.

I got hit getting our two machine guns back from a trench where our men had left them. I and another man, a Private Adams, did it together and I had to make five or six journeys under bullet and shell fire. A great lyddite landed in the trench when I was there but in a way the dust and smoke was rather a protection. We were

John Alfred Innes of The Greenings

holding the Germans on Tuesday neither side got much ground. Since last Tuesday I've simply been incapable of doing anything and until a day or so ago had to be fed like an infant. How are you all and all the family? Give them my love.

Ever your loving, Evelyn Broadwood.

Evelyn Joan Broadwood and Gerard Theodore Bray just prior to their wedding in 1911

Evelyn Joan Bray (née Broadwood) was the daughter of James Henry Tshudi and Margaret Broadwood and was born in 1886. In 1911 she married Gerard Theodore Bray in Vancouver and at the outbreak of the war she and her husband and children travelled back to England to join the forces. The family went to live with her sister Audrey Innes at The Greenings in Charlwood.

Barbara Marion Craster was the daughter of Edmund C. Craster, a judge in the Bengal Civil Service, and Katherine Margaret (née Broadwood) the daughter of Henry Fowler and Julianna Broadwood. Barbara was born in 1873 in Bengal and was Evelyn Broadwood's cousin. After Edmund's wife died in Bankipore in India in 1874, he lived for a time at Pleystowe which was part of the Lyne Estate on the Newdigate/Capel borders, with his two daughters, Katherine and Barbara and sons John and Herbert. They later moved to the family home in Northumberland. Barbara became a senior member of the WRNS and was a friend of Lucy Broadwood. She died in 1972 at a club for First World War service people in London. She never married.

Bertha Marion Broadwood (1846-1935) was Evelyn's aunt and was unmarried. She was renowned as a pioneer of village nursing care and cottage hospitals.

The Rector, in writing to his parishioners, was very concerned about the increased practice of treating, that is buying drinks for servicemen. This became such an important issue that an Act of Parliament, introducing licensing laws was passed.

The Rectory
October 28th, 1914

My dear Friends,

It would, I suppose, be hardly possible to exaggerate the seriousness or the importance of the battle now being fought in the N.W. of France. Who can count the numbers lost on both sides? It is too sad to think about it. Yet we are most grateful to be able to state that the Allies are holding their ground and in spite of the enemy being reinforced they have not been beaten. We must increase and increase and still increase our Army as greatly and as speedily as possible and render every help we can. The time has come when more of our young men should offer themselves to take their share in the great struggle. Far better to prevent the enemy from coming to England than to engage him when here. The Bishop of London said he would rather die than see England under German rule. For 1000 years our Country has not been stained by the foot of an enemy and it must not be so now. It will not if all do their duty.

I wish to draw your attention to the strong remarks made by Lord Kitchener, the Archbishop of Canterbury and others, respecting the immense harm done by treating men who are training to go to the Front. We know how strictly a man has to train for boating, football and even cricket, but these are nothing compared to what will be required of those who go to the Front. How essential is it then that they should be as fit as possible. I know it is done in kindness, but it is a very mistaken kindness and should be stopped at once. Extra gifts of socks, shirts, scarves, even tobacco and chocolates would be very acceptable and we can show our sympathy by giving these. We regret that the Choral Society will not be able to continue this winter in consequence of there not being sufficient tenors and basses. I am glad to hear the sopranos and altos intend to commence their practices after Christmas, but why should they lose the time before Christmas and allow the other competitors to get greatly in advance of them?

Everyone in Newdigate will read with deepest interest Lieutenant Broadwood's letter. We regret very much to hear of his injury but trust it is not of a very serious nature and that he will soon be better. He is now in the hospital at Boulogne, and when he is well again, will, we hope, be allowed to come to England to gain his strength. Strange to say Mr. Innes was at Boulogne and will be able to comfort his brother-in-law. We wish him every best wish and a very speedy recovery.

I am, your sincere friend, H. G. Bird.

Evelyn Forsyth, another aunt of Evelyn Broadwood, was travelling in Switzerland at the beginning of the war. She wrote to her niece, Audrey, from Hôtel Bellevue et du Parc in Thun on the 31st October 1914.

Dear Audrey,

We get English papers very irregularly and late and it was only last night that Jean and I read in the 'List of Casualties' that dear Evelyn had been wounded! We are <u>much</u> grieved but can only hope that it is not a serious case and that you may soon have good accounts of him. Do let us know by a post-card to, Hôtel Château Bellevue, Sierre, Valais, Suisse (where we are going on November 3rd), how he is going on and where he is. I have addressed a letter to him today to 'The Norfolk Regiment, Expeditionary Force, Armée Anglaise, France' on the chance of its reaching him.

Aunt Lucy wrote lately that you had only heard of him once since the war began, that he had dysentery but was better. Really if his wound is not severe and he is sent home, we shall all <u>rejoice</u> as he has quite fulfilled his duty in the service of English, French and Belgians in their fight for liberty! In one casualty list a month ago I read the names of <u>11</u> men belonging to families of our friends! And I see that young Mrs Oswald Walker is still advertising for news of her husband who was wounded but has not been heard of since mid-August! **(Marcia Eugenia Walker (née Mansel) searched in vain as her husband, Captain Oswald Bethel Walker, died on the 23rd August 1914 whilst serving with the 15th (The King's) Hussars. He was aged 39 and they had married at St George's, Hanover Square in London in 1910.)** – we see French, Swiss and German-Swiss papers and the Italian 'Corriere della Serra' daily. The latter is an excellent paper. The English papers are stale before they reach us – are very one-sided and of course are closely censored. As we gave up our London flat last June we are remaining in this neutral country as I shall not look out for another English house till the war is over and I know how my finances stand! Already one at least of my investments has needed payment, and most people will be much the poorer in consequence of the war all over Europe. Asia "civilised" Africa and America and Australia! We have written many letters but have received very few, and we think that our correspondence is opened and stopped on the way. For the spy-scare is universal. We spent a month in the mountain village of Ehn and returned here early in September and have stayed here because the hotel is so comfortable and we have a suite of three rooms, very cheap! But next week the hotel closes so we are going to join the Perrys at Sierre. Your Aunt Amy was at Ehn and at Thun for some time but is now at Hôtel de Paris in Montreux; we may perhaps ourselves go to Montreux in December. Thun is very beautiful but like all places on a lake, is damp and Jean as well as myself, has had rheumatism. Sierre however is supposed to be one of the driest and warmest places in Switzerland. The snow falls lower on the mountains day by day. Jean has made several pretty sketches from our sitting room window of these same mountains – the Jüngfrau Range – in bright and dull weather. She has also been busy knitting stockings like most of the English women – for the allied troops. We have had two Belgian and two French families here but they don't seem to trouble themselves in that way. But two German ladies who have left, were making stockings for <u>their</u> warriors! At Jeans's London suffrage office they are employing 45 'out of work' women in making 500 shirts by order of the War Office. How many widows and orphans there will be now in all the countries of the belligerents! I hope they will emigrate most of the poor little orphan girls to the Colonies where 'females' are wanted before they are old enough to form friendships in the old country and to feel one tick for England!

Much love from Jeanie and me to you all and to Joan when you write to her.

Your loving Aunt, Evelyn Forsyth

Evelyn Charlotte Broadwood (b.1851) married the barrister, William Edwardes Henniker Forsyth in 1878 and was another of Evelyn's aunts.

Lucy Etheldred Broadwood (1858-1929) was Evelyn's aunt and was a talented musician and famous collector of folk songs. She never married.

Amy Murray Broadwood (b. 1853) was also Evelyn's aunt.

Some 13,500 men were lost at the battles on the Marne and Aisne and on the 5th November the Allied line in front of Ypres lost the Messines Ridge. The French mounted a counter attack with great heroism but they met such withering fire that they had to withdraw. It was not until 1917 that the ridge was retaken by the British and they found rows upon rows of neat skeletons with red and blue tattered cloth still clinging to them, testament to the terrible bombardment which they had faced.

After the First Battle of Ypres, the Western Front froze. The Germans dug in to protect their gains and the allies constructed trenches from the North Sea to Switzerland. By this time British and French reinforcements had arrived and the remnants of the allied forces which had held back the fury of the German attack were withdrawn to take some badly needed rest.

On the 31st October Audrey wrote to her sister, Joan.

Dearest J,

Many thanks for your birthday letter of wondrous length! It was good of you to write such a long one. I enclose a letter to you from Evelyn (sent with a letter to me) the first since he was wounded. I also send you a copy of his to me.

The wound could not have been as slight as John's wire gave me to understand as apparently he was shot through or close to an artery and lost a tremendous lot of blood. He will probably not be moved for a little time. I had a card from Barbara Craster (who is working as a Red + nurse at Boulogne and has seen Evelyn several times) to say that he had to have a slight operation but that he stood it well. I hope now that he will get on all right. He is in the best hospital in Boulogne and in good hands which is a great comfort. In a way it is a great blessing the wound is not too slight as it will prevent him fighting again for a long time one hopes. He seems to have had wonderful luck all through as he has been under much shell and rifle fire. He is to come to England when better, first to a hospital I expect and then I hope to get him here which will be a great joy.

We go to Oakwood on Wednesday and I can come back here ready to receive him at any time. I have heard from John several times. He has been doing a lot of work taking wounded from the trains to hospitals at Boulogne and now he and others have gone nearer the front to work between Field Hospitals and the trains.

Wasn't it wonderful his getting out there just in time to find Evelyn at Boulogne? It has been such a comfort to me to get first hand news of him, and now Barbara can keep me posted up with news. This morning, November 1st, a registered parcel arrived from Halfords and inside was a bar broach, emerald in the middle and diamonds in each side. I imagine it is a birthday present from John! He says he may be able to get home for a bit in about a month's time.

I go to lunch today with the Powells at Goodwyns Place and drive myself over. I was much amused by "Goodness knows" etc! I enclose at last the long promised copy of Evelyn's letter describing the Battle of Mons. Forgive me for not sending it sooner. Will let you know how Evelyn goes on.

Your ever loving, A

The tenants were also concerned and wrote to the family.

> *Bonnetts Farm*
> *Capel, Surrey*
> *Nov. 15th 1914*

Dear Madam,

We were all very sorry to hear Mr. Broadwood, our landlord, has been wounded. We all hope he is better and are very anxious to hear how he is. What a terrible war it is. Hoping you and Mr. Innes and the dear little children are well. Hoping I am not troubling you too much but if you will kindly let me know I should be most thankful to know how Mr. Broadwood is.

Lady Scatton (?) wrote and told me he was wounded and sent on a paper with his photograph in, and said how sorry she was, she has three of her sons at the front.

I am madam, Yours faithfully, E. Stone

Ps. We were pleased to hear you have a little son our news came from Canada.

> *Rhome Wood*
> *Holbrook Route*
> *Near Horsham, Sussex*

Dear Madam

Have you heard any more news about Mr. Broadwood as we have heard that the bleeding from his wound cannot be stopped I know he was prayed for in Newdigate church on Sunday I do hope it is not so bad I should feel very greatfull (sic) if you will kindly just write a line to tell me Oh I do hope and pray all will be well with him also Mr. Innes for I hear he has gone out to help May God watch over them both and all others trusting you are all well.

Believe me your Humble Servant

Annie Holcombe

Annie Holcombe was 26 years old when she wrote this letter. She grew up at Cowix on the Lyne Estate where her father, Charles, was the estate carpenter.

By the 5th November Evelyn was feeling well enough to write to his aunt, Lucy Broadwood.

Thank you ever so much for the three letters, which you have written me since I was knocked out. I have enjoyed them and appreciate all the kind and affectionate things which you say more that you can imagine. I was in a very low way when I got the first hit, now I have picked up so well that I can write a more or less respectable letter and this morning I got back the use of my fingers. You would laugh I am sure if you saw me now and what limbs of myself I can see look like the limbs of those people in the pictures of the Great Indian famine. I have been through a bad time, but I really have had everything in my favour and I have to thank God from the very first for having really given me a miraculous number of consecutive pieces of fortune. I was hit through the thigh, the bullet touching both a vein and an artery!

I had a sharp burning sensation and heard the bullet at the same moment, and turned at once and hopped back round a house corner which was there. I felt myself going and had just time to uncover the place and put my finger tight on the spot to try to stop the frightful draining, shouting all the time for someone to come if there was anyone there (as I had made the last journey alone). There was one man and I at last induced him to come to me which took another 10 to 15 seconds and by that time I was unable to move. I made him tie my leg and thigh up as tight as he could pull and by that time some other men came up and they got me onto a door which had been blown out of the house by a shell. We had been under cover all this time but now they had to take me along a shell swept road. However the shelling stopped just then and I was taken back to the regular stretcher bearers, who immediately carried me back another half mile to the doctor as we had been far out in front. He attended me at once (which is great luck) and sent me off with another doctor and six orderlies all to myself to carry me to the nearest ambulance wagon. Before I was moved however I heard the Colonel ask the doctor next door some questions and the doctor answered in a very low voice and the colonel said 'dear, dear, dear!' – which was rather a cheerful thing to hear!! – and I had a special motor all to myself with a doctor in it and he kept now and then speaking to me. I knew why – Isn't it a ghastly idea! (to see whether E.H.T.B. was a corpse or not!) This is only to show what trouble everyone has been taking.

After successive stages I arrived at Boulogne and was taken to the best hospital with trained hospital nurses and Harley Street surgeons. They had a consultation and called in for his opinion Mr (here Colonel) Makings (?) who is the crack man in all London in this subject and is Consulting Surgeon to all the forces – so royalty couldn't have been better treated. I was rather bad for a day or two after my operation, which was rather a big one, but now here I am after a fortnight alive and cheerful and enjoying life. I cannot move but have plenty to read and the best position in the ward and I can lie and look out into the street and see things passing, and the weather these last few days has been lovely.

This is a more or less private enterprise, though officially recognised of course. It is a hospital got up by Lady Sarah Wilson and others and is a good work. There is accommodation for 200 sick and wounded. This floor contains only officers, I believe.

I've no news except about myself, so you must not mind this letter being about me. I love hearing from relations at home and hearing all the news.

The Colonel mentioned in the letter was Lt. Colonel, later Brig. General Colin Robert Ballard (1868-1941), commander of the 1st Battalion, Norfolk Regiment. His mother, Joanna, and her family lived for a time in the 1890s at Linkfield Lane, Reigate. She then went to live in Cheyne Walk, Chelsea with her brother, Colin C. Scott Moncreif, who was Under Secretary for Scotland, and his wife and daughter.

Lady Sarah Isabella Augusta Wilson (née Spencer-Churchill) was the daughter of the 7th Duke of Norfolk. She married Lt. Col. Gordon Chesney Wilson of the Royal Horse Guards who was killed in action in France on the 6th November 1914. During the Boer War she became the first ever female war correspondent and covered the Siege of Mafeking for the Daily Mail.

On November 10th Lucy Broadwood wrote to Audrey from her London home at 84 Carlisle Mansions in Victoria Street.

Dearest Audrey,

So many thanks for your delightful letter. I had taken a great affection for Colonel and Mrs Ballard already. Do you remember how he reported to his wife on a post-card the well being of 15 officers (including Jack Longfield and Evelyn), how she at his request published the news to their relations? And now comes Col. Ballards' good appreciation of Evelyn's work. How much the more I like him; how proud you must feel! And how proud I feel of Evelyn too!

SMS Emden, a German light cruiser which sank many allied ships and was finally destroyed by H.M.A.S. Sydney at the Cocos Islands in November 1914

I want to send you Evelyn's long letter to me, but John Craster carried it off to Chatham and so I can't. John, Norah and family look plump. They had to wait four days at Singapore because some of their ships crew declined to go further as the 'Emden' was near.

Poor Aunt Bertha! In answer to my <u>very</u> gentle representation that the Boulogne visit would hardly be appropriate, in view of the condition of the common hospitals and serious cases therein, I received a most <u>exceedingly</u> tart post-card, bristling with artillery, at the end of which she proposes to come between 5 and 6 and be preached to by me who 'set myself up to be her mentor'.

However I attend a course of lectures between 5 and 6.30 on Tuesdays, so I shall not be in, and hardly with self-respect <u>could</u> have received her after so violent a card.

When people live quite alone as she does they do become convinced that they alone are right. It is so sad that her great generosity and goodness are often overshadowed by her impetuous ways and words. I hope you are having good news of your John and that he is keeping warmer.

I am so grateful for the beautiful copy of Evelyn's letter.

Ever, dear Audrey, Your loving   Lucy Broadwood.

May I have Barbara's letter back?

Love to the Shearmes

(John Evelyn E. Craster (b.1874 in Bengal) married Norah Eileen Wheatley in 1905. He was the brother of Barbara Craster.)

Major Alfred Herbert Tyler was one of the sons of Sir Henry Whatley Tyler and used to visit the farm at High Trees in Newdigate with his wife and family. The Observer newspaper published the following letter under the headline – The Happy Warrior – "It is Heavenly"

We are permitted to quote the following passages from an officer's letter from the front:-

"Picture to yourself a small three-roomed cottage with a hole made by a shrapnel shell through its tiled roof. The match-boarded ceiling below is pitted with bullets, and some of the rafters are broken. It stands on the edge of a large fir wood, and just across the road the ground is honeycombed with cunningly contrived little holes covered over with earth. There are other similar cottages nearby, some entirely collapsed, and in the ground round are numerous holes made by the fall of the German shells. The door of the cottage bears the legend, ' – Coy., R.E. Officers' Mess,' and on the hearth is a perforated bucket containing glowing embers, which makes up for the windows having no glass in them, and makes the room a palace. There is a constant sound of gun firing on our side, and shells exploding from the other one every half-minute at least during most hours of the day.

Soon we shall have tea, and then as soon as it is dark we shall creep into the before mentioned burrows to wait... When that is over the sappers creep out... dig and improve trenches for the infantry and put them up barbed wire, and generally make themselves useful, returning when they have completed their task to their little burrows. It is heavenly but for goodness sake don't let K know (his wife).

Bi (his nephew) is doing the same thing less than a mile away in the –th Coy., which is the one belonging to this Division... Just back from evening's amusement and about to retire to my bunny-hole. Of course the shells and things sound much more dangerous than they really are. The company has only actually had 20 per cent. casualties to date, including earlier operations."

The writer, Major Tyler, Royal Engineers, was killed in action the next day, November 11, in the great battle of Ypres, and the nephew he mentions, Lieut. Albert Tyler R.E. was killed on the following day, November 12. Major Tyler was a grandson of General Sir Charles Pasley K.C.B., R.E. and one of the nine sons of the late Sir Henry Tyler, three of whom were in the Royal Engineers, three in the Royal Artillery, and one in the Indian Civil Service. Five are serving their country at the present moment.

2nd. Lieut. Alfred Herbert Tyler (Reproduced by kind permission of the Library of the Royal Engineers)

2nd. Lieut. Alfred Herbert Tyler in 1890 – far left (Reproduced by kind permission of the Library of the Royal Engineers)

The author, Frederick Ernest Green (1867-1922) was born in Hong Kong and for a time worked as a shipping clerk. He purchased Barings Field, a smallholding in Cudworth, Newdigate, in 1906 and married Carolina Beane in 1908. He became a prominent letter writer, boldly criticising the agricultural policies of succeeding governments whilst staying aloof from all political parties. He wrote a number of books including *A Few Acres and a Cottage, The Tyranny of the Countryside, The Settlement of ex-Servicemen Etc.* and sold the farm in 1921. He wrote to the Dorking Advertiser and the following was published in the letters column on the 21st November. Clearly the possibility of a German invasion was in people's minds.

The author, F.E. Green in his apiary

... and his men working in the fields at Barings Field

Those of us who cannot enlist owing to our age or to some slight physical disability, or to some strong restraining family tie, feel it our duty to relieve, however little, the tension endured by our brave lads now fighting in France and Belgium. We have no right to calmly accept a life of comparative security and comfort at home without being made to feel ourselves sure of the discomfort, if not the horrors of war. It is clear to most of us that every man now training in Kitchener's Army and the Territorial Forces will join their comrades in arms on the continent next year; and the more those of us who are obliged to remain at home make ourselves efficient by drilling and shooting, the more trained soldiers would the country be able to spare for foreign service. Most of us who have joined the National Volunteer Reserves are married men of early middle age with families. We do not wish to enrol strong young married men who might be expected to enlist, though one can hardly blame them for not doing so whilst the miserable pittance allowed to a soldier's childless widow remains at 7s 6d.

The movement has caught on with great rapidity about Horley, and has spread as far as Newdigate, where a certain amount of drilling and miniature rifle shooting has been performed for some time; but the difficulty with us of Newdigate is that of performing company drills and day marches at Horley, as it is a seven mile cross-country walk before beginning a strenuous day's march. If a company could be formed at Dorking the movement I am sure, would spread with enthusiasm through Capel, Ockley, Beare Green and Holmwood, where rail and motor bus would help to bring men together quickly. Indeed a centre might be formed at Holmwood and route marches performed over Leith Hill, down to Ockley, and back to Dorking along the Horsham road, men falling out at, say, Beare Green for their various village homes.

I cannot understand why a company has not been formed in Dorking, which has a reputation for being a patriotic town with a military tradition, apart from the trenchant fact that Dorking is looked upon as holding a strategic position along the line of the North Downs, and it is of primary importance to us, from a military point of view, to train ourselves for hill fighting. All that men are asked to do is give up a little of their time, say two evenings a week and an alternate Sunday, even that is little enough compared to what our brave boys are enduring at the Front in the cold and wet, day and night, under the pitiless fire of shrapnel.

If anyone will immediately call a meeting at Capel, Holmwood, Ockley or in Dorking, will they inform Mr Brodie Rowe of Hatchetts or myself.

PS. Since writing the above, I have learnt with pleasure that through the activity of Colonel Fisher Rowe, Mr. Aitken, and other gentlemen, a Volunteer Corps, affiliated with the Central Volunteers Association was formed at Dorking this week. I hope this will extend its operations so as to include those living in the villages lying on each side of the main road to Horsham, namely, Holmwood, Newdigate, Capel and Ockley.

W. H. Wilkins, A. W. Dean and A. W. Gibbs were enrolled as special constables at Newdigate. Capt. Alfred William Gibbs RN lived at Hillview (now Darragh House) and was Superintendent of the Sunday Schools. He was born at Portland in Dorset in 1859 and became an engineering student at the Royal Naval College at Greenwich.

Mabel Estelle Winfield lived with her husband Henry Groves Winfield and they had a smallholding at Brook Farm in Cudworth. They used to deliver milk around

the village and serve it directly from the churn. Henry sat on the Parish Council for many years and the council estate, Winfield Grove was named after him in 1947. He died in 1955 and his wife in 1959 and they are buried in the churchyard.

Mrs. Winfield wrote the following letter to the Rector.

Dear Mr Bird,

I should be grateful if you would make it known, through the medium of the Parish Magazine, that I am collecting bandages, pillow slips and linen to send to Calais, the field of action, or wherever most needed, each month during the war.

To those who are able to send bandages – 4-in., 5½-in., and 6-in. in width, and 6-yds in length are the most useful. They should be rolled tightly and fastened with a safety pin. I need not add that they should have no jagged edges and that all should be boiled beforehand, if made of new stuff. Lengths of roller towelling 1½-yards in length, hemmed, are also most useful.

The need of bandages is most urgent. A Doctor's friend, who is working at Calais, writes: "That the wounded arrive with pads of newspapers in their wounds and that garments have to be torn up to bind these wounds." To those who have not time to make bandages I shall be glad to receive either the stuff to make them or the money to get the stuff with. One dozen yards of unbleached calico will make quite a lot. An account will be sent to the Magazine from time to time to acknowledge anything sent and to show where the things have gone. I know that a great many in the Parish are working hard for the comfort of our soldiers and sailors, and I am sure that my plea for this crying need will not go unheard.

Yours sincerely, M. Winfield

Frank A. Clark notified villagers about an appeal for prisoners of war at the Doeberitz Camp (Doeberitz was a military camp with a permanent barracks, eight miles west of Berlin, and was initially used for interned British, French and Russian civilians).

A group of Englishmen at Doeberitz

An appeal has been made by a lady who is a subject of a neutral country living in Berlin, who recently paid a visit to our brave and courageous countrymen who are interned in the Doeberitz Camp as prisoners of war, much to their regret you may be sure. She says they have read and re-read all the English novels which kind-hearted compatriots in Germany sent to the Camp, one man having read the same novel for the eleventh time. So will our Parishioners and other friends in the Village of Newdigate please leave any books of light literature they may at the Post Office, or let Mr. Dean know and they will be called for. Already quite a splendid lot of well-bound novels and magazines have been given, and the collector takes the opportunity of thanking the following ladies and gentlemen for their kindness, viz:- Mrs. Pilbeam, Miss Hackwood, Miss Dean, Miss Bowring, Mrs. J. Rusbridge and Mr. H. Brodie Rowe. Many of us through circumstances are debarred from taking our part in the fighting line, but we can in so many ways help to relieve and cheer the lives of the Tommies who are so ungrudgingly giving their lives for their country's sake – the gift of books is one little way.

On the 27th November 1914 the Surrey Times reported the death of Albert Tyler – Lt. Albert Tyler was the only child of Col. H.E. Tyler R.E. and Mrs Tyler of Guildford. He was killed in action on November 12th.

Lieut. Albert Tyler (Reproduced by kind permission of the Library of the Royal Engineers)

Sir Henry Tyler and Bi at Hightrees Farm in Newdigate

Lieut. Albert Tyler – seated far left (Reproduced by kind permission of the Library of the Royal Engineers)

Lieutenant ALBERT TYLER
11th Field Company, Royal Engineers

Albert Tyler was born at Greenwich on the 1st February 1893 and was the only son of Colonel Henry Edward Tyler of the Royal Engineers and his Irish wife Martha Frances. He grew up at Sandown on the Isle of Wight before moving to Wetherden, Warwicks Bench, Guildford. His grandfather was Sir Henry Whatley Tyler also of the Royal Engineers so he grew up within a family steeped in army tradition. He was educated at Charterhouse School, became a gentleman cadet at the Royal Military Academy at Woolwich and was gazetted 2nd Lieutenant in the Royal Engineers on the 19th July 1912. Known as Bi, he served with the 11th Field Company and on the 26th October 1914 they were assisting the King's in assaulting houses supposed to contain German machine-guns. At 5.20 a.m. this section succeeded in taking four houses on the Paschendaele-Bercelaere road. The company worked through the nights improving trenches but on the 12th November, Lieut. Tyler was killed and his friend, Lieut. Bourdillon was wounded. His name is commemorated on the Menin Gate at Ypres and the Charterhouse Roll of Honour. In his will he left £4032. 3s. 11d.

Alfred with his wife and child

Alfred with his son, Desmond, Aged 9 months

Alfred Tyler and fellow officers

Major ALFRED HERBERT TYLER
Royal Engineers Commanding 5th Field Company

Alfred Herbert Tyler was the eleventh child of Sir Henry Whatley Tyler and Lady Margaret Tyler and was born at High Elms near Hampton Court on the 27th December 1870. Despite being part of a large family he had a privileged childhood and followed the family tradition by joining the Royal Engineers. He was gazetted 2nd Lieutenant on the 25th July 1890 and promoted Lieutenant on the 25th July 1893, Captain on the 25th July 1901 and Major on the 25th July 1910. He took part in the operations in Sierra Leone in 1898/99, the Karène Expedition when he was wounded (Medal with clasp); served in the South African War in 1900-02 as Special Service Officer, Rhodesian Field Force and took part in the Transvaal and Cape Colony operations when he was awarded two further clasps to his Queen's Medal and the King's Medal with two clasps. From the 10th January 1907 until the 25th April 1912 he was 1st Assistant Superintendent Building Works at the Royal Arsenal in Woolwich.

He married Ephrata Anna Kathleen Bremner (known as Kathleen) at the Garrison Church, Roberts' Heights, Pretoria whilst serving in South Africa. The happy couple left the reception in a carriage drawn by four horses with Royal Engineers as outriders. They had three sons and lived in Salisbury and visited his parents at High Trees in Newdigate.

At the start of the war he was based at Aldershot. He embarked for France with the 2nd Division on the 9th August 1914 where his company soon found themselves digging trenches at Mons to cover the retreating British army and offering some help to the hundreds of families who were evacuating their homes. The engineers worked almost non stop for 48 hours and finally slept in a field – weary and dirty.

By September the Royal Engineers were given the job of destroying bridges in order to stall the advancing German army. The 5th Field Company was detailed to blow up the bridge at Le Trilport near Meaux and then marched for nine miles. For three days no rations had been drawn as the supply column had gone missing.

The last two months of 43 year old Alfred Tyler's life were spent in desperate conditions far removed from the regimental finery of Queen Victoria's army. Often the men were up by 3.00 a.m. in the dark, cold and wet constructing barbed-wire entanglements. As fast as the trenches were dug they filled up with water due to the incessant rain and the soldiers were living in constant fear of artillery shells which were exploding all around constantly.

November found the sappers from the 5th Field Company digging trenches near Polygon Wood prior to what later became known as the First Battle of Ypres. The Germans knew that they were there as they fired magnesium flares which lit up the whole area like daytime. The horror experienced by these men was unspeakable and this just under three months from leaving summery England.

By the beginning of November casualties were heavy and fighting was taking place all day. The noise was deafening as they were surrounded by artillery fire, English, French and German. Two officers had been killed and Lieutenant A. R. J. Collins took temporary command of the company. On the 9th November, Major Tyler arrived at Polygon Wood and assumed command of the 5th Field Company.

The Germans intended taking possession of Ypres on the 11th November, the 100th day of the war, and when dawn broke the morning was grey and misty and strangely quiet. But the bombardment commenced in the early hours and by nine o'clock it had grown to a crescendo. When it was lifted the enemy began to stream across the fields.

The Corps History and War Diaries take up the story: For the first ten days of November, the 5th Field Company worked every night on improving the scanty defences. Two small redoubts were made at the corners of Polygon Wood. On the 11th November, at about 9.30 a.m., whilst the company was still bivouacking in the north-west corner of Polygon Wood, not far from the 5th Brigade Headquarters, the new O.C. (Major A. H. Tyler) was informed that the Germans had broken through the 1st Black Watch and the Cameron Highlanders. Sergeant Lethbridge, RE and some twenty sappers were sent to man the trenches on the south side of Polygon Wood, while Major Tyler took the rest of the company southwards into the open, occupying a disused trench and a short length of hedge on the left rear. This trench was enfiladed by enemy fire from the Nonne Bosschen on the right and Lieut. Collins was shot and mortally wounded whilst signalling for reinforcements. The Germans had set fire to a cottage on the edge of the Nonne Bosschen and the smoke from this obscured the view of the sappers in the trench. Also the right flank was in danger, as the Germans in the wood were well behind it. This caused Major Tyler to fall back to a second position, which had a similar right flank trench thrown back, from which Lieut. Gowlland's section, aided by some twenty or thirty infantrymen, was able in their turn to enfilade the Germans. At about 2.30 p.m., the Prussian Guard's attack having been stopped, the 2nd Oxford Light Infantry made a vigorous counter-attack, with two companies, and drove the Guards through the Nonne Bosschen. Seeing this success on his right, Major Tyler ordered his men forward. The company split up into parties; one under Lieut. Gowlland crossed over towards the left and followed a trench down the edge of Polygon Wood; another under 2nd Lieut. H.F. Renny-Tailyour moved across the open, and a third with Major Tyler and 2nd Lieut. N.M. Vibart moved along a communication trench towards the old British front trench. Fire from these parties accounted for about one hundred of the enemy running back outside the Nonne Bosschen. Soon afterwards, Major Tyler and Lt. Renny-Tailyour were killed and several other casualties were caused by heavy machine gun fire from a building on the right. At about 4.30 p.m. the remains of the 5th Company were withdrawn under orders from Brigade Headquarters. During the night the dead and wounded were collected. Major Tyler was buried a quarter of a mile north of the north west corner of Polygon Wood, Lieut. Collins was buried a quarter of a mile south of Polygon Wood and 2nd Lieut. Renny-Tailyour was buried south of Polygon Wood five yards from German trenches. About a quarter of the company had been casualties. The 5th Company gained seven DCMs for its exploits that day – a record for a small unit.

Major Tyler's grave was subsequently lost and his body was never recovered. His name is commemorated on Panel 9 of the Menin Gate and notices appeared in the Times, the Morning Post and the Daily Telegraph. In his will he left the considerable sum of £22,500. 12s 3d. Mrs Tyler moved to Westgate-on-Sea and presented the church with a brass cross and candlesticks which were inscribed to the memory of her husband and are still used to celebrate Holy Communion every week. His name also appears on the war memorials in the church and on the sea front.

Lieut. Collins received lasting fame in 1899 when as a thirteen year old schoolboy he scored the world record cricket score of 628 not out in a junior house match at Clifton College in Bristol.

Lieut. Geoffrey Cathcart Gowlland attained the rank of Captain and died in 1980 aged 95 years.

Alfred Tyler en route to France

Alfred Tyler in France

Souvenirs taken on the 11th November 1914, the day Alfred
Tyler was killed

Alfred Tyler's sons – this picture was recovered from
his body

The Rectory
November 27th, 1914

My Dear Friends,

By God's goodness we have again been spared to enter upon the most solemn season in the
Christian Year when we consider the two Comings of the Lord: First as a child to redeem the
world and secondly as the Judge of mankind. May I express the hope that you will all make an
endeavour to serve God more zealously than you have ever done before? The sad news that we
receive so frequently from the war of so many being taken from us ought to fill us with the deepest
sympathy for their friends and should make us doubly earnest in our own life.

Everyone in Newdigate will feel the deepest sympathy for the Misses Tyler who have lost at
the Front a Brother and Nephew on two consecutive days. We do not grieve for those who have
gone for they are, we are sure, much better off. They were fighting in a just cause and have laid
down their lives for our sakes. Surely we may say "Greater love hath no man than this, that a

man lay down his life for his friends". We do grieve most sincerely for their friends and trust that God will give them strength to bear this great trial which He has laid on them.

I am, your sincere friend, H. G. Bird

On the 28th November Barbara Craster wrote to Audrey Innes from the Hôtel de Paris, Boulogne.

Dear Audrey,

I don't know whether Evelyn was able to write and tell you that he was being sent home. I believe he left yesterday afternoon, but unfortunately I was in bed with a chill and could not go round to say good-bye to him. He had been down on the list to go for three days but had to wait for his turn. As to his further movements you will have to trust to hearing from him. I know he meant to let you know as soon as he arrived in England. I think all the hospital ships go to Southampton, which probably means a temporary rest at Netley, but I don't really know.

You will like to know that I have been hearing high praise of him from his Brigadier-Major, who is brother to one of our number and was here on sick-leave for a few days. Quite by chance we discovered that Evelyn belonged to his brigade and he immediately went to see him, which was the very best thing apparently, as he said Evelyn told him of something that he had been going to report when he was hit and which had been weighing on his mind ever since. He was able to assure him that it didn't in the least matter. He said Evelyn was an excellent officer, and that his Colonel was much attached to him and most grieved when he was wounded. He also said that his running had saved the situation at least once.

I haven't been able to make out quite what the doctors think as to his leg being at all permanently weakened. He seems able to move it alright now, and he said they told him there was nothing damaged that would not heal up, but as the principal artery is damaged I imagine the blood-supply may never be quite so good again, and at any rate the leg is going to be weak for a good time. He seemed pleased at your suggestion of taking a house in London later, but I expect he will have to be in some regular hospital or nursing home for some time yet.

Major Wethaby (his Brigade-Major) thought he seemed nervous and excited still. Personally I have thought him all along less nervy than I should have expected after all he has gone through, but of course one must expect a certain amount of strain, and it may show more as he gets stronger in other ways. He really has been through a very bad time, and probably you will notice the effects more than I as you know him so much better. Do let me know when you hear where he is. I don't suppose he will have the energy to write himself.

We go on with our rest-station at the Gare Centrale. The work of finding the wounded in the trains is very spasmodic, as they come so irregularly, but in between times we find plenty to do fitting up our five railway vans so as to have them all complete if we are moved elsewhere. We have a kitchen, dispensary, staff room (where we sit and have meals) and two stores. The whole thing causes much amusement and interest, and we have many visitors, besides all sorts of officials who come to inspect.

I hope you have good news of John. I hear of him occasionally through Mr Paget.

Love to the Shearmes if you are still with them.

Your affectionate cousin, B.M. Craster

Netley Hospital or the Royal Victoria, overlooking Southampton Water, was opened in 1863 and was a quarter of a mile long. During the war it was manned by the Red Cross and over 50,000 patients were treated. It was demolished in 1966 and only the chapel remains.

Audrey went to stay with her aunt and uncle, the Shearmes at the rectory in Oakwood Hill, and she received a telegram in the afternoon on the 30th November.

Innes, Vicarage, Oakwood, Dorking Arrived yesterday safe 17 Park Lane visiting hours 3 to 5.30. Evelyn

The Parish Magazine of December 1914 kept villagers up to date with the latest news although the details were not always accurate.

... Further news has come respecting Lieutenant Broadwood who is in one of the hospitals in Boulogne. He is very weak from much loss of blood as he was shot right through the leg and close to an artery, but apart from that he is getting on well. He was hit whilst carrying a wounded man from the trenches. All praise to him. He is to come to England when he can be moved. How delighted we should be to get a glimpse of him at Newdigate.

Mrs. E. C.Janson from Newdigate Place has organised the programme for the Newdigate and Charlwood Useful Services Brigade. Drills supervised by Mr. H. Rowland are being held in the schools every Tuesday and hat and armlet badges can be purchased for 2s. 8½d.

A Committee Meeting of the Choral Society was held in the Library, but owing to the inclement weather the attendance was small. A general discussion took place with regard to finance, and the continuation of the Society. The financial statement of the Society shows a deficiency of some pounds, but this has been met by the kindness of the Rector, who is our conductor, and to whom the Society is deeply grateful. We also thank Mrs. Janson, Mrs. Hawkes, Mrs. Palmer and Miss Goldberg for their generous support. It has been decided that owing to the War, which is creating many raids on the members' time, the society should not meet until after Christmas, when it is then hoped that the lady members will compete with their parts in the Leith Hill Musical Festival at which we scored so well in the last competition. A concert will be given after the season in the Schools when it is hoped the proceeds will put the Society on a stronger footing.

Mr. Innes who is the Secretary of the local branch of the Soldiers and Sailors Families Association has gone to the Front in his Car. He is working very hard conveying wounded from the Field Hospitals to the trains.

Henry Rowland (1848-1919) lived with his wife, Mary Ann, at Yew Tree Cottage. He was the Parish Clerk.

The Leith Hill Musical Festival was founded in 1905 by the composer, Ralph Vaughan-Williams, and is still a major event within the musical calendar.

Yew Tree Cottage in Newdigate

Brickyard Cottages – now Kettle's Cottages

Captain Gibbs R.N., the Superintendent of the Sunday Schools, has been called up to be engaged in important work with the Navy.

Raymond Potter, son of Mr. F. Potter of Brickyard Cottages, has secured first prize for general proficiency and second prize for bayonet exercises at Chatham. He was a regular worshipper at St. Peter's, the 1913 billiard champion at the Institute and a member of the Carving class at Newdigate Place.

Congratulations are also in order to R. W. Garman a former member of Newdigate Church choir, who enlisted in the King's Royal Rifles on September 5th and received his sergeant's stripes within a month.

Roland William Garman (b.1895 in Beare Green) was the son of Henry and Jessie Garman and married Eileen Buckley in Guildford in 1926. Henry was the coachman at Arnolds in Capel.

December 6th – Holy Baptism. John Albert French, son of William Birdwood Martin and May Martin

Within the village various organisations and classes were being arranged. Dr. Robertson was teaching principles of First Aid and some of the ladies in the needle class were working more than eight hours a day making articles to send to the soldiers and sailors. A Drum and Fife Band was being formed under the direction of Mr. G. C. Headland, the church sexton, and Mrs. Winfield was collecting bandages, pillow slips and linen to send to Calais. Mrs. Janson had formed the Useful Service Brigade and the Dorking Advertiser printed the following report.

The Newdigate Useful Service Brigade had its first church parade on Sunday, Nov. 29th. Since the formation by Mrs. Janson, whose genius is always showing itself in some shape or form, the Brigade has magnified in importance; a drill master in the person of Sgt. H. Rowland has been engaged by Mrs. Janson, and drilling and shooting takes place in the schools and grounds twice a week, so that it is becoming an efficient body of men, which now numbers forty six members. It has the approval of the Social Service League, the National Service League, Sir Arthur Conan Doyle and local clergy and gentry.

The Brigade mustered on Workhouse Green at 2.15 and looked very fit, spick and span in their khaki hats and conspicuous badges. After inspection they 'formed fours' and with the Newdigate Scouts in front, under Scoutmaster J. A. Steeds, and the Newdigate Service Drum and Fife Band, marched through the village to the strains of 'Onward Christian Soldiers' and 'What a friend we have in Jesus', a body of men and lads that any town might be proud of. The church was filled to its utmost limit, many people being unable to gain admission. The service was conducted by the Rev. H. G. Bird who gave a very useful address. At the close of the service Mrs. Irwine, who possesses a grand musical talent, sang 'Recessional' by Kipling. The Rector also sang 'Send him Victorious'. Miss Maggie Broughton officiated at the organ and played several musical selections with great touch and finish. The service throughout was impressive, and the congregation joined very heartily in singing the old fashioned hymns appropriately selected for the occasion. A collection was taken up in aid of the funds of the local War Disaster Fund. After the service the Brigade formed up in front of the church and proceeded by way of Church Road and New Barn Lane, halting slightly while passing the house of the veteran church warden, Mr. H. Hackwood, who, although confined to his bed, came to the window and saluted the procession as it passed.

At the Workhouse Green the men were dismissed, and then a most pleasant and soul-inspiring afternoon terminated. Mention might be made of the inception of the 'Newdigate Service Drum and Fife Band'. A meeting was called only a week previous to the church parade by Mr. F. A. Clark, at which it was unanimously decided to form a band. The matter was entered into very heartily by all present, and a committee consisting of Messrs. F. A. Clark, M. Hall, E. Powell and H. Rowland was formed. Mr. G. C. Headland, who has a very varied and wide knowledge of band training and conducting, was asked to act as band master, and the band are to be congratulated upon securing his services.

Margaret Broughton was born in Stoke Newington in 1880 and moved to Newdigate with her parents. She lived for a while at Dean House Farm. She was the church organist and gave piano lessons from her new bungalow in what is now known as Underhill Road.

Sir Arthur Conan Doyle (1859-1930) was the author of the Sherlock Holmes stories. He was convinced for some time that war was inevitable and wrote to newspapers urging the Government to make suitable preparations. In 1913 he wrote to the Fortnightly Review concerning untested methods of warfare such as the airship and submarine. At the outbreak of war, and at the age of 55, he tried to enlist and was turned down, but he organised a civilian battalion of over a hundred volunteers. He was given permission to visit the front in 1916 and he said that he would never be able to forget the horrors of 'the tangle of mutilated horses, their necks rising and sinking lying amidst the blood soaked remains of soldiers'. The war was cruel to Conan Doyle. He lost his son, Kingsley, his brother, two brothers-in-law and two nephews.

This initiative in Newdigate was not without its critics and 'A Constant Reader' wrote to the paper anonymously.

I gather from a report of a society in Newdigate called the Useful Service Brigade that the men who form it appear to be under the false impression that the War Office will recognise it as a unit. I learn that three quarters of the membership consists of young men of recruiting age, which would, of course be a quite sufficient reason for the War Office to turn round and say 'We cannot recognise you because we consider the majority of your members ought to be in the Regular Army, and those who are above the recruiting age should be in a recognised volunteers corps, which we consider large enough to form a unit. Such corps are being formed at Horley and at Dorking'. I do not think that Dr. Conan Doyle would approve of the Useful Service Brigade run on the lines of the one formed at Newdigate. I think I am right in saying that he approved of societies being formed to do any useful civilian work in an emergency and not to supplant military organisations.

Sir Arthur Conan Doyle also wrote to the paper.

Windlesham, Crowborough
Dec. 9th 1914.
In your last issue you quote me as approving of the above. So far as I know I have never heard of it. But if it fulfils the conditions which make it eligible for affiliation to the Central Association

of Volunteers Training Corps, then I entirely approve of it, since I am on the committee of that body. The all important condition is that save in most exceptional cases the members of the corps shall be under 38 years of age. If that condition is impinged upon then the Corps is certainly doing harm, not good. One recruit is worth the whole of it from a national point of view.

The controversy rumbled on with Frank A. Clark and H. Brodie Rowe writing indignantly to the paper claiming that Sir Arthur Conan Doyle, 'a man of whom our country has a most profound respect, has a bad memory' but Mrs. Janson sent a request to the paper to set the record straight.

THE USEFUL SERVICE BRIGADE

Mrs. Janson, who is responsible for the above; wishes it to be distinctly understood that she had nothing to do with the description of the Church Parade of the Brigade printed in your edition of December 5th; if she had been consulted beforehand she would not have allowed names to be mentioned without first having asked special permission, or quite such an eulogistic notice, though the men had certainly earned all the praise they had been given. She thinks, however, from the paragraph written by Sir Arthur Conan Doyle that he must have forgotten the interview he accorded her in September, when she certainly understood he approved of the Useful Service Brigade drilling, but advised that members should not be taught to shoot, and were urged to enlist, which advice has been followed.

The names of the men below who have been recruited, who formerly were members of the Brigade, prove that enlistment has been advocated, and though many of the remaining men have rather a youthful appearance, in several cases it is because they are under the age of 17; some are rejected recruits, others the sole bread-winners of their families, and a few have not the inclination to join, though all will gladly render help should emergency arise, as will the rest who are over age. The men are very keen, walk long distances to drill, and under the able and patient instruction of Sergt. H. Rowland, are already fairly efficient, while in connection a drum and fife band has been started by Mr. F. A. Clark, and taught by the sexton of Newdigate Church, who is quite an experienced band master, so that any way occupation is given four evenings a week, and a smart, orderly body of men collected together, many of whom, no doubt, will eventually be pleased to be affiliated to the Central Volunteer Reserve in Dorking.

Recruits enlisted from the 'Newdigate Useful Service Brigade':
Arthur Monk, John Burberry, Stephen Harber and Harry Harber, all Queen's Royal West Surrey Regiment. Chas. Harber – Army Service Corp. Sydney Brett – Royal Army Medical Corps – Raymond Potter – Royal Engineers. William Dentitt, Henry Peake, McQueen, N. Monk – Naval Reserve, G. Wey – Killed in Action, W. Still.

Men of the Useful Service Brigade who enlisted, or offered service and were rejected:
Jack Spiller, Luke Gadd, A. Wooltorton, R. Wooltorton, Ernest Barrett, F. Grundy, George Streeter, Alec Weller.

To show that Mrs. Janson's own family have not been backward her son, G. F. Herron has joined and now instructs the Naval Automobile Reserve, while waiting to go to the Front, in charge of ten men with two Maxim guns and a three pounder, her son W. F. Herron, joined the 4th Cavalry Reserve and is now teaching cavalry recruits at Tidworth and may be sent to reinforce the Dragoon Guards at the Front, her son Kenneth C. Herron tried for the Essex Yeomanry, but was rejected because he had no previous Yeomanry experience, so he is now training scouts; her grandson, Cyril D. Herron (aged 19) is now at Ypres with his regiment, the 2nd Dragoon Guards, 'Queen's Bays'; and her nephew Douglas Fenton de Wend (age 24) late Lieutenant Duke of Wellington's Regiment, was killed in action on November 11th at Ypres.

L.N. Stanborough, Adjt. 8th Heavy Brigade, 8th Division, B.V.E. had received clothing and gifts from Miss Bird (age 24) and he wrote to her on December 11th, 1914.

Dear Miss Bird,

A large sack containing 28 shirts, 8 pairs of socks, 2 helmets, and 2 woollen wraps has reached me, and I could not make out whom it was from till I found your paper with name and address, and also the 2/6 from the old lady in the village. I am now concluding that you are Wilfred Bird's sister, and I am writing to thank you very much indeed for your kind and welcome gift, which is very much appreciated by the men. I think they appreciate the kind thoughts that prompt the gifts, almost more than the gifts themselves; it shows that they are not forgotten, at least that is what I find from looking through the letters which I have to do as a censor. One of the men is writing especially to thank the old lady, and I enclose his letter. We are now living in a thick mist, but the country is not so flooded out as usual at this time of the year, at least that is what the local authorities tell us. The country here is so low that one sees nothing of what is going on, and practically never sees an enemy, except occasional prisoners or spies, though we have experienced a certain amount of shelling; for the last three or four days their guns have been extraordinarily quiet in these parts, possibly getting short of ammunition. The men are very well fed and are very cheery. The infantry in the trenches have the worst time, they have three days in and then three days rest, back in billets. I wish we could make a push here and get on to higher ground.

With very many thanks to you for your kind gift and hoping that some day I may thank you personally

The Royal Victoria Hospital at Netley was sent a parcel and a letter of thanks was duly received.

The Matron acknowledges with very many thanks the beautiful gift of garments so kindly sent by Miss Bird from her village working party. Everything is so acceptable and so warm and well made, the wounded soldiers are always so grateful for the warm garments given to them, and would like to thank the givers themselves if it were possible.

On the 16th December, German cruisers crossed the North Sea and shelled Hartlepool, Whitby and Scarborough. 137 people were killed and 592 injured. This was seen as an example of unscrupulous German aggression which contravened all forms of human decency. Stories of German atrocities in Belgium and France were widespread but an officer in the Lincolns writing to his uncle in Leigh, a village close to Newdigate, probably held a more balanced and truthful view. The Dorking Advertiser précised the letter.

Whilst the Germans had treated this officer well there was another side to the picture. In the village of Chessy, from which the Germans had been driven out, he himself saw quite a young girl with her body slit open from the throat downwards. In the same village he saw a man of 75 with his brains knocked out, and a broken rifle by his side. " In my association with the Germans they have been most humane, gentlemanly and considerate" adds the officer, "I believe the atrocities have been committed by men blind with liquor, and not by the officers in higher authority. I don't believe a word of a lot of the allegations which have appeared".

Corporal Wyatt, age 26, wrote to the rector's daughter, Ethel Bird, on the 19th December.

I am writing to thank you for your kind letter and shirts which I safely received. As you know during the first part of the war such things could not be got but you will be pleased to know we are well looked after now, although we have had a rough time we are not downhearted but are ready for harder times if necessary. The weather is very miserable at present, raining every day. The guns I think are the cause of it. As regards myself, I never felt better or fitter in my life. Everybody thought the war would be over by Christmas, but I had my doubts. As regards news, people in England get more news than we do. We only get news from the papers that are sent out which are generally five or six days old. But only get to know the news of our own little place in the fighting line. One thing I am sure they are a beaten army but are only holding out to do as much destruction as they can.

I hope Mr Bird is in good health and I wish all a happy Xmas. You may be sure we shall make the best we can of it.

I remain, yours sincerely, Corpl. Wyatt

Miss Clark Jones of Bath House sent gifts and tobacco to all who had gone to the front and she received the following letters.

From G. Batchelor in H.M.S. Vernon (This was an establishment which concentrated on torpedo trials and the training, research and development of anti-submarine devices)

I am at a loss to know how to thank you enough as I am a poor hand at writing and we do not have much time. We are out in all weathers sweeping the anchorage at Spithead and the approaches to the harbour for any chance mines that may have managed to get through. We have had some very bad weather here lately, in fact the worst I have seen for a good many years.

Still through it all we have a great deal to be thankful for. There are a great many poor chaps worse off than we are and we must not grumble as it is for a just cause and the defence of home and country. Again thanking you very much for your kindness and trusting you are keeping in good health, I must close with the hopes of a speedy termination of the war and down with the Kaiser.

From Pte. T.R. Bourne
Thank you very much for the kindness in sending me those cigarettes which I received quite safely.

From Sapper Anthony Potter of the Royal Engineers
Thanks for the gifts. It was most kind of both of you and the good old village. Hope I can soon be back to see you.

Postcards were the most popular and efficient means of communication

From Purdey Johns, Liscard
Thank you for the socks. It is very kind of you.

From Geo. Hudson, 9th Batt. Queens
I am very pleased indeed with your present you have sent me.

From Arthur Still, HMS Lynx, 4th Destroyer Flotilla
Thank you for the box of cigarettes which I was very pleased to receive this morning; you may be sure they will be very acceptable.

From Pte. R.F. Potter, R.W.S.
Just a line to thank you for the cigarettes. It is very good of you I am sure, to think of us poor soldiers. Of course, they will be very nice smokes after being packed by such charming young ladies.

From G. Monk
I am writing you these few lines to let you know I am getting on fine and I hope you are the same. Thank you very much for the box of cigarettes you sent us.

Military Appointments – 3rd Battalion, Queen's Royal West Surrey Regiment – Francis Shorland Ball, Lieutenant.

Francis Shorland Ball was born on the 6th December 1879 in Lancashire and married Ada Ethel (Flossie) Goldberg of the Red House, Newdigate in 1909. They lived at 17 Chester Terrace, Eaton Square, London SW1. He was promoted to the rank of captain, was gassed and became a prisoner of war.

Leslie and Francis Shorland Ball in a 20 hp Lanchester in 1909

Francis Shorland Ball

With the approach of Christmas, Princess Mary, the seventeen-year-old daughter of George V and Queen Mary, came up with an idea to provide the troops and the sailors with a special gift. Money was raised through public and private funding and 500,000 embossed, brass 'Princess Mary' boxes containing a combination of a pipe, lighter, 1oz of tobacco and twenty cigarettes were distributed. In sections across the Western Front, soldiers of both sides fraternised and exchanged food and souvenirs. This caused much concern at headquarters and was never allowed to happen again.

Much has been written about the Christmas truce but this letter which appeared in one of the English papers from 2nd Lieutenant A.R. Sinkinson of the Lancashire Fusiliers describes the event.

The sight of Germans wandering about in front of their trenches made our men itch to do likewise, and, finally, though it was strictly against orders, one or two of our men got out and met the Germans half-way and exchanged newspapers or cigarettes. In order to put a stop to a situation which was proving impossible, on Christmas morning we received orders not to shoot unless it was absolutely necessary. This injunction seemed to "wireless" across to the Germans, for they stopped sniping altogether, and an unearthly stillness reigned over the scene. This, coupled with the fact that it was actually not raining or snowing, proved too much for the patience of the men, and in a short time we had the unwanted spectacle of the entire personnel of the rival trenches standing on their respective parapets waving and shouting at each other. I need hardly tell you what a relief it was to everyone; it was not war, but it was certainly magnificent. Later on the Germans obtained permission to get out into the debatable ground and collect three of their dead for Christian burial. I went out myself after a time with a copy of 'Punch' which I presented to a dingy Saxon in exchange for a packet of excellent cigars and cigarettes. I explained to him that it was verboten (I talked to him in his own tongue) for our men to come out, and wished him a Merry Christmas, whereupon he gave me a smart military salute and withdrew. As I walked slowly back to our trenches I thought of Mr. Asquith's sentence about not sheathing the sword until the enemy be finally crushed. It is all very well for Englishmen living comfortably at home to talk in flowing periods, but when you are out here you begin to realize that sustained hatred is impossible. Of course it will all break out again, but at present we are enjoying a kind of truce till New Year's Day. When we were relieved on the 28th we were quite unmolested by snipers.

Christmas came and for the folks at home not so much had changed. The shops were full and there was plenty of food for everyone, even luxuries were available. This was the landmark that everyone looked forward to in August – 'it will be over by Christmas'. The war was just beginning, but for one young Newdigate lad, Sidney John Burberry, it was already over. The Dorking Advertiser of December 26th, 1914 printed this obituary.

The realisation of the horrors of the terrible European War which is now raging with so much wanton destruction and brutality and with such unthinkable consequences, comes home very vividly to us when we hear that it has reached the very threshold of a home in our village, in the death of Sidney John Burberry, a lad of only 19 last July, who has succumbed to his wounds, another victim sacrificed on the altar of that vile monstrosity, nay demi-god, the German Kaiser. Poor 'Jack' as we called him, was well known to all in the village. A lad in the flower of his youth, he was one of the first in the village to obey his country's call; he unhesitatingly, with his bosom chum, Arthur Monk, toed the line whilst ones with a sense of timidity held back. Jack had a quick ear and a sure eye and his intelligent disposition soon gained him a place in the ranks of the fighting line in the Queens. Unhappily the circumstances that surround his death and the place where he was killed are not known; he died on November 21st, 1914.

On the battlefield of life he only ranked as an ordinary soldier, just doing his bit to stem the onrush of the Uhlans, but in death he ranks with the highest officer in the Army who has shared his fate. To him the village owes an everlasting debt of gratitude for taking part in preventing the people of these islands from the same mutilation as has been meted out to the plucky little Belgians. Our deepest sympathy goes out to Mr & Mrs Burberry and to the brothers and sisters – a family much respected by all Newdigate.

(The Uhlans were an elite corps of light cavalry originally armed with lances)

Harriett & Sidney Burberry outside their home at Woodshill Cottage in Newdigate   *Two pals – Jack Burberry & Arthur Monk*

25th December 1914, and the little church at Newdigate was beautifully and tastefully decorated for Christmas, and the services were extremely bright, though in consequence of serious losses in the village the choir and congregation were small. The number of communicants, however, was in excess of former years.

With Christmas over the Rector quietly retired to his study. Two years had passed since his wife had died and he had one son in the army and another mentally retarded and in an institution. He was comforted by his two daughters but the news was bad. He was worried about the former schoolmaster, Mr. Hackwood, and details had just arrived concerning the death of Jack Burberry.

Private SIDNEY JOHN BURBERRY, L/10692
2nd Battalion, The Queen's
(Royal West Surrey Regiment)

Sidney John Burberry (or Jack as he was known) was one of the very first young men from Newdigate to enlist. He was born in 1895 and grew up at Woods Hill Cottage where he lived with his elderly grandparents, William and Fanny Lapworth, and his brother and sister. He became a baker's assistant but joined up at the outbreak of the war and by November he found himself in the trenches at La Boutillerie. He died on the 21st November 1914. According to the regimental diaries the day had been spent improving the fire trenches and making racks for rifles which was very important as they so easily became clogged by mud.

No-man's land at La Boutillerie (Ref. Q49102) Reproduced by kind permission of the Imperial War Museum

Strangely just two men were reported as wounded that day but Jack was killed and his body was never found. He is remembered on the Ploegsteert Memorial. The memorial reads 'To the glory of God and to the memory of 1147 officers and men of the forces of the British Empire, who fell fighting in the years 1914-1918 between the River Douve and the towns of Estaires and Furnes, whose names are here recorded but to whom the fortune of war denied the known and honoured burial given to their comrades in death'.

The Rectory,
December 28th, 1914.

My dear Friends,

We must all of us regret most deeply the illness of Mr. Hackwood who you have known so well for so many years. We hope that God may spare him to us for some years yet. It was a great shock to us on Sunday morning to hear of the death of Mrs. Trow, who had been ill for such a short time and we feel the deepest sympathy for all the members of the family. We have also had our first loss from the war. Sidney John Burberry was one of the first from this parish to enlist and joined the Queen's West Surrey Regiment. During his training he quite distinguished himself and so was sent to the front earlier than some others who enlisted at about the same time as he did. We wish to offer our deep sympathy to the members of his family and trust they will be comforted by the thought that he died for his Country and Home.

With every best wish for the New Year.

I am, yours most sincerely, H.G. Bird

Kate Trow (née Weller) lived all her life in Newdigate. She married James Trow, a bricklayer, when she was 18. She was 49 when she died suddenly in 1914.

Mrs Trow and her daughter outside their home at Reffolds

For many years the school children had been entertained at Christmas time at The Red House by the Misses Goldbergs and this year was no exception. Their father, the eminent solicitor Leopold Goldberg was Prussian although a naturalised British subject. He moved to London although his daughters remained in Newdigate.

The Red House – The home of the Goldberg family

The interior of the Red House

A most delightful tea was given on December 30th by the Miss Goldbergs of the Red House to the children attending Day School. In addition to the excellent tea, which needless to say was much enjoyed by the dear ones, every child received one or more presents. We are very much obliged to the Miss Goldbergs for their great kindness. Very hearty cheers were given when they left the room.

1915

There was still much enthusiasm for the war and people were ever more convinced that the Germans had to be defeated. Dorking had become pretty much a garrison town and one 12 year old lad wrote a poem for the paper.

> *Our Dorking was a dull old town*
> *Until the soldiers came our way,*
> *But now the streets are bright and gay*
> *Because of all the lads in brown.*
> *For when they swagger up and down*
> *All very eager for the fray*
> *And they, we hope, will win renown*
> *Upon the all important day.*
> *Trade was dull, and often nil*
> *Before the soldiers made it bright*
> *And shopmen have a bulging till*
> *From early morning till late at night.*
> *And many a pretty Dorking maid*
> *Has lost her heart I am afraid.*

The days of January and February 1915 were generally unproductive and the months passed absorbing thousands of newly trained troops into position. The advantage lay with the Germans who had gained the higher ridges and the best that could be hoped for was to hold the ground already occupied. It was at this time that the 'raid' was increasingly employed. This often meant the loss of officers and men with the sole result of 'putting the wind up the enemy' and keeping him tied to his position. The British public heartened to the news of the so-called victory at the Battle of Dogger Bank on the 24th January. Owing to poor communications the three German battle cruisers escaped leaving only the blazing Blücher to her fate.

There was much excitement for the Newdigate schoolchildren on the 14th January. The school log reports:

A biplane having descended in a field close to school, the teachers took the children out for a closer inspection of the machine during the morning. After taking on board fresh supplies of petrol and oil, the airman again ascended, flying in the direction of Aldershot.

The Rector, in his first communication of the New Year, wrote about T. M. Quartley. 2nd Lieut. Thomas Warner Quartley was actually killed on the 15th January 1915 whilst serving with the 3rd Battalion King's Own (Royal Lancaster Regiment) attached to the 2nd Battalion South Lancaster Regiment. He matriculated from London University in 1914 and was in fact 18 years of age when he was buried at the Wulverghem-Lindenhoek Road Military Cemetery. His father, Selwyn W. Quartley, was a doctor in Harley Street and a friend of the Broadwood family.

The Rectory
January 26th, 1915

My dear Friends,
Everyone will feel most deeply the loss the Parish has sustained by the death of their old friend, Mr Hackwood, who for so many years had taken the greatest interest in everything connected with the welfare of the Church and Parish. He will be sadly missed by all.

May I also add how much we sympathize with the friends of the late T. M. Quartley, who received his commission lately and was killed in action on January 14th. He had probably only reached the front about Christmas Day, so that only a little more than a fortnight was spared to him in the fighting line. He was an unselfish nice lad and only 19 years of age and we can only think of him as being better off in God's Kingdom above.

Before the issue of the next Magazine we shall have entered upon the Season of Lent which I most sincerely hope will be better spent by us than ever before. We are told of the wonderful impression made by the war on our soldiers at the Front — of the hundreds and hundreds who receive Holy Communion Sunday after Sunday and of the prayers offered up in the trenches. Can we say there has been a considerable change for the better over those who are left behind? I feel not and to me it is a great grief that whilst the war is raging abroad many here are quite indifferent and care so little! The Day of Intercession was fairly well observed in this Parish but why could not every one have made a point of being present at one at least of the services to supplicate Almighty God for a cessation of this awful war?

Miss Bird gave the children attending her Sunday School class a charming tea on January 4th. In addition to the tea Father Christmas came and brought such an abundance of presents that every one again had something to take home. Surely the Newdigate children ought to be exceptionally good for in my experience which is of very long duration I have never seen nicer treats.

With every good wish, I am, dear people,
Your Sincere Friend, H.G. Bird.

Following the death of 2nd Lieut. Quartley his commanding officer, Major W. F. Sweny, Royal Fusiliers, O.C. 2nd South Lancashire Regiment wrote to Beatrice Ferard at Ockley Lodge.

Dear Miss Ferard,

I am more than sorry to have the sad duty of thanking you for sending out the oil for Mr Quartley's Machine Gunners.

It was in keeping with the rest of his conduct here that he should have gone out of his way, even to the extent of getting his friends to share his efforts, to have made every effort to ensure the efficiency and comfort of his men. He was such a keen boy and always cheery, it seems hard to realise that he has gone from this short life. He came to this Battalion when officers were much needed and very scarce and did most splendid work the whole time, and no doubt his keenness led to his being taken so soon. He was going down to superintend the work which was necessary in his Trench, owing to the enemies enfilade or flanking fire when, in his haste or interest, he forgot to take cover at a bend and the sniper found his mark. He died quite peacefully shortly after, never regaining consciousness, having been hit through the top of his hat. He was buried near where he fell and a cross was put up marking his grave. He was very popular with his men and absolutely fearless under fire and therefore a fine leader.

The Dorking Advertiser printed the following notices:

Henry Hackwood

January 16th – Death of Mr. Hackwood – We regret to report the death, which took place on Thursday afternoon at Newdigate, of Mr. Henry Hackwood, the veteran schoolmaster. The news of his demise will be received by his many pupils and colleagues in this part of the country with genuine regret, and nowhere will his death be more lamented than in the parish of Newdigate, where among all the classes of parishioners, he was held in the highest esteem and respect. Mr. Hackwood had been schoolmaster at Newdigate for some forty years and had long accepted the office of Churchwarden. He leaves two sons and one daughter to mourn their loss. The funeral is fixed to take place on Sunday afternoon, the cortege leaving the house at 3.30 p.m.

January 23rd – Henry Hackwood Obituary – On the 14th January a biplane which was out with others scouting for a German aircraft of some kind, settled for the night at the rear of Mr. Hackwood's cottage. The next morning practically the whole of the village turned out to view it. It remained in the field all morning and it was remarked how Mr. Hackwood would have gloried to have been there and what an honour he would have thought it to have entertained and given his hospitality to the lieutenant-commander and his sergeant. At twelve o'clock the biplane was ready to fly. It seemed the harbinger of death, for as it flew away the spirit of the dying man went after it in quick succession.

The parish magazine published the following letter:

January 21st, 1915

It is with gratitude that I write to thank those who have so generously responded to my appeal for bandages, and through whose aid I have been enabled to send two boxes of bandages, shirts, and linen, to the "Sophie Berthelôt Hospital" for wounded Belgian soldiers, at Calais. Dr. Cecil Hewer, who is one of the surgeons there, has come across some very sad cases; what has struck him so much is the touching way in which the poor fellows place themselves entirely in his hands for operations in such a confiding way, they are so brave and grateful. Dr. Hewer thinks we little understand how awful are the scenes abroad, and how thankful we should be to have even a roof over our head. He also says that one hears of many getting blessing at this terrible time and that for this one should be thankful to God.

I am anxious to continue sending bandages etc. each month and shall be glad of any help. I append a list of names of those whom my warmest thanks are due.

M. Estelle Winfield

Mrs. Ted Butcher, Mrs. Gadd, Mrs. Clarke Jones, Miss Bird, Miss Seward Hill, Miss Jones (Cudworth Gate), Miss Bankes, Miss Herron, Mrs. Middleton, Mrs. Coomber, Mrs. Janson, Mrs. Palmer, Mrs B. Rusbridge, Miss Sedgewick, Mrs. Wooltorton, A Widow.

At about this time, Maud Fortescue Sutton-Pickard, a 35 year old Red Cross Nurse with the British Troops, describes this hospital in her book 'France in Wartime'.

The next place I visited was the Sophie Berthelôt Hospital which is situated in the rue Gambetta, in the St. Pierre part of the town. It is one of the most interesting hospitals in Calais. The first floor belongs to the Dames de France and is quite separate from the second floor which is run by the English. Both floors are devoted exclusively to Belgian and French wounded. The British section is immaculately clean with snow-white walls and cheerful crimson blankets. The matron, Miss Cauldwell, told me that the orderlies and assistants are voluntary workers, English bank clerks and city men who gladly give their services for the wounded Allies, often sacrificing good positions to do so. Tea, which was quite a friendly meal, was served in the dining-hall downstairs, the nurses sat on the other side, quite like a Quaker meeting, except that there was a distinct atmosphere of cheerfulness pervading the place.

Many pupils at the Newdigate School were unable to attend owing to heavy snow storms which fell on the 24th and 25th January leaving the roads practically impassable.

A soldier wrote home to say that he had only had two cigarettes in five days and the editor of the Dorking Advertiser was moved to set up a fund. He published the following advertisement illustrated with a cheerful artillery man happily puffing away on a pipe as the guns were pounding.

Smokers Advertisement

The shopkeepers Alfred and Selina Dean had two daughters, Lilian and Susan. One of them had arranged for parcels to be sent for the troops and the following letter was published to illustrate how deeply the gifts were appreciated.

> 6, Visrue Brizeur
> Guimper
> 8th Janvier 1915

Dear Mademoiselle,
I have just received a parcel containing four good shirts, two pairs of socks, one pair of mittens, one pair of cuffs, and twelve bandages. I thank you from the bottom of my heart for your great kindness. My dear soldiers will be glad to wear these warm and comfortable garments.
With deep gratitude and the best of good wishes.
Fanny Jones.

The rector had received a letter from Margaret Lucy Tyler thanking him for the note he had sent sympathising most deeply with her and her sister in their great affliction following the deaths of their brother, Major Alfred Herbert Tyler, Royal Engineers on the 11th November 1914, and their nephew, Lieut. Albert Tyler, also of the Royal Engineers, who died the following day.

Sir Henry & Lady Tyler inspecting their new reaping maching

High Trees – the country home of the Tyler Family

Dear Mr Bird,

So many thanks for your kind sympathy in our sorrow. 'The best of two generations' was what one of the brothers says. But both did their duty and died the ideal death, in the best of health and happiness, without suffering; and for home and country – to save us from things too bad to be written. In each case the infantry had been driven in and the Engineers were sent to retake the trenches which they did, and in that case they died in the moment of victory. It was the Prussian Guard attacking when eleven German Army Corps were sent against our one army corps – just the pick of their troops – 550,000 men. We were said to have accounted for 100,000 of them in four days' fighting!

Yours Truly, M.L. Tyler

The population was moved by stirring events from the front and not only did most of the soldiers die painlessly, (courtesy of Commanding Officers, not wishing to add to the stress already felt by grieving families) but events were being grossly exaggerated as can be seen from Margaret Tyler's letter. The stories about alleged German atrocities to the Belgian population would not abate.

Maud Sutton-Pickhard was warned by a senior doctor that he had never seen any evidence of the widespread cruelty exacted by the German troops – only what would normally be expected at wartime. However, she was moved to write the following after meeting an Irish soldier who told the following story from his own observation:

When in Belgium he and another man had taken their horses to water, and while engaged in this occupation they saw two white objects among the bushes in the distance. At first they were puzzled and wondered if some dead soldiers had been robbed of their clothes by ghouls. Suddenly it dawned on them that the white objects were a couple of women, as the narrator expressed it: "I said to meself 'they do be faymales I believe!' His friend refused to go and see, saying as an excuse that he was a single man. But my Irishman replied that he was married and the father of three, "two boys and a lass"; so giving the other man his horse, he started to investigate. He said quite simply, "I went for the love of God." (I was quite touched at this quiet reverence of a humble sincere soul.) The white objects turned out to be two young Belgian girls whom the Germans had outraged and stripped of all their clothing, carrying off the latter, so that the unfortunate creatures would have nothing with which to cover themselves. The poor girls were frightened and tried to crawl under the bushes when we came near, so he went back and got his Captain, who spoke French, and the latter brought them clothes and heard their wretched tale of abuse by over a dozen Germans! (It seems too dreadful to contemplate) The beasts tore off their beads and other medals that Roman Catholics wear, and outraged them while they held a loaded revolver to each poor girl's head. The unfortunate victims were in a pitiable condition of shock and collapse. The good Captain finally found some Belgian relatives with whom to place them.

Parish Council Meeting – Wednesday, 20th January 1915

Present: F.G. Rose (Chairman), A. Dean, G.J. Butcher, W. Greenfield, H.G. Winfield. (R. Rusbridge, clerk)

A vote of condolence was passed in silence expressing deep sympathy for Miss Hackwood in her bereavement. The great loss which the Council has sustained in the death of the Chairman, Mr. Hackwood.

Letter received from Mr. Clark Jones complaining of the hedge overhanging in the bridle road leading to Home Farm.

The clerk was instructed to write to Messrs. White & Sons calling their attention to the state of the stiles leading through the Bookhouse Meadow.

DR. MARGARET LUCY TYLER,
M.D.BRUX., L.R.C.P., L.R.C.S. EDIN., L.R.F.P.S. GLAS.
(1859 – 1943)

Margaret Lucy Tyler was the fourth child of Sir Capt. Henry Whatley Tyler (1827-1908) and Lady Margaret Tyler (née Pasley) and grew up within a large family which had a long army tradition.

Her father was born in Mayfair on the 7th March 1827 and after passing through the Royal Artillery Academy at Woolwich he joined the Royal Engineers in 1854. He was stationed in St. Lucia in the West Indies, where he became a corresponding member of the Zoological Society, he sent species to the Society and had papers published. Many of his specimens were used at the Great Exhibition of 1851 and he was given the responsibility for assembling the prospectuses. He donated a sixteen volume set in 1860 to the State Library of Victoria in Australia. The specimens were later used for the initial exhibits at the Natural History Museum. He remained in Government service until 1877, his last post being that of Inspector of Railways under the Board of Trade, a position he held for twenty-four years, during which time he was sent to inspect railway systems in France and Italy, with a view to the adoption of Brundisi for the Indian mail. After he retired from Government service his skills were in great demand by other countries and he travelled as far afield as Panama and Peru, for which the New York Times reported that he received 'almost fabulous fees'. He served as President of the Grand Trunk Railway of Canada for eighteen years, Chairman of the Westinghouse Brake Co., The Peruvian Corp., The Rhymney Iron Co., and Deputy Chairman of GERC. He became Member of Parliament for Harwich (1880-1885) and then Great Yarmouth (1885-1892).

He married Margaret Pasley (1826-1912) at Kensington in 1852. Her father General Sir Charles William Pasley (1780-1861) was born in Eskdalemuir in Dumfries and learned Latin, Greek and French at an early age. He was commissioned into the Royal Artillery in 1797 but transferred to the Royal Engineers in 1798. He served in the British Army for over fifty years and introduced a course in military engineering which developed into the School of Military Engineering at Chatham. He was appointed Inspector General of Railways on the 2nd December 1840.

Margaret's brother, Major General Charles Pasley (1824 – 1890) was commissioned into the Royal Engineers in 1843 and served in Canada and Bermuda. In 1851 he too was on the staff of the Great Exhibition but was posted to Australia where he was involved in quelling the unrest at the Ballarat goldfield. He was an official nominee of the Legislative Council in Melbourne and was involved in many of the new works projects such as the Parliament House and the Victoria Barracks many of which reflected his own personal taste whereby he favoured using local materials and encouraging local designers. He became superintendent engineer of the naval dockyard at Chatham at a time when it was undergoing major extension work. He retired from the army in 1881.

Following Henry's marriage to Margaret they lived at Wivenhoe Hall in Essex which Margaret Lucy described as 'an old Domesday Book house'. It was demolished in 1929. Just after 1878 the growing family moved to High Elms at Hampton Court and then on to Pymmes Park at Edmonton before moving to Linden House in Highgate which was a substantial house requiring a large staff. In 1898 they bought High Trees Farm and other properties in Newdigate

Margaret Lucy Tyler

to use as a country retreat. They substantially modernised the house and were said to have had one of the first motor cars in Surrey. In 1905 Sir Henry donated £500 towards the organ fund and to enlarge the vestry at the church and a plaque recording this event can still be seen. He died in 1908 leaving effects to the value of £162,000 and Lady Margaret died in 1912.

They had a very large family consisting of Amelia Charlotte (1854-1934), Lt. Col. John Charles Tyler, Royal Engineers (b. 1855) whose son 2nd. Lt. John Collett Tyler, Royal Artillery, was killed in 1915, Maj. Henry Edward Tyler, Royal Engineers, (b. 1856) whose son, Lieut. Albert Tyler, Royal Engineers was killed in 1914, Margaret Lucy Tyler (1859-1943), Madeleine Georgina Tyler (1861-1939), Charles William Tyler, Royal Artillery (b. 1863), William Pasley Tyler (b. 1864), Edward Ernest Tyler (b.1865), Brig. Gen. Arthur Malcolm Tyler, Royal Artillery (1866-1950), Brig. Gen. James Arbuthnot Tyler, Royal Artillery (1867-1945), Major Alfred Herbert Tyler, Royal Engineers (1871-1914) and Hector Granville Sutherland Tyler (1872-1941) who was with the Indian Civil Service and became Secretary to the Governor of Agra and Oudh in 1902. Twelve children in all.

Margaret Lucy studied medicine, she graduated as an M.D. in Brussels in 1893 and was first registered in England on the 30th July 1903. She took an early interest in homoeopathy and recalled that her Scottish grandfather, Sir Charles Pasley K.C.B. became a very keen homoeopath because he was a man of rare intellect and his life had been saved by Lachesis (a snake poison) when he was desperately ill with pneumonia. She also said that her mother and father were keen homoeopaths and described how her mother had saved the life of one of her children. He had been suffering from broncho-pneumonia and was supposed to be dying. The doctor had been unable to relieve the symptoms and her desperate mother 'came in with her wee globules of Ant. Tart. – that marvellous remedy for little children and old people, when the lungs are filling up, and the end is near. When the doctor returned a few hours later, the change was so amazing. That infant survived to command the Heavy Artillery of one of the Divisions in the Great War, and homoeopathy in the nursery saved a Brig. General for the nation's hour of life and death struggle.'

Sir Henry donated large sums of money to extend the London Homoeopathic Hospital in London and said to his daughter, 'I have done my part in enlarging the hospital – you must do the rest!' At the outbreak of the war she was Assistant Physician at the London Homoeopathic hospital and continued working there for nearly all the rest of her life. She declared that the out patients department was the happiest place of her life where she always looked forward to meeting her friends (as she termed her patients).

She had an able pen though she declared that she wrote with great difficulty and much correction. The novels 'Lost Identities' and ' Miss Lydd' and the drama 'Anne Boleyn' were written by her and this was one of her early poems:

IN ONE IMAGE; AFTER ONE LIKENESS!

The whispering corn is crisp and golden now;
And deeply laden, every crimson bough.
Earth yields to man her store – her gift from Thee! –
We take it meekly, Lord, on bended knee.

Each flower that sunward lifts a fragrant face
Exhales her thanks, in perfume, colour, grace;
These are Thy creatures, all; to Thee they raise
By perfect life, the perfect Hymn of Praise.

But we, too, Lord, are Thine; and more is ours
Than lavished by Thy love on grass and flowers:

Lord of the Harvest, Thee, we too, would bless,
But from the depths of our unworthiness.

For we have smirched Thine image very sore,
Until it praises Thee on earth no more;
In us, Thyself Thou can'st no longer see:
How shall we yield our harvest unto Thee?

We'll crowd Thy courts with flowery loveliness;
Thy works shall praise Thee, in Thy Holy Place;
While, kneeling lowly, in our humbler ways,
We give Thee penitence in lieu of praise.

After the end of the Boer War she wrote the following verses with shades of the pain to follow in just twelve years time.

'War and Peace'
'By their fruits ye shall know them'

1899
Of Peace we prated still:
We feared to break her sway.
War in each heart, and lust to kill –
How could peace stay?...
Or, was she ever Peace, except in name ? –
All hearts consuming in the battle flame.

Peace! – these, in arms, that fear
An hour of vengeance nigh;
That brag, and goad and jeer,
And sting with tyranny,
A grim, Imperial, trampled foe;
Teeth-set to avenge his shame and woe...
These spit! Those curse! –
Lord God of Hosts, can war be worse?

Peace lost, we prate of War,
Daring to brand her 'sin?'
From boom and crash recoil with awe,
Scared by the murd'rous din!

All eyes averted, every visage pale,
For death, and trickling wound, and widow's wail.

Yet – Self and Pelf forgot,
Virtues grow queenly, where
Earth cowers beneath the stinging storm of shot,
While Heaven is deaved with prayer!
And angels smile where pity masters strife;
And greatest love for friend lays down his life!

And noble foeman heaps on wounded foe
The tenderest care...
Can He, the 'Captain of the Host' (you know)
Himself be there?
Spittings and curses cease!
Driven on the very blast of War, He sends His peace.

1902
Up! greet the promise of a wider Peace,
Daughter of War!
She bids the ancient, sullen scorn to cease;
She will establish, for all time, the Law.
Peace (thin-masked war) is dead! War too shall cease!
He wields the battle thunders Who is *Prince of Peace*.

According to the Medical Register, Margaret remained at Linden House until at least 1923 but by 1927 she had moved to 23 Welbeck Street, London W1. From 1932 to 1942 she was the editor of the Journal of Homoeopathy which had a world wide influence. In an issue of the American journal, Homoeopathy Recorder, she was described as 'one of the grandest, greatest and most beloved of teachers and workers of the day'. In 1942 she published Homoeopathic Drug Pictures which dealt with homoeopathic remedies, culled from every possible source, and it became standard reading for students.

Margaret Tyler and her sister Madeleine loved to retreat to their country house at High Trees, and she felt deep affection for the people of Newdigate. She died on the 21st June 1943 and an obituary written in the British Homoeopathic Journal by Sir John Weir KCVO read as follows:

Behind the physician was the woman who was deeply imbued with the ultimate religious values of life. In that spirit she did her work, trusted and respected by many, for her fine character, personal integrity and complete lack of all selfish ambition. She will rank with that good Victorian company in which we honour the name of many richly endowed adventurous souls who saw 'the future in the instant' and clung to their faith and, for right or wrong, brooked no interference in their concept. Despite failing health she worked to the very end, and died in service. It is typical that almost her last quotation was 'At the end of life we shall not be asked how much pleasure we have had in it, but how much of service we gave to it; not how full of success, but how full of sacrifice, not how happy we were, but how helpful we were.'

With Germany committed on two Fronts in January 1915 Sir John French wrote to the War Office: 'In view of numbers and German commitments in Russia, it seems of the utmost importance that we should strike at the earliest possible moment with all our strength'.

Having been marooned in defensive positions for the winter the soldiers were keen to launch an attack and get out of their own sodden trenches. Intelligence reports suggested that the German forces were at their most vulnerable at Neuve Chapelle. This was a logical target because once the village had been taken then the Aubers Ridge, which protected Lille, could be captured and the allies would gain the treasured higher ground. French was very concerned about the lack of shells coming from the factories in England. For years the trades unions had struggled for the rights of the working men, and they were not going to give up their hard fought for improved working conditions. Thus restrictive practices continued with one man per machine. The men believed that the employers were making huge profits from war work, and although prices were rising, wages remained static. Together with the loss of many skilled men who had joined the army in the initial rush, and the general disquiet and distrust, arms production was well below the figures expected and promised. Thus the guns were quiet in the period leading up to the battle but at 7.15 a.m. on Wednesday, 10th March 1915, the British guns started ranging and the Battle of Neuve Chapelle commenced. Accurate fire in the centre meant early success for the allies and soon the village had been taken, but on the flanks the enemies' defences remained intact and, as the infantry advanced, they were simply swept away by accurate machine gun fire. The Middlesex and Scottish Rifles suffered terribly. When nobody came back to report it was assumed that their objectives had been captured. The bodies of this first wave were later found lying dead in the formations in which they advanced, and by the 13th March nearly 13,000 officers and men were wounded or dead as the attack stalled and the initiative was lost.

The Rectory
March 1915

My dear Friends,
We take this opportunity of thanking Captain Gibbs very much for all he has done in our Sunday Schools for many years, and we trust he may be spared by God's goodness to come back to us again. He is doing most important work for the Navy. Mr. Clark, who has been in the choir

for some years, is also greatly missed. Mrs. Winfield has become Superintendent of the Sunday School. A meeting of Parishioners is to be held on Wednesday next in the Parish Room at 3.30 to consider what steps shall be taken to erect a memorial to the late Mr. Hackwood. We do not know what the meeting may wish, but it has been suggested that an Altar for the Lady Chapel carved by members of the Carving Class, who owe so much to the interest taken in the Class by Mr. Hackwood, would be a very suitable memorial. It would be very delightful if this could be done, and if the sanction of the Bishop can be obtained for its erection, I cannot imagine a more suitable memorial to one who has done so much for the young people of the Parish. The class will do the work gratuitously, but from £20 to £60 would be required to purchase fittings such as Cross, Candlesticks, Wings etc.

With every good wish, I am, yours very sincerely, H.G.Bird

The meeting of parishioners in the Village Club was duly held to decide what form the memorial to the late Mr. Henry Hackwood should take. The Rector was in the chair. Among the suggestions offered was a school bell, a stained glass window, an altar in the south aisle or a stone at the graveside. It was unanimously decided in favour of the altar, the carving of which was to be done by the members of the class at Newdigate Place. A small committee was appointed to carry out the arrangements with Mrs. Janson as treasurer.

Many people were suffering from sore throats and on the 13th March the Dorking Advertiser gave some advice:

Sunlight Advertisement 1915

Sunlight Soap

'*Influenza Throat*' *is very prevalent in Dorking just now. According to a doctor, it is the result of the constant change in weather.* '*Home treatment*' *said the doctor* '*should include an even temperature, the abstention from smoking, and occasional nitre balls, which should be sucked at intervals of an hour or two until relief is felt.*'

The complications which may arise from even the mildest form of '*flu throat*' *are so many that the patient should be particularly careful to remain at home in the warm until the symptoms have disappeared.*

Just now in some of the towns where soldiers are billeted, the '*flu throat*' *is very prevalent. The soldiers contract the malady through exposure in all sorts of weather, and they pass it on to civilians who are susceptible, or in other words, who are not in the very best of health.*

Stalemate across the Western Front meant that new initiatives were required. The British felt that if the Dardanelles could be forced by the navy then the army could be landed and swiftly take Constantinople, thus removing Turkey from the war, and allowing British troops to attack through the back door. The loss of several capital warships with great loss of life in the straits, and the failure to open the Sea of Marmara, meant that the plan had to be modified, so in April 1915 troops were landed at Gallipoli.

A new and deadly form of warfare took place as Germany renewed their attack around Ypres. At 5.00 p.m. on the 22nd April, at what was to be known as the Second Battle of Ypres, the Germans opened the gas cylinders. The gas flowed down wind in a low lying greenish and yellowy cloud and remained thick on the ground. First the soldiers' eyes smarted then the deadly chlorine acted on the membrane of their throats which thickened and caused choking. Finally the chlorine reached the lungs eating them away with a torturing, burning effect and leaving the victims helpless in the trenches. Behind the gas clouds came the swarms of enemy troops.

Dr Frederick George Chandler MA., MD., FRCP (1885-1942) was an officer in the Royal Army Medical Corps and after the war, together with his wife Marjorie, bought Little Gaterounds in Newdigate as a weekend home. In the London Hospital Gazette he described the results of a gas attack:

We drove into the courtyard of a college and got out. There filling most of the court were fine, stalwart men, lying, gasping and heaving and fighting for breath, some red with bloodshot eyes, others black in the face with their chests struggling to get more air; others with their faces disfigured by yellow chemical; many with

Dr. Frederick George Chandler RAMC

terrible wounds to add to their torture; many dying, some already dead, others fully conscious struggling for the air which their lungs could not absorb. One went white and sick. Inside was the same thing, room after room filled with the same gasping, breathless asphyxiated men. Wounds were nothing to this, not the ghastliest. From that moment I hated the Germans and shall always remember what I saw on May 4th, 1915.

He also wrote about the misery of flooded trenches:

When the battalion returned to the trenches a thaw had set in, after the frosts of Christmas, and the conditions became appalling. The country was very flat, chiefly arable land, and intersected in all directions by ditches and streams, which flowed lazily into the Lys. The trenches had been cut indiscriminately through and across these, cutting field drains and blocking up ditches which were an essential part of the drainage system. As every hollow place got fuller and fuller of water, dams were made to keep the water out, and the wretched men had to pump and bale. Every device was attempted to keep the rising water out of the dug-outs. Higher and higher rose the water, filled sand-bags were piled up in front of dug-outs, and as anyone walked along the trench the water would overflow and come flopping in. Holes were dug in the dug-outs only to be filled almost immediately with water, when the baling process had to commence, and people had to sleep on boards over this if they were lucky enough to have even boards. Finally, a dam burst, and a number of men were nearly drowned. Rifles, ammunition, and kit were lost, and the men had to be called out of the trench. There was no cover whatever, and that particular night the men had to make a thin low parapet of earth, working all night, and through the next day lie on the sodden plough behind it, exposed to the most awful weather, with no effective protection at all against bullets. They were too exhausted and wretched even to wish to fetch their rations. The only thing that prevented the complete annihilation of everybody was that the Germans were, as subsequent events showed, in a similar plight.

In a contemplative moment he added:

It is a mixture of merriness and grimness, where the contemplation of a sunset is interrupted by the flight of bullets, where a merry party may be blown into the heavens or the hells at any moment, where brooding horror spreads his raven wings and the night-owl sings, to misquote Milton, and indeed the night-owl does sing and cheer me vastly.

Newdigate Parish Magazine – April 1915

The Pew and Litany Desk are both placed in the Church in memory of the late Mr. & Mrs. Frank Cooper, of 'The Knowle' Newdigate, a small tribute to the memory of two dear people who were loved and respected by all who knew them.

Mrs. Winfield requested that the following letter should be published:

I have again to thank the many kind and generous donors of bandages, etc. for the Belgian soldiers. Dr. Picton, one of the surgeons of the Sophie Berthelôt Hospital, Calais, writes 'It is you, we have to thank for some welcome and invaluable presents and dressings sent to the Sophie Berthelôt. I well recall some lots of bandages which were your speciality, broad ones, firmly rolled.

Permit me, in the name of the officer commanding (Major Stedman) to thank you sincerely for your welcome gifts.' I have written to Dr. Picton and told him how generously the people of our little village have helped in sending the things. The next lot of bandages are going to Capt. E.N. Bennett, whose cry for help for the Serbs is in the 'Daily Mail', it makes one long to do more, the need is great, he says that 'Uskul is a veritable valley of death' and specially asks us, who next Sunday may implore the Divine pity on 'prisoners and captives' to bear in mind the necessities of these stricken men. Six doctors and twelve orderlies in one case, have the control of 1,800 sick and wounded. They have fought a gallant fight against terrific odds, but typhus has beaten them, at this moment two orderlies are dead, three have been invalided home, three are laid low with typhus, two doctors are suffering from the same disease, and the work at the hospital has been temporarily abandoned, men died of sepsis because their wounds could not be dressed. Capt. Bennett cries for help of all friends, he says for Heaven's sake let something be done soon.

I append a list of those who so kindly helped.

M. Estelle Winfield

Mrs. Woods (Broad Lane), Mrs. Palmer, Mrs. Janson, Mrs. Rose, Mrs. Overton, Mrs. Bishop, Mrs. Martin, Mrs. Gadd, Miss Dean, Mrs. Spiller, Mrs. Ted Butcher, Mrs. Spencer Lucas.

Children of the time – Christopher & Madge Lucas in 1914

Margaret Tyler had been corresponding with one of her brothers who was serving in France. It became quite clear to her that sandbags were desperately needed at the Front and she was determined to do something about it. She wrote to the Hampstead and Highgate Express from the family home at Linden House, Highgate Road and they published this letter on the 3rd April 1915.

"Will you tell the women of England that they can themselves make defences for their loved ones at the Front. What they are asking for is a million of sandbags, empty of course". Her brother at the Front says: "It is quite mild spring weather with us now. Now we do not want any more mufflers or caps for warmth, but we always want sandbags, by the million: and if the kind people who have helped us so greatly during the winter with warm knitted things wanted still to help, they could not do better than make sandbags for our protection. To make a nice commodious house for a few officers in their gun position, for instance, will require some 2000 sandbags, and the number wanted for a single battery for protection for the guns, men, officers, and telegraph officers will run into tens of thousands – a mile of trenches will require perhaps 100,000 and each little post, observation station, or shelter of any kind behind those trenches requires many more. When we advance we have not time to empty out old sandbags and carry them on. We require fresh ones. The size of them should be about 3ft by 2ft and the material, I should say, coarse linen or canvas. White is usual". The bags should be sent to Miss Tyler.

The response was encouraging and the paper published another letter from Margaret Tyler on the 17th April.

Millions of Sandbags
May I again ask your help? We want to thank so many people for sandbags, suggestions, cheques that provide material for those who can only afford to work, and for postal orders, and extra stamps that help with postage of pattern bags &c; and thanks also to the wounded soldiers who are sewing in hospital defences for their comrades at the Front. We are trying hard to reply and acknowledge everything, but find it impossible to identify them, dealing as we are with thousands in the day. It would help us very much if such letters were always enclosed in the parcels.

The Parish Magazine recorded letters which the Rector had received from his son in France.

The Rectory
April 26th 1915

My dear Friends,
First let me thank you most heartily for so kindly giving me your offerings at Easter. Those in church, with two cheques sent to me since, amount to £11 1s. 6½d. It is very kind of you and I value your offerings very much.
I am, Your very affectionate Pastor, H.G. Bird.

As the dependants of those who have gone to the Front are receiving allotments from their husbands and sons, which are increased by sums granted by the Government, the Soldiers and Sailors Families Association which has done so much for the dependants in Newdigate, will not be able to help in future except in very exceptional cases.

Extracts from letters received from the Rector's son, Lieutenant W.S. Bird from France:

In the train between Havre and the Trenches.

10/4/15

I am now definitely in for it, and it won't be long before I am with my old Regiment again. Should like to be in the 4th Batt. as I know so many friends in it, but I shall like the 2nd very much. Charles Eyre is in it. I must try and give you an account of the journey. We were paraded by the adjutant at 2.30. I have 109 loyal North Lancs. to look after and deliver over to their Colonel at headquarters. One has to be very careful men don't get out of the carriages and get left behind. We had a three mile march to the station, where the men were entrained, 8 mostly in a carriage. Then rations, consisting of a tin of pressed beef, a tin of tea, sugar, biscuits, jam and cheese were issued in double quantities to last the journey, the officers have the same as the men. Luckily I had half Capt. Drummond's hamper which had all sorts of delicacies in it, a tongue, hard boiled eggs, butter, sardines, wine and apples, while I bought a yard or so of bread – you can imagine three of us picnicing on the train! In ordinary circumstances one would hate a meal under such conditions but we all enjoyed our breakfast and dinner immensely. At 6.30 a.m. the train stopped and we procured hot water from the engine and made some tea. I fancy we detrained somewhere about eight in the evening and it is now only 8 a.m. (Friday). Heavy rain again during the night but I slept pretty well. Two nice officers in the carriage, one was at Neuve Chapelle and his accounts of that affair are terrifying. He tells me he has parcels sent out weekly. I should like some khaki handkerchiefs, chocolate <u>most essential</u>, tobacco (log cabin) and a military note book for pocket use with pencil attached etc. etc.

11/4/15

Here I am in a dug-out with Charles Eyre. It is delightful being with my own Regiment again, but although I know only two or three of the 18 officers, all are so nice that I feel quite at home. Have been more or less under shell fire twice today, in fact we are getting here for safety, as some German guns have been trying to locate a battery of our own which is close to Eyre's company's quarters. Shells have been bursting between 80 to 300 yards of us. Two this morning went through the house where Eyre lives, one penetrating into his bedroom, but he was not in. 11.30 a shrapnel bullet actually going where his head lies. I slept fully dressed in a barn last night, didn't take boots off as we have to be ready for emergencies. Meals splendid – had such a good lunch – tongue, jellied chicken, sardines and cake. (Shelling begun again but with bigger guns and over our heads). Am feeling quite happy out here but weather so lovely and haven't yet been in the firing line.

13/4/15

Yesterday, and before we were in what are called Reserve Trenches, something like 1000 yards from the Germans; of course under shell fire. There has not been much doing of late, though a *few shells have fallen 100 yards or so from me on different occasions, an interesting experience at a comfortable distance, but the real thing is in the firing trenches and must be very different. So far the life has been an idle one but what we are going to do now I don't quite know. Yesterday evening we marched back into reserve billets. Started from the trenches at dark and were relieved by another battalion. Then we marched away from Yea Raye – about 10 or 12 miles and got into barns for the men, houses for ourselves. I am with a French miner. He works from 3 a.m. to 5 p.m. Seven children in the family but the people are very nice. A room and bed extraordinarily clean. I had a good sleep in <u>bed,</u> and a bath in a large tub in the kitchen – A weird experience! We found the march rather fagging, largely over cobbles, but my feet lasted well, pack and equipment, haversack, revolver and ammunition are so heavy to carry at first. I am going to play a game of football with my platoon against another. If you ever want to know what to send the men, I shall always be thankful for socks to distribute to those under me.*

I expect to move forward at once but when I am to go I do not know and if I did I should not be allowed to tell you.

Just under four weeks later Lt. Wilfred S. Bird was lying dead in no-man's land.

The Rector visited the school on the 16th April to tell the boys in the upper classes about some of the local boy scouts who were just about to go on patrol duties on the South Coast. A month afterwards the school was closed from the 19th May to the 14th June due to an outbreak of whooping cough.

As well as her normal, long hospital duties Margaret Lucy Tyler had immersed herself in collecting sandbags at Linden House. Following on from her letters to the Hampstead and Highgate Express, on the 1st May 1915 she wrote to the Dorking Advertiser. She repeated the message from her brother.

People are asking 'What do they want sandbags for?' 'Have you enough sandbags yet or do you want more?' It is doubtful whether anyone not actually in the Field at all realises what the word 'sandbags' means to the soldier in the firing line or how urgently millions of sandbags are needed to stem the casualty lists. Are enough being sent?

The mother of a Captain, Royal Field Artillery writes, 'I have sent my son 350 sandbags. He is delighted with them and says his observation post has been safe for the first time since the last shift. He talks about the shortage.'

The wife of an officer in the RFA writes that her husband 'has asked me to make an urgent appeal on his behalf for sandbags because the Artillery are almost more in need of sandbags than the infantry, for they have the huge guns to cover as well, and the men are not 'dug in' to the extent that the men in the trenches are.'

An infantry lieutenant writes, 'We want a tremendous lot of sandbags. Our division alone has been using a million a month. For our battalions alone we usually require about 2,000 a day for their present trenches, but we have not been able to get them in sufficient quantities lately. If you saw a shell burst on a parapet of sandbags and one without, you would soon see how many lives they save and if it is to be a war of attrition, we want to take every possible means of avoiding loss of men in the trenches.'

A Colonel commanding a Brigade Royal Field Artillery, writes, 'It is quite mild spring weather with us now. We do not want any more mufflers or caps for warmth, but we always want sandbags by the million, and if the kind people who have helped us so greatly during the winter with warm knitted things want to still help, they could not do better than make sandbags for our protection. We must have hundreds of millions of sandbags in use and we always want them. To make a nice commodious house for a few officers in their gun position for instance, will require some two thousand sandbags and the number wanted for a single battery, for protection for the guns, men, offices, telephone operators, will run into tens of thousands. A mile of trenches will require perhaps a hundred thousand and each little post, observation station or shelter of any kind behind these trenches, requires many more. Then every house, barn or other locality occupied in the area in which shells fall for a depth of two or three miles behind our trenches ought to have its own dug-out for use when necessary, into the making of which the sandbag enters, and when we advance we have not time to empty out old sandbags and carry them on, we require fresh ones.'

A Captain, RFA, describes the way in which the Infantry advance. Each man takes ten sandbags under his arm as he runs out. When fired at he drops and fills a bag as he lies, for cover. Then he dashes on again with his nine remaining bags, to repeat the manoeuvre again and again, always leaving the filled bag to cover some man behind him. In this way the whole line advances with temporary cover, until they can dig themselves in. We are told that 'the men will do almost anything if only they can have enough sandbags.'

With a million men in the field, ten million sandbags will only mean ten per man and new bags are needed as fast as they move. The supply required is endless.

All bags sent to us are inspected, acknowledged (so far as possible), with instructions where defective, re-made when necessary and forwarded without delay to the Front. The size of the sandbags should be 33" x 14". War Office restriction does not apply to us – we are sending out thousands daily direct to the Front – so please send all you can.

She kept the appeal going and on the 1st May 1915 the Journal of Nursing reported:
Sandbags Stop Bullets
Miss M.L. Tyler of Linden House, Highgate Road, London NW sends us the latest instructions and official measurements for sandbags:- Material in Hessian (jute), Size 33in. by 14in. when made up. Seams: Put edges together, turn them up once, together; sew over strongly with string or stout linen thread (or machine twice with thread, not chain stitch). Take deep stitches. One end to be left open (lightly caught or raw edged). Turn bag inside out, and tie on a piece of stout string to close sack when filled. N.B. – Wide turnings, strong seams. The bags are tossed about, and must stand strain. Empty bags sent to Miss Tyler are sent to the front without delay. Millions of bags wanted.

Before this piece the Journal also informed its readers about a very useful combination knife and fork that had been designed whereby wounded soldiers who only had one arm could easily feed themselves.

H.O. Dallas of Innisfail, Crawley supported Miss Tyler and noted that she was sending over 4000 sandbags a day from Linden House.

Miss Tyler would have been staggered to hear of the loss of another nephew – the third member of her family to have died.

2nd Lieutenant JOHN COLLETT TYLER
122nd Battery, Royal Field Artillery

John Collett Tyler was born on the 9th December 1893 in the foothills of the Himalayas at Roorkee, which is in the northern Indian state of Uttarakhand. He was the second son of Col. John Charles Tyler, Royal Engineers, and Florence Mary, and a grandson of Sir Henry Whatley Tyler. The family owned Woodlands Farm in Newdigate and it was here that a daughter, Rosamund, was born in

1905. John Collett Tyler was educated at Wellington College from 1909-1911 where he was head of the school and captain of football, and at the Royal Military Academy where he was senior under-officer and obtained the Sword of Honour in July 1914. The Commandant in his report, on that occasion, observed that he would especially mention Senior Under-Officer J.C.Tyler, who had shown in his present responsible position that he possessed in a high degree those qualities which were looked for in the best type of officer. He was gazetted 2nd Lieutenant, RFA on the 17th July 1914 and joined at Woolwich on the 9th August, left for Dundalk, Ireland on the 10th and embarked for France on the 17th.

Lieut. John Collett Tyler (Reproduced by kind permission of the National Newspaper Library)

Hill 60 was an artificial ridge, 60 metres high, made from the spoil from a railway cutting which had been dug many years before. It had been captured by the Germans in December 1914 and the British were determined to regain it as it afforded a good observation point. Tunnels had been dug under the hill by the 171st Tunnelling Company and a charge of 2700 pounds was laid in each chamber. At 19.00 hours on the 17th April the plunger was hit and debris flew 300 yards into the air. The British took the hill – only to lose it again that night when the Germans counter-attacked. The next day the hill was again retaken but during this attack 2nd Lieut.Tyler was killed. The Major commanding his battery wrote on the 21st April, 'There is a big battle going on here now which started at 7 p.m. on the 17th, John and I went forward that day to observe. I had to send John and a signaller on by night, to the newly captured trench to let me know if the

Germans were counter-attacking and to observe by day. This job he did in his usual gallant way. Three times he came back to me under heavy fire and great difficulties to mend the telephone lines. He was shot at dawn, a rifle bullet clean through the forehead. He died as he lived, doing his duty gallantly and well. Had he lived he would have certainly had the D.S.O. He was killed in the foremost trench captured from the Germans. Just after he was killed the Germans retook the trench and held it for about twelve hours. We then took it back'. The General Officer Commanding wrote a few days later, 'I had already sent in his name for good service. His cheery, gallant example was worth everything at these times'.

His name is recorded on the Menin Gate, the Colchester War Memorial and the Wellington College Roll of Honour.

Panorama showing Hill 60 (Ref. Q44172) Reproduced by kind permission of the Imperial War Museum

The Lusitania, one of the world's largest liners, was torpedoed and sunk by a German submarine off the Old Head of Kinsale on the 7th May 1915. She had on board nearly two thousand people of whom 1195 lost their lives, including Alfred Gwynne Vanderbilt (1877-1915), who was a familiar figure as he used to drive his coach along his 'favourite piece of road' by Holmwood Common. (An inscribed granite slab, protected by railings, can be seen by the A24 road at Holmwood). This event led to an uproar amongst the public who exacted their revenge on German residents and businesses. The Dorking Advertiser noted,

RMS Lusitania

People will not talk of Mr. Vanderbilt in future as the millionaire sportsman and man of pleasure. He will be remembered as the 'Children's Hero' and men and women will salute his name.

When death was nearing him he showed gallantry which no words can adequately describe. He stood outside the palm saloon on the starboard side, with Ronald Denyer (his valet) by his side. He looked at the scene of horror and despair with pitying eyes. 'Find all the kiddies you can, boy' he said to his valet.

The man rushed off immediately, collecting the children, and as he brought them to Mr Vanderbilt the latter dashed to the boats with them two at a time. When he could find no more children he went to the assistance of the women, and placed as many as he could in safety.

In all this work he was gallantly assisted by Ronald Denyer, and the two continued their efforts until the very end. Mr Vanderbilt was unable to swim but he took off his lifebelt and handed it to an old woman. Alfred Gwynne Vanderbilt left a fortune of $26,375,000.

Winston Churchill gloomily surveyed the current position, 'We were in the presence of the fact that Sir Ian Hamilton's army had been definitely brought to a standstill on the Gallipoli Peninsula, was suspended there in great peril, was difficult to reinforce and still more, difficult to withdraw ..... At the same time the failure of the British attacks in France on the Aubers Ridge could not be denied.'

Locally it was announced that under the sanction of the Lord Lieutenant, a Public Meeting would be held at the School-room at Newdigate, on Wednesday, May 12th at 8 p.m. when Percy A. Harris Esq. LCLC (Hon. Secretary of the Central Association of Volunteer Training Corps) would address the meeting on 'Volunteer Training'. The meeting would be supervised by General Sir Josceline Heneage Wodehouse (1852-1930) GCB, CMG, PA, Regimental Commandant of the Surrey V.T. Corps and a veteran of the Zulu Wars and former Governor of Bermuda, and Mr. H.H. Gordon Clark, Commandant of the 10th (Dorking and District) Battalion V.T. Corps. Chairman: The Rev. H.G. Bird MA, TD. Admission free.

There was much enthusiasm at the meeting and the School-room was packed. The Dorking Detachment of the Volunteer Training Corps under the command of Mr. A.J. Rivett attended in full force and they marched through the village headed by the Newdigate Band. The procession will live in the memory of those who turned out and we hope that the result will be the means of organising a first-class platoon with sections.

The Rector said they were certainly in a time of very grave responsibility. Never before had England had such a hard task as she had to-day. They began to fight by fighting for a weak state – Belgium – but now we were fighting for their very existence. It was a matter of life or death for them. After referring to the sacrifices of the youth of England in going to fight for England, the Chairman said there were hundreds and thousands of young men who would not be missed in this country if they went to fight for them. They could not all go to the front. He would be there if they would let him go (applause). Every one of them should be doing something for their country, otherwise they could see England extinct. The Bishop of London said he would rather be dead than be under German rulers. They must do their duty in the parish. A good many had joined the V.T. Corps and he was told that 30 had joined in Capel. They were not going to be second to Capel. There must be 31 members at Newdigate. They must make up their minds they would be second to no one (applause).

Mr Percy Harris gave a stirring speech and Mr. Gordon Clark said that Newdigate was one of the first villages to form a corps of its own. They all knew Mrs. Janson had infused much spirit into the object and now the V.T.C. had been formed and re-organised by the Government the only way for them to serve their country was by enrolling themselves into that corps.

Mr. F.E. Green proposed a vote of thanks to the speakers.

Three days before this meeting the rector's son Wilfrid was killed in France. The telegram advising him was dated the 12th May and probably arrived the day after the meeting. The Dorking Advertiser carried this obituary:

Another well known figure in the world of sport has thus passed away and his loss will be keenly felt, especially among cricketers. He was educated at the Grange, Eastbourne, where he was captain of the cricket and football XI, and afterwards at Malvern where he represented the school at cricket, football and fives, and was head of the School House. Whilst Lieutenant of the School House Corps his squad won the School Cup. He afterwards went to New College, Oxford, where he captained the Oxford cricket XI. Since then he has played at Lords for Middlesex and for the Gentlemen versus the Players, and he represented England versus South Africa. For eight years he was a master at Ludgrove School where he won respect and affection of masters and boys, and indeed all who came in contact with him. His example was that of a true and upright gentleman and will have its mark on many in the years to come. His commanding officer wrote of him 'Bird was a splendid fellow and a very promising officer. He was popular with us all and I am more than sorry to lose him.' Lieutenant Bird was shot through the heart whilst leading his platoon into action. His loss will be greatly felt in Newdigate where he has always been a keen and generous supporter of the local cricket and football clubs and indeed any society which tended to the improvement and good of the village. The sympathy of the whole neighbourhood will go out to Mr Bird and his family in their great sorrow.

Wilfred Stanley Bird, Lieutenant 5th Battalion King's Royal Rifle Corps, who was killed in action on May 9th, was the son of the Rev. H.G. Bird, Rector of Newdigate.

Ludgrove School was founded in 1892 and moved from London to Wokingham in 1937. William and Harry, the sons of Prince Charles were pupils there. The school obituary was in a similar vein to the Dorking Advertiser but was headed:
'*Whosoever leads such a life need not care upon how short warning it be taken from him*'

Mr. G.O. Smith (1872-1943) the headmaster of Ludgrove School received the following letter from Lt. Charles Howard Eyre. The headmaster was a former

captain and centre forward for the England football team and liked to employ staff with a sporting prowess. Note that the obituary stated that he was shot in the heart whilst Charles Eyre said that he had been shot in the head!

11th May 1915

Dear Joe,

Just a few lines to tell you the sad, sad news about poor old Wilfred Bird. By the time you get this, you will probably have seen his name in the papers. He was shot through the head while leading his men in an attack on a German trench, and fell without another word. It is perhaps the death one would most prefer to have – absolutely painless. To be shot by a stray bullet in a trench or on a working party by night or by a stray shell miles behind the lines – these are the things we all dread. But to die at the head of your men, while they are looking towards you for guidance and inspiration, that is a great thing and I do believe that Wilfred – in fact I know, he told me so – that, if he had to die, he would prefer to die so. His captain told me that he was carrying out his orders to the letter, when he fell. He took his men over our earthworks, across an old disused British trench, through some barbed wire and was leading them over the 300 yards of open, when a maxim caught him. His body, I believe is still there. Although one of the wounded brought in his wristwatch, which has been sent to his father, to whom our CO has written a letter.

Every officer who left the earthworks that day was killed or wounded. In spite of disguises – Wilfred was wearing webbing equipment and carried a rifle with bayonet fixed – the Germans seem to spot an officer at once. I can't write more, but I thought you would like to learn something. After all, the loss is ours, not his.

Give my love and sympathy to all at Ludgrove.

Yours ever, Charles Eyre

Charles Eyre was born in Liverpool in 1883 and his father the Rev. John Rasdall Eyre was vicar of St. Peter's in Tiverton. He attended Harrow School and was himself killed on the 25th September 1915. He is buried at Dud Corner Cemetery in Loos.

Ludgrove School

Lieutenant WILFRED STANLEY BIRD
5th Battalion attached to the 2nd Battalion
King's Royal Rifle Corps

Wilfred Bird was born on the 28th September 1883 at Yiewsley in Middlesex. He was the eldest child of the Rev. Henry G. Bird M.A. and his wife Henrietta Maria (née Greenham). He had two sisters, Muriel Henrietta (1885-1964) and Ethel Mary (1890-1962) and a brother, Charles Henry Greenham Bird (1887-1919). He was brought up at the vicarage of St Andrews in Hillingdon where his father was rector. He was educated at The Grange in Eastbourne and afterwards at Malvern where he was in the cricket eleven from 1900-1902 at the time Canon Sidney James came to be headmaster. He went up to New College, Oxford where he kept wicket in 1904-05-06 and was captain in his last year. He kept wicket for the Gentlemen at Lord's in 1908 and 1912 and played several games for Middlesex. He was an extremely careful and good batsman, but specially excelled as a wicket keeper. One of the best known captains of England said; 'He is the best wicket keeper I ever saw.' He had been a member of the MCC since 1905. His father became

rector of Newdigate in 1913, just a year after his mother had died, and he used to bring teams down to Newdigate to play against the village. He became a master at Ludgrove School where he was immensely happy and it was a terrific struggle to answer the call, but he never failed to recognise his duty. A member of the Officers Training Corps, he was gazetted to the 5th Battalion of the King's Royal Rifles on the 29th December 1914.

Wilfred Stanley Bird at Ludgrove School

Wilfred Bird was attached to the 2nd Battalion who on the 9th May 1915 were moved up into reserve from the La Bassée Canal sector. It was planned that a combined French and British attack would capture the strategically important Vimy Ridge. The surrounding area was flat and intersected by drainage ditches, some being too wide to jump. There was little natural cover and it was difficult to see the enemy positions. It was a fine and sunny day after several days of heavy rain, but there was a mist caused by the heat so the attack was duly planned. The battalion consisted of 27 officers and 1000 men. They had tea at 1.30 a.m. and rested until 5.00 a.m. when a heavy bombardment opened, with field guns firing shrapnel at the German wire and howitzers directing high explosives at the front lines. The bombardment intensified and the KRRC went

Ruins of the church at Richebourg St. Vast (Ref. Q17323) Reproduced by kind permission of the Imperial War Museum

over the top facing heavy machine gun fire. At 5.40 a.m. the line of fire was lifted by 600 yards and the infantry assault began. They were met by intense cross-fire from the German machine guns which could be seen virtually undamaged in their protective emplacements. At 6.00 a.m. the advance halted with hundreds of men pinned down in no-man's land, unable to advance or fall back. A report was sent to Brigade H.Q. and a further bombardment was ordered without much effect. Eventually at about 7.30 a.m. the battalion received orders to withdraw to the north side of the Rue du Bois. The battalion had four officers killed, Capt. The Hon. E.M.J.Upton, Lieut. W. Hodges, Lieut. W.S.Bird and 2nd Lieut. C.W. Morris, and 42 men killed, plus a total of 123 wounded and 82 missing. On the 12th May the G.O.C. 2nd Brigade inspected the battalion who received a very complimentary appreciation of their services on the 9th May. His Major wrote of him, 'Bird was gallantly leading his men when he was shot, and died instantly. Bird was a splendid fellow, and a very promising officer and very popular with officers and men alike. I am more than sorry to lose him.'

Overall the battle had been a total disaster for the British Army, with no ground won and no tactical advantage gained. On that day there were 11,000 British casualties. Wilfred Bird's body lay somewhere in the mud at Richebourg St. Vaast where he had led the charge across 300 yards of exposed ground. His wrist-watch was found, and returned to his father, and apparently his body was buried because in November 1915 the Rev. H.G.Bird wrote ' Thank you so much for kindly sending me particulars of the position of my late son's grave. It is a great comfort to my daughters and myself to know the exact spot which, if I am well enough, I hope I may be able to visit after the war is over'. It is unknown what happened to the grave because his name, along with many of his comrades who fell that day, is remembered on the Le Touret Memorial which records soldiers with no known grave. His name can also be found on memorials at Lord's and at Uxbridge Cricket Club. A clock was erected in his memory on the cricket pavilion at Ludgrove School, but it was later destroyed when vandals set light to the building.

The Dorking Advertiser of the 15th May 1915 reported on the British Industries Fair:-

At the British Industries Fair, now being held at the Agricultural Hall, Islington, the Newdigate Wood Carving Class, stand F20, has a very attractive display of carvings for Church and architectural pieces down to small furniture, frames, stools etc., which were much admired by her Majesty Queen Mary. She asked many questions concerning the class and particularly praised a carved altar central panel, church screen pediment and coat of arms carved by J. Sanders, an over mantel with dolphins and gilded Tudor frame, carved by W.Broughton, a rose, shamrock and thistle design tripod photo frame by A. Beck, and a sideboard panel and cake stand by George Horley, one of the Newdigate postmen.

Newdigate school was closed from the 19th May until the 14th June due to an outbreak of whooping cough which at one time was affecting over 25% of the pupils.

On the 18th May Lord Kitchener announced that British troops must be adequately protected from asphyxiating gases by the use of similar methods. Also 300,000 more recruits were required.

Five hundred soldiers of the 7th Battalion of the Scots Guards were travelling on a troop train on the 22nd May when it was involved in a devastating crash at Quintinshill near Gretna. Old rolling stock had been pressed into service and the carriages were wooden framed. The interiors were panelled with gas lighting, so – upon impact – fire rapidly spread throughout the train. In total 226 people were killed, including 214 Scots Guards, in a disaster which recorded the greatest ever loss of life in a rail accident in the United Kingdom.

Bad news arrived at Newdigate Place when Mrs Janson was informed of the death of 19 year old Cyril Herron:-

Ruins of Château Potijze (Ref. Q52018) Reproduced by kind permission of the Imperial War Museum

2nd Lieutenant CYRIL DOUGLAS HERRON
2nd Dragoon Guards (Queen's Bays)

Cyril Douglas Herron was born near Canterbury, Kent in 1895 and educated at Wellington College from 1909-1912. His father, Robert Douglas Herron was a Captain in the 2nd Dragoon Guards (Queen's Bays). Cyril lived with his mother Emily Sophia Bloor Herron, née Bradwell (1864-1941), who was known as Ella, and his younger brother, Robert Roy Herron, at Manor Farm House on Eggars Hill in Aldershot, close to where his father's regiment was stationed. The Queen's Bays were ordered to prepare themselves for overseas service and on the 16th November 1901 they left Aldershot and sailed for South Africa with Capt. Robert D. Herron the squadron leader of 'A' Squadron. At dawn on the 1st April 1902 the regiment rode into a laager of 500 Boers, a number far greater than anticipated, and during the ensuing struggle Capt. Herron was amongst 80 men who were killed that day at Holspruit.

It was therefore no surprise that Cyril joined his father's regiment, and he was commissioned on the 15th August 1914. They sailed for France on the 16th November 1914 as a component of the 1st Cavalry. In May 1915 an officer described the conditions in France at that time: ' Cavalry has been in the trenches on and off for the past three weeks and have had severe casualties. The Germans attacked with gas and large numbers of men were asphyxiated. The respirators do not have the desired effect and unless we make an effort to produce noxious gasses quickly then we will be fighting at an enormous disadvantage.' The last 24 hours of Lt Herron's life can only be described as hell; the following extract from the regiment's war diary and history illustrates this. 'The regiment remained in billets until the 9th May when it was ordered into reserve trenches south of Potijze, relieving the 9th Lancers. On the 12th May the Bays moved into the first line trenches, taking over from the 19th Hussars. These trenches were in a very bad condition, being shallow and straight, and as the men improved them at night they were digging through decomposing corpses. The noise, too, attracted some snipers and the RSM, Mr Turner, was killed by a bullet through the neck. On the 13th May, from 3.00 a.m. to 7.00 a.m. the Germans opened a bombardment of heavy howitzer shells, 'coal boxes' and 'Jack Johnsons'. All telephone lines were cut and the trenches of 'B' squadron on the left were largely destroyed. One troop on the extreme left had only Sergeant Isles and one trooper left. 2nd Lieutenant Herron being killed and all others of his men killed or wounded, some of them buried in the wreckage of the trench. Even so a mouth-organ concert was improvised during the continual bombardment.'

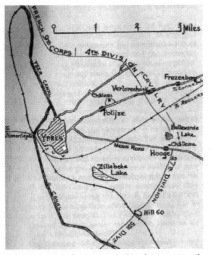

Map showing the position of 2nd Lieut. Cyril D Herron's Company on the day he was killed (History of the Queen's Bays)

2nd. Lieut. Cyril D. Herron

2nd Lieut. Cyril Douglas Herron did not hear the mouth-organ as he was killed on that day and is buried in the Potijze Chateau Grounds Cemetery. A memorial to him and his father can be seen in Newdigate Church and he is remembered on the Wellington College Roll of Honour.

In September 1918 Cyril's brother Robert became a 2nd Lieutenant in the 1st Dragoon Guards and was stationed in India. He later transferred to the Royal Field Artillery and survived the war.

A memorial service for Lieut. Wilfred S. Bird was held at Newdigate Church on the 26th May and was reported as follows:

We know we are only giving public expression to a feeling that is uppermost in the minds of all our readers. Lieut. Bird died, not only for the safety of our homes, but for the maintenance of civilisation and liberty against the greatest days that have menaced these priceless possessions for centuries. Our soldiers face the hazards of the battlefield without flinching and the death of such heroes as Lieut. W.S. Bird will for ever have a place of honour in the national records. Surrey will never cease to cherish the names of her sons who fall fighting and their names will be forever fragrant. Major Phillips, who was in command of Lieut. Bird's battalion, writes of his subaltern as follows: ... 'He fell whilst gallantly leading his platoon, being shot through the heart. He was a great favourite with all, both fellow officers and men, and gave promise of being an able officer. I am more than deeply grieved at his loss'.

When we read of this gallant officer leading his men to victory before he succumbed to the fire of the enemy, we are reminded of Macauley's lines:

> *For how can man die better*
> *Than facing fearful odds*
> *For the ashes of his father*
> *And the temples of the Gods*

The local paper had published many stories written from the front telling of relentless horrors and this letter from Private T. Miles of Grove Road, Redhill tells of the time he went over the top with the Royal West Surreys. He wrote it from the Canadian General Hospital in Le Treport. Later the authorities decided to 'sanitise' the war and this sort of letter no longer appeared. In fact it took many years before books about the war would publish pictures of dead and mutilated bodies.

I have got a bullet in the thigh. It was terrible the morning we made the charge. The shot and shell burst in every direction, in fact it was like being in hell. I do not know how Ted (brother) got on because I did not see him after we charged, but I hope he got through alright. The German dog who shot me had to pay dearly for it, for no sooner had he done me than my mate shot him right through the body. I have got the bullet as a souvenir, and I live in hope of getting another go at the German dogs. Our battalion suffered heavily, my company being the first to get over the parapets of the trenches and we lost a lot of men.

On the 9th June Mr. Asquith announced that the total number of British casualties up to the 31st May 1915 was 258,069. Killed 50,342 (officers 3,327), wounded 153,980 (officers 64,980) and missing 53,747 (officers 1,130).

The Dorking Advertiser carried a small piece about David Green who was born in Sydenham, Kent in 1895. He grew up at Etheldene, Station Road, Limpsfield with

his father, the author F. E. Green. David Green served with the Suffolk Regiment in Egypt and after the war worked for the Hong Kong & Shanghai Bank in Shanghai. On the 26th June 1915 the Advertiser reported:

Mr. David Green, only son of Mr. F.E. Green of Barings Field, Newdigate has taken his B.A. degree with honours at Trinity College, Cambridge, in spite of the handicap of training with the O.T.C. two or three times a week in winter and spring. He is now waiting for a commission. Mr. Green was educated at Reigate Grammar School.

Just a few weeks following the death of his son the Rector was clearly resentful of men who were not 'doing their bit' and urged everyone to join the common cause. He also, probably to add a feeling of guilt to those still at home, published a list of those from the parish on active service.

The Rectory
June 30th, 1915

My dear Friends,
There seems not much to write about this month. It is sad to think that the war still rages and will probably continue to do so for some time to come. The majority in England, however, do not even yet, I fear, grasp the great seriousness of it and all that it means to us. As I have said before each one must ask himself what he is doing to help in the greatest of all struggles which the world has ever known. You will be surprised and shocked to hear that someone said to me he did not consider he had anything to fight for since he had not an inch of land in the country to call his own. What an awakening such a man would have if he could be taken to the 'dug outs' and so gain experience of the reality of the struggle – or if he could spend a week or two in Belgium and hear the sad stories that are told there of the suffering and starvation of the people, as well as the terrible atrocities that have been committed on innocent women and children. His eyes would indeed be opened and he would see things differently from what he does now, and if England were defeated (which may God prevent) our position would be made worse than the Belgians. This however, is only one side of the question. We are taking part in this great struggle because we know it is a just and right course to pursue. We could not, even to save our lives, stand by and see others wronged. Every man, woman and child must make it a matter of conscience to 'do his bit' for the common cause. If there is anyone who is not doing this I venture to think he is not worthy to be called an Englishman. We are being told on all sides of the duty of practising great thrift by the rich and poor alike throughout the Country. The enormous expenses of the war will cripple this country for many years to come and we must all do what we can to help by denying ourselves in every way possible and especially of those things imported into the country.
I should like to congratulate those who have joined the Voluntary Training Corps. and to wish them 'good luck'. We think more might join and come to the drills. I know many think it will be impossible for the Germans to land in England in large numbers. They may, however, be able to land at some unexpected moment a certain number of trained men who would do much

harm and should Calais be taken by the Germans they will possibly be able to do much more than we imagine.

We have been ordered to close our Schools for a time in consequence of the prevalence of whooping cough which I am thankful to say now appears to be nearly extinct.

Some will be interested in reading the following account of my son's last moments as sent by an officer to the editor of The Malvernian. 'He was ordered to lead his men out of the trenches across an exposed 300 yards and was killed instantaneously by machine gun fire whilst cheering them on. Every officer in the charge was either wounded or killed.'

I publish the list of those from our own parish and a few who are relatives of parishioners who are on active service either in England or abroad. Our list is quite a good one though there are Parishes with a smaller population which beat us. I shall be most grateful to be told of any omissions or inaccuracies in the list.

I expect to be away from the 13th July for one or two Sundays. During my absence the Sunday work will be taken by the Rev. A. E. Clark-Kennedy, from Ewhurst, and Mr. Howell has most kindly promised to attend to any urgent cases in the parish on the week days.

With every best wish, I am your affectionate Pastor, H. G. Bird

Francis Shorland Ball
Alfred William Gibbs
Frederick Goldberg
Herbert Walter Goldberg
Geoffrey Comber Griffiths
George Frederick Herron
Walter Fitzroy Herron
Frank Bandy
Henry Bandy
Bert Batchelor
George Batchelor
Herbert Bedding
Sidney Brett
Ernest William Henry Bourne
Sydney Rupert Bourne
Cyril Bourne
Matthew Cassell
Frank Arthur Clark
William Luther Dean
Arthur Dennis
Arthur Ede
James Frederick Elliott
John Elliott
William Elliott
Alfred Freeland Gibbs

George Hudson
Henry Harber
John Robert Harber
Stephen Charles Harber
Cecil Thomas Hills
William Robert Henry Hopkins
Walter Johns
George Monk
Arthur Henry Monk
Anthony William Potter
Frederick Raymond Potter
Joseph Potter
Edward Rowland
Frederick Rowland
Percy W. Edward Rowland
John Sanders (sic)
Arthur Still
Charles Taylor
James Taylor
Albert Trow
Walter Henry West
George Woltorton (sic)
William George Waytt (sic)
James Weller

Charlie Harewood
Alfred Henry Horley
Albert Horley
<u>*Honour List*</u> *– W.S. Bird, Cyril Herron, William Burberry*
<u>*Boy Scouts*</u> *– Roy Goldsack, William Hale, Albert White.*

James William Sanders

Pte. William Robert Henry Hopkins

Doris Bedding [of Ash Farm, Cudworth] aged 10 years, passed on the 2nd June the second Trinity College Examination in Pianoforte Playing. Miss Broughton, our organist, who taught Miss Bedding, is to be congratulated on the success gained by her pupil.

Ten-year-old Arthur Hogsflesh from Chaffolds Farm wrote the following in the Parish Magazine:

I hope all the boys enjoyed the outing to Leith Hill as well as I did. We had such a glorious day. We started from Newdigate at 11 o'clock and the Rector came to see us off. We reached Cold Harbour at quarter past twelve and put the horse and trap up there. Then we all made our way to the tower. When we got up there we had lunch, that Joe had brought with him; we had beef, tongue, bread and cheese and ginger beer.

Then we all went up to the top of the tower; when we came down we had games. While we were at our games, Mrs. Janson and the Rector came. Then we had tea and while we were having it Mrs. Janson hid apples and oranges and we had to find them and I found two apples. Then we had scrambles of sweets; soon after we went up the tower again. Then we had just one more game and then the lady said that we could go up to the top of the tower again free. When we came down we had to see about home. When we were going home we sang our favourite songs and I think all the boys will agree with me in thanking Mrs Janson most heartily for a happy day.

On the 21st July the school headmaster, John Steeds, noted that attendance had been very poor owing to the older children helping in the hayfields.

On the 27th July Mr. Asquith, in Parliament, stated total British military casualties to July 18th numbered 330,995 and total naval casualties to July 20th as 9,106.

On the Western Front the war continued to rage with a series of attacks, retreats and counter attacks. Often there were only two hundred yards between the British and German trenches and in many places the sandbag barricades, built head high, were close enough for the opposing troops to hear each other talk. The various assaults were held up by German machine-gun fire, the lack of support at the vital moment and the lack of artillery which alone could reduce the machine-gun emplacements. On the 30th July, early in the morning, the Germans exploded a huge mine under the British trenches at Hooge. Immediately afterwards they attacked, for the first time, with a new deadly weapon – the flame thrower. This was followed closely by trench mortars.

Dorking Advertiser – July 31st, 1915

We regret to hear that Lt. H. W. Goldberg has been very seriously wounded in France and is now in the No. 2 British Red Cross Hospital at Rouen. Lt. Goldberg joined the Inns of Court Officers Training Corps last Christmas. He obtained a commission in the 1st Battalion Royal West Surrey Regiment and went over to France in June. He was wounded on July 24th in the arm and leg by shrapnel and it is feared that he will have to lose an arm. Both the injured officer and his family, who reside at the Red House, Newdigate, will have the deepest sympathy of their many friends. Lt. Goldberg was the Liberal candidate for the Reigate Division at the two elections in 1910. In the December election he lost to the Conservative, Col. Rawson, 7710 to 5194 votes.

On the 7th August the Advertiser announced that 7799 Pte. W. Hopkins, East Surrey Regiment was wounded and it also announced the death of Lt. Goldberg.

It can only be with the deepest sympathy with his family and with the greatest regret that his many friends in Surrey will learn of the death from wounds of 2nd. Lt. Herbert Walter Goldberg, son of Mr. Leopold Goldberg of Newdigate. It was at first hoped that his wounds, though serious, would not prove fatal and he himself was, indeed, able to write home to say that he expected soon to be invalided to

Pte. William Hopkins

England. This hope, unfortunately, was not realised and he died, very peacefully, at the British Red Cross Hospital at Rouen on July 31st.

Lt. Goldberg was born in 1880 and was educated at Charterhouse and at University College, Oxford. There he had a distinguished career. He was the only man of his year to have a first class in jurisprudence. On leaving Oxford he was called to the Bar and became a pupil of the late Mr. Leigh Clare, afterwards Vice Chancellor of the County Palatine of Lancashire. His mental powers and especially perhaps a great gift for analysis and a genius for hard work, fitted him particularly for the Chancery bar and he gradually built up for himself the reputation of being a junior of exceptional ability and great promise.

Lieut. Herbert Goldberg with his
nephew, Anthony Shorland Ball
in 1915

Lieut. Herbert Walter Goldberg

Always a keen politician, he contested the Reigate Division of Surrey in 1910 in the Liberal interest and though he was defeated he proved a most popular candidate with strong political beliefs and the power to set them forth clearly and convincingly. Though his rapidly increasing work at the bar compelled him to resign his candidature not very long after this election, politics had so great an attraction for him that there can be little doubt that later on he would again have entered that field. He was married only a few days before the outbreak of the war, to Miss Angela Vernon Sanderson, daughter of the late Rev. Lancelot Sanderson, headmaster of Elstree School. At Christmas he joined the Inns of Court O.T.C. where he obtained a commission in the 3rd Battalion of the Queen's Royal West Surrey Regiment in April. On June 1st he left for France and was attached to the 1st Battalion with which he was serving when he met his death.

His loss will be very deeply and very sincerely regretted by the host of friends whom he had gained in the political, the legal and the social world. For he was a man of broad sympathies and many attainments. His literary taste was refined, cultivated and scholarly and there is little that is good in the literature of England and of France with which he was not intimately acquainted. He was an excellent all round sportsman and at football, lawn tennis and at golf his performances were all distinctly above the average. He had what is, perhaps, one of the rarest of all gifts, that of staunch and constant friendship and it is as a true and greatly valued friend that he will be most widely missed.

His life and his death are a fine shining example.

2nd Lieutenant HERBERT WALTER GOLDBERG
3rd Battalion attd. 1st Battalion, The 'Queens'
(Royal West Surrey Regiment)

Herbert Walter Goldberg was born on the 12th January 1880, the son of Leopold and Louisa Goldberg. His father, a solicitor, was born in Prussia but was a naturalised British subject. The family lived at 10 Clapton Common and later in Folkestone before he established a practice in London. They had a London home at 23 Cadogan Gardens and in the 1890s they bought an estate in Newdigate, building The Red House. Herbert, or Bertie as he was known, was educated at Charterhouse and University College, Oxford, where in 1898 he gained a first in jurisprudence. On leaving Oxford he was called to the bar at the Inner Temple where he became a pupil of Mr Leigh Clare. In the elections of 1910 he unsuccessfully stood as a Liberal candidate for the Reigate Division and his interest in politics led to him publishing a book entitled 'Politics for the Pocket'. Just before the war he married Angela Vernon Sanderson (1883-1959), the daughter of the Rev. Lancelot Sanderson who was formerly the headmaster of Elstree School.

Herbert joined the Inns of Court Officers Training Corps at Christmas 1914 and gained his commission with the 3rd Battalion, The Queens in April 1915. He went to France on the 1st June with the 1st Battalion and on the 21st July he was wounded in the leg and arm by shrapnel from a bomb accident whilst at Beuvry. He was taken to No 2 British Red Cross Hospital at Rouen. The hand grenade then in use had a dangerous method of ignition and many accidents occurred; it was not until the arrival of the Mills bomb that this type of weapon was considered to be safe. In the same incident, nineteen year old 2nd Lieut. Alfred Cecil Armitage from Worcester Park was killed along with another man. Herbert wrote to his father saying that he expected to be invalided back to England very soon but that he might lose an arm. His hopes of returning were not realised as he died from his wounds on the 31st July.

He was buried at the St. Sever Cemetery in Rouen and his name is recorded on memorials at Charterhouse, Temple Church in London and in the Newdigate churchyard. On the gravestone his name appears with those of his mother, father, and brother, Frederick William. At the time of his death his wife is described as living at Glenbourne, West End, Southampton but they also kept a London address at 11 Victoria Grove in Kensington. The famous English cricketer, C.B. Fry, lived at Glenbourne from 1898-1908.

That Wednesday evening there was a great demonstration on Redhill Common where Col. R.H. Rawson M.P. made reference to Lt. Goldberg's death. Col. Richard Hamilton Rawson M.P. (1863-1918) was educated at Eton and Oxford and won the two parliamentary elections as a Conservative candidate for Reigate in 1910 which explains his knowledge of Lt. Goldberg. He was formerly a Colonel in the 1st Life Guards and lived at Woodhurst in Slaugham which later became the home of Dame Margot Fonteyn. Col. Rawson said he hoped they would allow him to refer and perhaps it would come from him more appropriately than others, to the untimely death of Mr. H. W. Goldberg, who was well known to many there. He, at any rate, had given for his country the greatest offering that any man can possibly give – he had given his life for his country. His name, he was sure, would be remembered with respect and admiration by everybody who was acquainted with him in Reigate D.V.

The reports in the paper and the parish magazine simply mention that Lt. Goldberg had been wounded by shrapnel and at no time do they state that his injuries were caused by an accident. Perhaps Leopold Goldberg used his influence to give his son's death more gravitas. Although the reports state that the injury occurred on the 24th July the official war diary gives the date as the 21st July. The diaries also give his initials as G.B. Goldberg, but as H.W. Goldberg was the only person with this surname to die in 1915 it must be assumed that this was an error. When his will was published he left property to the value of £1,645.

The Rectory
August 2nd, 1915

My dear Friends,
I will only write a few words this month. We are all of us so grieved to hear of the sad death of Second Lieutenant Goldberg and you will wish, I am sure, to extend to all at the Red House, our deepest sympathy. After twelve months of most terrible losses we seem to be making but little progress and it appears as if the war would continue for sometime yet. We must do all in our power to hasten its end and the very best way of doing this is by earnest repentance and prayer. We must find out our own faults and those common to the nation and repent of them, and we must pray as we have never prayed before.
I am, your affectionate Pastor, H.G. Bird.

The editor of the Parish Magazine added:
Everyone in Newdigate will sympathise most deeply with Mr. Goldberg for the great loss he has sustained by the death of his eldest son. All know how kind Mr. Goldberg and his daughters have been to so many in Newdigate and we can only pray that God may give them all strength to bear this great trial laid upon them.

On the 3rd August Livingstone Haig, from his home at Beam Brook in Newdigate, wrote the following letter to the rector.

Dear Mr. Bird,

On the Field Day of the C V T Corps, which took place last Monday, it was humiliating to find Newdigate represented by but two members. There is a sufficient number of able-bodied men in and around our village from which to form two or three sections but it is pretty plain that the will for this is conspicuous by its absence and that the only chance for those Newdigate members who wish to qualify for military usefulness is to join one or other of the neighbouring village corps.

That this is the case will be a matter of regret, I think, by any patriotic and thoughtful person.

Suggestions by a Working Man
Causes of the War:

Soon after the war commenced there were large placards up giving four or five good reasons why we were at War. They were all good, sound reasons, but they were secondary.

The primary and most important reason for the War is the scarcity of religious worship, the comparatively few who attempt to worship God. When the Children of Israel neglected to worship God enemies came and fought against them. We English who, as many think, are descended from some of the lost Ten Tribes of Israel, so long as we neglect to worship God must expect to be recalled to our duty to God in the same way.

We might look upon this War as a merciful call to repentance from a loving Father rather than as a punishment for sins; but let us beware how we neglect this warning lest a worse calamity befall us. So shall this War, dreadful though it is, become a blessing to England.

Helping the Enemy

When the Children of Israel were fighting against the Amalekites, Moses was on a hill where he could be seen from the battlefield, praying to God. While Moses continued to pray the Israelites gained, but when he ceased through exhaustion the enemy gained. This was so noticeable that Aaron and Hur, who were with him, held up his hands that he might continue in the attitude of prayer after he was too exhausted to do so without help. So you see, that when Moses ceased to pray he was practically helping the enemy. In like manner, we are helping the enemy while we neglect to pray to and to worship God. But, you say, some thousands of people have been regularly praying to God for peace ever since the War began; how is it that their prayers are not answered? Because God's purpose is not yet achieved. He wishes for the prayers and worship of millions who have not yet turned to Him. Fellow working men! Do not help the enemy any longer. Pull yourselves together; attend public worship regularly and take your wives and families with you. Fill all the Churches and Chapels to overflowing and when you are in God's House pray earnestly for the blessing on our soldiers and sailors that they may not, after they have risked their lives for our sakes to save England from invasion, be called unprepared to the Great Judgement Throne.

In the early morning of the 9th August 1915 the Acasta Class destroyer, HMS Lynx, struck a mine in Moray Firth and immediately sank. Her captain, Commander J. Cole, was lost along with seventy three crew members. The twenty six survivors were picked up by the SS Volcano. Newdigate lad Arthur Still was not on board as he had been transferred. There was however some confusion. One mother writing from Gravesend, upon receiving notification

HMS Lynx in 1914 (Reproduced by kind permission from the National Maritime Museum)

of her son's death, was certain that a mistake had been made as the last time she had heard from him he was on board another ship. Sadly he had lately been posted to the Lynx. Another wife writing from Eastney near Portsmouth was told that her husband had been killed only to learn that he was not, in fact, on board but had been transferred to another ship. Another widow, after being informed of her husband's death, wrote to the Admiralty advising them that her husband was a chief stoker and not just a stoker as described in the notification. This, she explained, would have an effect upon the amount of pension she would receive.

The desperate need for shells, which contributed to the fall of Herbert Asquith's Liberal Government, led to one of Lloyd George's measures which still survives today. Excessive drinking and time lost through hangovers was affecting the war effort. 'Drink is doing us more damage in the war than all the German submarines put together'. Licensing laws were introduced and 'treating' (buying drinks for other people, especially soldiers) was forbidden.

2nd Lieutenant GERARD THEODORE BRAY
"D" Company, 2/4th Battalion, formerly 5th Battalion,
The Queen's (Royal West Surrey Regiment)

Gerard Theodore Bray was born in 1885 in Kensington. As a young boy he lived with his brothers and sisters in some opulence at 18 Cottesmore Gardens in Kensington. His father was a barrister who was later to become His Honour Judge Sir Edward Bray, and was descended from the Bray family of Shere in Surrey, whilst his mother Edith was the daughter of the Rev. Thomas Hubbard who was vicar of St John's in Newbury. Gerard was educated at Charterhouse and later took a position as Engineer on the Great Northern Railway. He emigrated to Vancouver and there he married Evelyn Joan Broadwood (known as Joan) on the 28th November 1911. They had two daughters, Madeleine and Audrey. At the outbreak of the war he enlisted as a private in the 2nd Canadian Contingent but decided to return to England. He, his wife and two daughters then aged 2 and 1, together with their nannie, Elsa Vants, left their home in Burquitlam, New Westminster and travelled overland to New York where they boarded the Atlantic Transport Line's 'Minnehaha'. (Built by Harland & Wolff in 1901 and torpedoed and sunk off Fastnet on the 7th September 1917 with the loss of 43 lives).

The Minnehaha docked at London on the 15th December 1914. Upon his return to England Gerard was given a commission in the 5th Battalion the Queen's which became the 2/4th. He settled his family in with his sister-in-law, Audrey Innes, at their home at The Greenings, a large house on the road between Newdigate and Charlwood. In the May, the Hon. Sir Henry Cubitt, C.R. Lord Lieutenant of Surrey, motored to Jesus College Close in Cambridge to inspect the Queen's (Composite) Battalion which had been formed from the 2/4th and 2/5th Battalions of the Queen's Regiment. Upon alighting from his car he was met by the Commanding Officer, Col. Frank Watney. This was the first Territorial Battalion from Surrey to be selected for active service and amongst the officers taking part in the inspection was 2nd Lt. G. T. Bray.

The battalion entrained to Devonport, and at 8.00 p.m. on the 17th July 1915, the SS Ulysses left Devonport en route for Gallipoli and Lt. Bray waved farewell to England for the last time. The Commander-in-Chief, sensing that the men were not as buoyant as the group involved in the original landings in April, tried to raise morale by saying, 'As to you, soldiers of the new formations, you are privileged indeed to have the chance vouchsafed you of playing a decisive part in events which may herald the birth of a new and happier world. You stand for the great cause of freedom. In the hour of trial remember this, and the faith that is in you will bring you victoriously through.'

The 2nd/4th became part of the 53rd Division and landed on 'C' Beach at Suvla Bay on 9th August where they were immediately thrown piecemeal into action along the British line. The landing was hazardous and when the beach was finally reached there was general chaos due to a lack of maps and briefing. This was coupled with the curses of heat, thirst, exhaustion and flies. Orders were immediately given to proceed to a line south-west of Chocolate Hill (Hill 53). They crossed the dry salt lake and as they were going up a hill they came under fire chiefly from Turkish snipers. It was here that Lt. Bray was mortally wounded, less than twenty-four hours after landing.

Joan Bray received news and cabled her sister Audrey from Charlwood on the 23rd August – 'Gerard reported wounded please ask War Office for information and how to get information and wire here'. Evelyn Broadwood wrote to his sister Audrey from Taylors in Capel on the 11th September:

Dearest A,
I am sorry to say that Joan has just received a wire from Mrs. Bray: 'Wire from Alexandria to War Office wounded and missing.' Aunt Helen and Aunt Mary arrived for a day or two this evening before this news arrived. Joan went up to her room at once and I have not seen her since. I hope that something definite will come to light. Since writing this Joan has appeared and seems to take it very well so that's a great thing.
Your loving, E.H.T. Broadwood.

Joan used the family influence in an attempt to obtain more definite information. During the month of September, Lucy Broadwood recorded in her diary that they had enlisted the help of Lord Shuttleworth (a former Liberal MP and Lord Lieutenant of Lancashire) who had made enquiries through the American Embassy concerning prisoners of war in Turkey. Lucy Broadwood wrote on the 26th September,

'Wrote to Joan Bray in answer to her letter enclosing a copy of a letter to her from 2nd Lieut. Ball who saw Gerard Bray apparently only slightly wounded in the leg near Chocolate Hill, Dardanelles and supposed he must be taken prisoner as he is not traced in hospitals. Two other accounts from privates told Joan that they believed Gerard was wounded in the foot or low down in the leg and thought our men had taken him on a stretcher. Another (I hope mistaken) account came through the Colonel of Gerard's regiment. This they have not repeated to Joan viz that amongst the colonel's wounded men, one in hospital at Eastbourne gave a circumstantial account of Gerard's death, how he was carrying a wounded soldier and was shot through the heart, dying a brave man's death. The soldier says that he crawled up to him and found him dead.'

2nd Lieut. Gerard T. Bray   *2nd Lieut. Gerard T. Bray*

On the 3rd October, John Innes wrote,

My dear Joan,

Audrey writes me that there is now very little hope of Gerard having survived the battle in Gallipoli and I write to say how very sorry I am. If what Mrs. Bray has heard is unfortunately true he must have died quite painlessly doing a very brave action and could not have known what happened to him.

We shall all miss him very much and Audrey and I will be only too pleased to help you and the children as far as possible both now and in the future.

Yours affectionately, John Innes

Joan did not give up hope especially after she had received a report from a Private Pink dated the 11th October 1915. Pink was in Lieut. Bray's company but not his platoon.

'We got orders to land at 1.30 a.m. Sunday morning. Ashore we were given a ration of bully beef. While eating it we had orders to advance. We crossed the dry lake. We were going up a hill on the other side when we came under fire. About 6.00 a.m. we rested where we were, then advanced again under more fire, could see no Turks. The fire chiefly from snipers. I saw Lieut. Bray hit, on the outside of the thigh. I bound up his leg with a handkerchief. Lieut. Bray gave them the range of some Turks, some small figures going up a hill at some distance off. A retirement was made. The men asked Lieut. Bray to retire, he said "No, never mind me".

He seemed to have more pluck than anyone else there. There was a slight trench cover from rifle fire on the shore. Colonel Watney was there when the men got back. Someone reported Lieut. Bray as having been taken to the dressing station on Chocolate Hill, a station established there two days before. An officer said, that makes the number of all our officers. The ground where Lieut. Bray was hit was only some four hundred yards from the landing point. It remained in our hands and the Turks were never there. The ground where the crops were burnt was away to the left. The men were astonished to hear that Lieut. Bray was missing.'

Joan continued to use contacts in high places all to no avail. As late as August 1916 she received a card from Major H.A. Brett, himself a prisoner of war – through the Croissant-Rouge Ottoman, a Swiss agency for prisoners of war – stating 'In reply to your letter via the Red Cross re. 2nd Lt G.T.Bray, I am afraid there is no hope. I have met, I believe, all the officers taken on the Dardanelles fronts, if he had been made a prisoner I certainly should have heard of him.' In November she received a similar negative reply from the Bureau Zuricois pour la Recherche des Disparus.

Finally, a Pte. A. Stanford reported Lieut. Bray's death, having been shown photographs of him. The Surrey Advertiser of the 16th December 1916 published the details:

'We were advancing to take the Turks' position beyond Chocolate Hill. Losing my company, I got mixed up with Lieut. Bray's platoon. We were under heavy rifle and machine-gun fire, a lot of our fellows getting hit, so Lieut. Bray gave us the order to retire, while he was attending to a wounded man. We had to retire across an open corn field. While going across this, I was wounded, and as I was lying wounded I saw Lieut. Bray coming across carrying a wounded man. As he was

A view of the beach at Suvla Bay showing Salt Lake and Chocolate Hill (Ref. Q50472) Reproduced by kind permission of the Imperial War Museum

passing me, I called out to him that I was hit, and he replied that he would come back for me if I waited. Immediately after, Lieut. Bray was hit and fell. I crawled over to him, but found that he was dead. I did not look to see where he was hit, but I think it was through the heart. I must say he died a brave man.'

45000 Allied soldiers fell during those August battles for, as a general put it, 'five hundred acres of bad grazing ground'.

The official citation for Lieut. Bray states that his death took place on Scimitar Hill though Joan wrote to the War Graves Commission in 1927 asking for the words to be substituted with, 'whilst carrying a wounded man on the slope towards Anafarta village, Suvla.' This amendment presumably never happened.

Gerard Bray's name is remembered on the Helles Memorial at Gallipoli and the Charterhouse Roll of Honour. Joan Bray never remarried and she lived the rest of her life in the locality. She died in 1972 and a memorial in Rusper church states 'Mother, Grandmother, Great Grandmother. Daughter of James H.T. Broadwood of Lyne and married to Gerard Theodore Bray of Shere.' His name is spelt as 'Gerald 'on the Newdigate War Memorial but, since the error was found, his name is always recounted correctly on Remembrance Day.

Officers of the Queen's (Composite Battalion)

Note written by Gerard Bray on the 17th July 1915 as he was en route to Gallipoli

Suvla Bay and Chocolate Hill – these photographs were taken by Gerard Bray and were probably recovered with the rest of his personal items which he would have left in safety before going forward.

Unbeknown to his wife and family Gerard Bray was killed almost as soon as he had arrived in Gallipoli – it took many months before confirmation of his death was received.

The Parish Magazine of September 1915 reported:

A service in memory of Lieutenant H.W. Goldberg, son of L. Goldberg Esq., Red House, was held on Saturday, August 14th. The officiating clergy were Canon Banister (Canon of Hereford), Rev. W. Urquhart (brother-in-law of the deceased), Rev. V. Ridgeway, son of the Bishop of Salisbury, and brother-in-law of deceased's wife, and the Rector. A beautiful address was given by Canon Banister. As an old friend of Lieutenant Goldberg's, he spoke of him as one indeed to be mourned by the nation. A man of exceptional intellectual power, who as far as his short life had gone had achieved great things and his family had justly looked forward to a brilliant future for him.

Combined with his great ability, Lieutenant Goldberg possessed a charm of manners and geniality that had endeared him to all with whom he came into contact. Canon Banister sought to give comfort to those who mourned by declaring his conviction that a life like that indeed is not ended but merely begun. He himself felt sure that those who are gone are progressing and carrying on in some way the work they had begun here.

After the address, Hymn 428 was sung, followed by the Blessing, and then the Nunc Dimittis was solemnly sung kneeling.

The chief mourners were: Mrs. Bertie Goldberg (wife), Mr. Goldberg, the Misses Goldberg, Mr. Frederick Goldberg, Rev. & Mrs. Urquhart, and Lieut. and Mrs. (sister) T.F. Shorland Ball. A large number of friends and villagers attended the service, who all wished to extend their deepest sympathy to those bereaved.

The Choir Boys had a very enjoyable tea in the Rectory Garden on Monday, August 10th, to which due justice was done. After this they adjourned to the Cricket Field, where a most exciting match was played.

Meetings will be held in the Institute on Wednesday afternoons, for the purpose of making sandbags for the Army. Hundreds of thousands of these are required on the Front and we hope to send a large number from Newdigate. Mrs. Irwine is organising these meetings and will be glad of any help.

A very pretty wedding took place in our dear little Church on Tuesday August 17th, when Miss Iris Irwine was married to 2nd Lieutenant Geoffrey Comber Griffith. Mr. Griffith gave up his important work and came to England and trained for the Army and was soon given a Commission. What a splendid example! We wish every happiness and trust by God's goodness they may be spared to live many happy years together.

Geoffrey Comber Griffith (b. 1889) was an engineer working in Brazil. He arrived in England on the Alcantara on the 17th October 1914 and gained a commission with the Seaforth Highlanders. He survived the war and at the time he applied for his medals in 1921 he was working for the Ceylon Goot Railway in Colombo.

The Rectory
August 23rd, 1915

My dear Friends,

I am sorry the August Magazines were so late in being delivered but I think no one is to be blamed. It was really caused by the war. We must try however not to let it happen again.

Just recently, we have been thinking much of the sad reverses suffered by the brave Russians, for undoubtably the Germans have made great and rapid progress in Poland. We trust the day will soon come when the Russians will be able to more than gain what they have lost, and it was most refreshing to read this morning of the great victory achieved by them in the Baltic – the importance of which can hardly be exaggerated. It is certainly the bounden duty of every one to ask himself what is he doing and whether he cannot do even more for the great cause of England and her Allies at this time.

It is very sad to read Mr. Haig's letter. I do hope there will be a large number who will join the Voluntary Training Corps, and so prepare themselves for any emergency. Forgive me if I make a remark which may seem harsh, and yet I feel it has much truth in it. It is this: I feel there are many of us who when asked to undertake any duty say, 'What shall I gain by it?' Surely dear people, we ought rather to say, 'What can I give – what sacrifice can I make?'

I am your affectionate Pastor, H.G. Bird.

In Gallipoli events were taking a turn for the worse for the allies, but all across the peninsula losses on both sides were appalling. In one incident the victorious Turks charged into the gully south of Rhododendron Ridge and, as the Anzac lines broke, colonels and generals fought side by side with privates in hand to hand combat in an attempt to stop the gap. The Turks then charged in four dense lines, and their impetus as they sped down the mountain was so great that they could not stop or turn back. They kept stumbling on in the face of fierce machine gun fire and barely a Turk returned to the hills. Back in Britain people started getting an inkling that things were not right as local soldiers returned home to tell their story.

Pte. Jack Pullen

Pte. Jack Pullen of Arnolds Cottages, Beare Green wrote vividly about the landings at Suvla Bay. He was attached to the 5th Queen's and after being shot in the thigh he was immediately removed to England. Writing from the Alexandra Hospital in Cosham near Portsmouth he said:

'I only had twelve hours on land, and that was quite enough too. It was something awful out there. We were at the new landing (Suvla Bay) and it was like taking Leith Hill, only a jolly sight worse, thousands got killed and wounded. I never thought they would send us back to England so soon. When we woke in the morning we could hear the firing, so we soon guessed where we *were off to. The same night we landed, had two hours sleep and then we were soon at it. The Turks had just had reinforcements, so we 'copped' it hot. I shall never forget as long as I live. Their snipers were a lot of trouble to us. Some of them were painted the same colours as the trees, consequently they were difficult to find.'*

Jack Pullen's brother, William, was also wounded.

Neither brother survived the war. Pte. William John Pullen, G/2236, of the 7th Battalion Royal West Surrey Regiment, was killed on the first day of the Battle of the Somme on the 1st July 1916. His brother Jack, Pte. H. Pullen was killed in December 1917.

The Dorking Advertiser published another dramatic report from a Private South of 'A' Company of the Composite Battalion which had been formed by amalgamating the 2nd/4th and 2nd/5th Battalions of the Queen's in April 1915.

The landing at Suvla Bay took place between 11.30 p.m. and 2.00 a.m. and we then had a two hours 'shake down' on the beach. At the end of that time we were told to advance, and we advanced to the bottom of Chocolate Hill. It was something cruel with the bullets whizzing all around us, but we reached the hill with the loss of only a few men. The Turks fired at us from three directions, from the front, and on the right and left. 'A' Company, commanded by Captain Bennett, led the advance. Captain Bennett has proved to be a splendid officer as have all the Queen's officers. We got to work round to the bottom of Chocolate Hill and advanced towards the left, the Turks being entrenched behind the hill.

We were next given the order to fix our bayonets and load our rifles. We were given the front position and told to take it the best we could. The men fairly leapt to the charge. It was every man for himself, and we were mad to get into it. We shouted and cheered as we dashed towards the hill, but we advanced too far, so that we came under a terrific gun fire, added to which the gorse caught fire. The order to retire was given, and we retired to a line of Turkish trenches just behind us and occupied these. Once inside we set to work digging to improve the trenches, the Turks 'throwing lead' at us all the time. We stopped in the trenches all the night, but none of us had any sleep, as we were continuously under fire. The firing calmed down about six o'clock the next morning. The snipers caused great concern. The women appear to be between 25 and 30 years of age and the men between 45 and 50. They are all painted green and are excellent shots.'

The Parish Magazine reported a couple of local news items:
The Newdigate headmaster, John Alfred Steeds, reported that attendances were very low owing to children absenting themselves to help with the harvest.

Ada Roffey from Sot's Hole celebrated her one hundredth birthday and many villagers visited her cottage to send their greetings.

...and the Dorking Advertiser reported that Gerard Bray was missing:

Ada Roffey, chatting to Maud and Lizzie Goldberg, outside her cottage at Sot's Hole on the occasion of her 100th birthday in 1915.

On the 28th August it was reported that 2nd Lt. G.T. Bray of the 5th Royal West Surrey Regiment, son of Mr. Edward Bray, Bloomsbury County Court Judge, brother of Sir Reginald M. Bray of the Manor House, Shere was wounded in action and a later report stated that he was now missing. His wife, Mrs. E. Bray of 26 Queens Gate Gardens, London SW, made a request for any information concerning the missing officer.

Alfred William Gibbs was leaving the village so he wrote a good-bye message:

Wood's Hill
Newdigate
25th August

My Dear Teachers and Scholars,
Will you please accept my heartfelt thanks for the lovely present which Miss Bird has given me in your name?

It was indeed a pleasant surprise and I would have liked to personally thank you all at the Sunday School Treat to-morrow, but important duties call me away. Let me take this opportunity of saying how much I have appreciated the privilege of being associated with the Sunday Schools and, perhaps after this terrible war is over, I may be permitted to take up my old work among you – a work I have loved and one in which I have received every encouragement from teachers and scholars alike.

Yours most sincerely, Alfred Wm. Gibbs.

Colonel Frank Dormay Watney CBE had been retired since 1909 and lived at a house called Copleys in Reigate. At the age of 45 he became the commander of the Composite Battalion in

Gallipoli and was very popular with the men and was described as a 'gallant officer'. On the 4th September he wrote the following tribute:

'The Queen's never wavered, and their dash and enthusiasm is marvellous ..... we had an awful experience, guns and rifle fire going off incessantly, but we did very well. No one fought further than we did, and at one time we were furthest forward, and we held our position at all costs, and have strengthened it, so that they will not take it now .... Of course, we were all shaken by want of sleep and want of water and food, but we shall pull right through, I hope.'

On Tuesday, 7th September, Mrs. Bourne of Bakershaw, Newdigate, received intimation that her son, Pte. S.R. Bourne (No. 2319) of the Queen's Royal West Surrey Regiment, was lying seriously ill at the Alexandra Hospital, Cosham. Pte. Bourne was severely wounded at the Dardanelles.

Arthur Francis Palmer Phillips of Newdigate was fined a pound at Horsham Petty Sessions on the 11th September for using excessive lights on his motor car.

Everybody feared the knock on the door, the pounding heart, the churning stomach – was it the dreaded telegram or was it the milkman? A mother, who had perhaps received such a telegram, wrote this poignant, rambling and bitter piece entitled 'My Only Son':

> *He writes 'I have great distinction won'.*
> *My darling, my stay, my only son.*
> *I prayed to God to keep him from harm,*
> *But my heart was daily filled with alarm.*
> *I was stricken dumb, it sapped my breath –*
> *'Wounded severely, but not unto death'*
> *Then came the news, he was 'maimed for life'*
> *But he fought most gallantly in the strife –*
> *'For you dear mother, I almost cried,*
> *But think how many brave men died'*
> *He tried to write me as in boyish glee –*
> *'I'm a Colonel mother, I have won the V.C.*
> *I saved a poor chap the foe struck down,*
> *And carried him safely back to town.*
> *He was safe, thank God, but alas! I fell*
> *Wounded and maimed by a screeching shell.*
> *Never mind, mother, your son will come home;*
> *All that is left of him, no more to roam.*
> *I can buy a leg, I'm not really a fright,*
> *And the arm that is left, you see is the right.*
> *So the left is the right, and the right the left,*
> *And I'm not altogether of arms bereft.*
> *You see, dear Mother, I have my sword.*

And his Majesty's kindly, heartfelt word.
'Promoted for gallantry, Colonel, and
For noble daring has won the V.C.'
So pray, cheer up, dearest mother mine;
I am still only 'that boy of thine';
I shall soon be well, then home again,
To see my Mother will cure my pain
Oh! Then, won't we have glorious days,
When my dear, brave Mother sings my praise.
She'll tell of the wonderful deeds he's done
And you'll make a hero of your only son.'

My darling son, I smile as I sigh,
Thank God, though maimed, you are not to die;
Truly, I'll welcome you home with cheer!
You never shall know of those hours so drear;
I'll comfort and bless you, my only son,
And help you to say 'God's will be done'.

However, there was still room for the patriotic verse,

If I should fall, grieve not that one so weak
and poor as I should die.
Nay, though thy heart should break.
Think only this. That when at dusk they speak
Of sons and brothers of another one
Then thou cans't say 'I too had a son,
He died for England's sake ....!

The Rector, writing towards the end of September, seems to be more optimistic as at last some better news was filtering in from the various fronts. The Russians were having success in Tarnopol in Galicia when on the 7th September it was reported 8000 men and thirty guns had been captured, and the French had some success when they gained a footing on the Aisne-Marne Canal. He does not mention the Zeppelin raids which were causing terror amongst the population. On the 8th September there were one hundred and six casualties; twenty killed during a raid over London.

The Rectory
September 27th, 1915

My dear Friends,
We are thankful today for the good news received from the Front after five months of depression

and anxiety. The French and our own soldiers have gained decided victories in the West and have taken many prisoners. The Russians are, most valiantly, holding their own in the East. We thank God for this, and pray that these successes may be the beginning of really more important ones. It gives me great pleasure to be told of the great interest that is being taken in making sandbags, for we are told that any number will be required in future. We must all do something to help in this great struggle. I am sorry to say we are still anxious about Rupert Bourne's wound, but the other cases of the sick and wounded are, I think, better.

I have received two or three letters from Lady Goodrich, who I greatly regret to say is leaving this neighbourhood, respecting the Choral Society. Most parishes in the district intend to practise the music selected by the Committee (parts of the Messiah) during the winter evenings and she begs Newdigate to do the same. I can only say that if a sufficiently large number wish to have these practices I shall be pleased to do my best – but unless a fairly large number express their intention of continuing the Society, I think it wiser not to attempt it.

The Sunday School Treat, which was held in the Rectory meadow on Sept. 3rd, was one of the most enjoyable ever attended; everyone was so happy and helpful.

The senior members of the choir expressed a wish some time ago, as it is war time, not to have their usual outing this year. We appreciate their decision very much. I hope we may be able to have a quiet evening together later on.

I am your sincere friend, H.G. Bird.

We understand that the memorial to the late Mr. Henry Hackwood, which will take the form of an Altar in the Lady Chapel, is nearly completed and it is hoped will shortly be erected in our dear old Church. We hear the carving has been most beautifully done by members of the local Carving Class, under the superintendence of Mrs. Janson.

The work has been entrusted to Joe Sanders (centre panel and part of frieze), William Broughton (inscription panels and part of frieze), George Horley (lily panel), P. Trow (lily panel), and Arthur Beck, Percy Trow and Norman Andrews (table).

Joseph James Sanders was born in Capel in 1889 and shortly afterwards his father, also Joseph, moved to Newdigate and farmed at Pancross Rolls Farm (now Melton Half). His father died in 1901, aged 38. The family later lived at Marshlands Cottages. Joe became a coachman for Mrs. Janson at Newdigate Place and this was considered to be a reserved occupation. He married Alice Bowring in 1919.

Joe Sanders

William Broughton was the son and fourth child of John Broughton, basket-maker, and Emily of Kingsland and was born in 1897.

George Horley was born in Newdigate in 1886, one of the seven children of Henry Horley, wood merchant of High Trees Farm. He became the village postman and a stalwart of the village, serving as churchwarden and bell ringer for over fifty years and in total holding over thirty village positions. He served in the Territorial Army and was in the Army Service Corps. George Horley Place is named after him.

Percy Victor Trow (13601) was the son of James and Kate Trow and lived at Brook Cottage, Workhouse Green. He served in the Royal Army Medical Corps from the 22nd November 1915 until his discharge on the 15th August 1919. A younger brother, Reginald (1901-1986) recalled ' My brother Ernest was seriously injured (Private Ernest Trow, G/6933, 3rd Battalion Royal West Surrey Regiment. Born 1886 and enlisted on the 22nd November 1915. He went to France on the 30th March 1916 and was seriously injured on the 13th September 1916 when he was shipped home. He was formally discharged on the 22nd August 1917 as physically unfit). A bomb exploded and out of the six men in the vicinity five were killed. Although badly injured, Ern lay there pretending to be dead until picked up by a search party. He was only thirty yards from the German trench. He was taken to a field hospital with forty pieces of shrapnel in his body. My father, James, was allowed to visit him for two days and didn't have to pay a penny. It was the only time he had been on a boat, let alone abroad. Five weeks later Ern was transferred to a London hospital and made a complete recovery, although pieces of metal kept coming out of his body for the rest of his life'.

Arthur Beck lived at The Lodge at Ockley Lodge.

Norman Andrews was born in the Isle of Wight in 1898 and lived with his parents at Russ Hill Cottages in Charlwood. He joined the Royal Field Artillery and was killed in September 1918.

The Battle of Loos, in late September, saw the first British gas attack but owing to the wind blowing in the wrong direction, it was not entirely successful. The British lost at Loos (in less than three weeks fighting in September and October) 2013 officers and 48,367 other ranks. These were the troops of Kitchener's New Army so optimistically raised in 1914.

By the Autumn of 1915, the question of how to maintain a regular supply of recruits was causing great anxiety. Casualties in Gallipoli were very high and in Flanders thirty thousand men per week were needed to take up the wastage. There were still over two million men of military age in the country who had not offered themselves for enlistment.

Lord Derby (1865-1948) was appointed Director of Recruitment and the last months of 1915 were a final chance of enlistment before conscription.

On October 12th, Edith Cavell, an English nurse, was shot by the Germans in Brussels. She was accused of being a spy and of aiding and abetting the escape of captured troops. The news was greeted with outrage, even by a British public who had grown used to reading about German 'atrocities' in the newspapers.

It was reported in the Dorking Advertiser on the 2nd October that Mr. David Green, the son of Mr F.E. Green of Barings Field, Newdigate had been gazetted 2nd Lieutenant in the 2/5th Suffolk Regiment.

Soldiers were in desperately short supply and a great recruiting rally was held at Redhill Common where there were processions and public meetings involving local dignitaries, urging for more young men to answer the call. In Newdigate the Voluntary Training Corps was meeting on Mondays at 7.30 p.m. for squad drill in the school playground, and on Thursdays for shooting at the rifle range. Lord Derby was entrusted with the task of canvassing recruits, and committees were set up in towns and villages throughout the country. F.G. Rose was appointed chairman of the Newdigate Committee.

The King was also enlisted to issue an appeal:

THE CALL OF THE KING

Buckingham Palace

To my People,
At this grave moment in the struggle between my people and a highly organised enemy who has transgressed the Laws of Nations and changed the ordinance that binds civilised Europe together, I appeal to you.

I rejoice in my Empire's effort, and I feel pride in the voluntary response from my Subjects all over the world who have sacrificed home, fortune and life itself, in order that another may not inherit the free Empire which their ancestors and mine have built.

I ask you to make good these sacrifices.

The end is not in sight. More men and yet more men are wanted to keep my Armies in the Field, and through them to secure Victory and enduring Peace.

In ancient days the darkest moment has ever produced in men of our race the sternest resolve.

I ask you, men of all classes, to come forward voluntarily and take your share in the fight.

In freely responding to my appeal, you will be giving your support to our brothers, who, for long months, have nobly upheld Britain's past traditions, and the glory of their Arms.

George R I

The Rectory
October 27th, 1915

My dear Friends,
We can hardly say that the attendance at the Harvest Thanksgiving Services came up to our expectations except that held on Sunday evening.

We cannot but think of the large number, no less than 100,000 Britons alone who have laid down their lives during the past 14 months of the War for their King and Country. May they rest in peace. They are better off we trust but our loss is irreparable. ' The souls of the righteous are in the hand of God and there shall no torment touch them. In the sight of the unwise they seemed to die and their departure was taken for misery. But they are at peace.'

Your sincere friend, H.G. Bird.

Mrs. Irwine of Hallings Hatch has sent the last of the sandbags from Newdigate to Miss Tyler, of Linden House, Highgate Road, London and High Trees, Newdigate. 1665 bags in all have been sent to her. Mrs. Irwine is very grateful to all those who so kindly helped her, by generous subscriptions and in cutting out and making the sandbags. It has evidently been a labour of love for everyone, as we all have the safety of our dear soldiers and sailors so much at heart. The meetings were well attended and very bright, but most of the work was done at home. Special thanks are due to Mrs. Palmer for her generous contributions of money and material. Also to those who came so often to help Mrs. Irwine to cut out and prepare the bags, to Mrs. Vine for her great help on every occasion, to Miss Dean for collecting money and for all her helpful suggestions and to Messrs. Butt, Monk and Bedding for kindly conveying the hessian and completed bags from and to Holmwood Station free of charge.

At our first meeting Mrs. Palmer kindly promised a bonus to the one who made the most sandbags. It was not needed as an incentive, but was offered as a recognition and all will be pleased to hear that it has been awarded to an old lady of 76 who has made, quite unaided, 161 bags.

The following letter has been received from Miss Tyler:

Dear Mrs. Irwine,

Newdigate is amazing! 1700 bags. I will send your letter to France to my brother. He was down every Sunday at High Trees last autumn when waiting for his Brigade to arrive from India. It seems years ago. I have not been down to Newdigate since he went out to the Front, I think. Certainly not since sandbags. I simply work at them, writing for them every moment I can get away from the Hospital till late at night, or late next morning rather, and all Sunday. I comfort myself, that to labour is to pray. It is to save life; and we have the Divine sanction here. I think we are doing what He would have done.

Will you thank everybody in Newdigate for their splendid help to the Army in the Field. I am having a few extracts from a few of the officers' recent letters printed, that the thanks may go to the people who deserve them. I think we shall all be proud, so long as we live, of having taken a real active part in defeating the enemy by saving soldiers' lives in France. And every life or limb saved means a man, trained and armed, given to the service of his King and Country. We should have been proud had we raised and equipped a Regiment. We should be more so for having saved one! Suffering and death and bereavement averted. Lives, the bravest and best of the Nation, preserved. The Germans fight over our sandbags. They turn their machine guns on to them.

Thank the Newdigate people. We do belong to them and they to us. My father did love the little farm, and my mother too. So many memories are there! I was never reconciled to their passing on till this war. Now I thank God they have been spared all this.

Of our five at the Front, so far, three are killed, and one wounded and long ago back in the worst of it. Three more to go — perhaps five. What will be left when it all ends? It is always the best that go! Why? And it is strange how they go in a moment, and without a pang! Are they wanted elsewhere ? Is the fight in other spheres too? One wonders. Satan was to be loosed for a *season .... Certainly the devil is in this war. I always look upon it that we are fighting him. It is no ordinary war – war in all its elements – on earth, sea, in air and under the sea!*

   Yours gratefully, M.L. Tyler.

On the 26th November a violent thunderstorm broke over the peninsula at Gallipoli and after just one hour some of the trenches were three feet deep in water. This continued for twelve hours. The water poured from the saps and the trenches were filled to the parapets forcing men to swim or be drowned. As they climbed to higher ground they were cut down by machine-gun fire. Next night a northern wind swept across the hills in angry snowstorms and the snow settled in the soaking clothes of the men – then froze. Soldiers who scarcely a month before had been warm in the tropical summer were caught and frozen as they lay in the trenches. Cecil Hills, the son of Arthur and Emma Hills of High Trees Farm, who had emigrated to Australia, was wounded two days after the storm had struck and was evacuated to Malta. When it thawed in December, bodies came floating down in the gullies – the same gullies where in August British soldiers had been desperate for water. Rupert Brooke had died in the Gallipoli campaign from blood poisoning, on the island of Skyros, eight months previously. His 'corner of a foreign field that is forever England' must surely have referred to Skyros and not the morass that had become Gallipoli. The romantic dream was over.

The Rectory
November 29th, 1915

My dear Friends,
The Archbishops have appointed January 2nd to be observed as a day of humble intercession to Almighty God for the War. I hope that we shall observe it well in Newdigate.

   I have received a very warm letter of thanks from Miss Tyler thanking Newdigate for the sandbags. I am sorry I cannot print all sent to me but these two or three quotations from officers at the front show us what immense benefit these sandbags have been to them – "I can safely say our casualties to guns and men would have been quadrupled had it not been for them. I know I am understating this statement rather than otherwise, as the splinters flying about the first day were very thick." Again, " If the Government refuses to let sandbags come out to us from Miss Tyler, they are making a great mistake, as sandbags are the life and soul of any unit in the firing line and one can never have too many." Again, "You (i.e. Newdigate, 76 years old Mrs. Elsey of Kingsland and Co.) helped to win the Battle of Loos." Newdigate will, I am sure, make more if they are required.

   The high price of coal has created a difficulty in fulfilling our contract with the members of the Coal Club, which is to supply half a ton of coal to all who deposit not less than 10/- during the year. The price for half a ton of coal delivered at the cottages is 17/3d. Five shillings for each contributor has been granted from Smith's Charity, so that 2/3d has to be found for each member as there are 42 who have made full payments, there remains a deficiency of £4.14s.6d. towards this Mrs. Janson has given a £1 and Mr. Goldberg a guinea, and I have very great pleasure in giving 10/-. We should be very glad to receive any contributions towards the deficiency that still remains.

   I am, yours sincerely, H.G. Bird.

Miss L. Seward Hill of Fairholme wishes to take the opportunity of thanking all those who so kindly contributed to the Bovril Fund she collected for, she realised the sum of £4.14s.6d which she forwarded to Miss Gladys Storey (the head of the work). The fund provides hot cups of Bovril to our soldiers when they come out tired and weary from the trenches.

Gladys Storey was the daughter of the painter George Adolphus Storey and was a friend of Kate Dickens, the daughter of Charles. She was awarded an OBE for her work in supplying the troops with Bovril during both World Wars.

Attached to the Parish Magazine each month was a periodical called 'The Sign'. Advertisers, conscious of the war, praised their own goods patriotically:

"For the boys at the Front just put a cake or two of Pears in the next parcel of presents you are sending."
For the men in khaki, for men in blue, for men in mufti, for women too! The Swan Fountain Pen."

A decision had been taken to evacuate Gallipoli. The Australian, Lieutenant Colonel C.B. White, devised complete periods of silence to fool the Turks and starting from the 8th December the withdrawal began at nightime. The forces at Anzac and Suvla were gradually reduced until 'Z' night on the 20th December when there were just 20,000 more to go. At some places the British trenches were only twenty yards away from the Turks, and still the men had to be extracted from right under their noses. Self-firing rifles were installed and by 3 a.m. the last men were leaving the trenches. An hour later the dumps on the beach were set alight. Apart from two injuries the entire force had been safely evacuated. For many people it has been assumed that Gallipoli was an Anzac operation but according to Alan Moorehead in his book 'Gallipoli', the Australian War Memorial in 1978 quoted the following lives lost:
British – 21,255, French – 9,874, Australian – 8,709, Indian – 7,594, New Zealand – 2,701 and Turkish – 86,692.
General Sir Charles Munro BT, GCB, GCSI, GCMG, Colonel of the Queen's Regiment, who predicted up to 40% casualties, described the evacuation as 'an achievement without parallel in the annals of war. To disengage and to withdraw from a bold and active enemy is the most difficult of all military operations; and in this case the withdrawal was effected by surprise, with the opposing forces at close grips – in many cases within a few yards of each other. Such an operation when succeeded by a re-embarkation from an open beach, is one for which military history contains no precedent'.

The ordinary British Tommy saw things differently. He felt cheated and that the operation was a complete waste of human life and resources. Driver P. Donovan of the 11th Signal Co. Royal Engineers wrote to his home in Dorking:

Do you remember Suvla Bay, Sir?
Yes Lime Tree Gully and Anzac, too
Also the beach at Lalla Baba
Where the shrapnel often flew

I remember the night we landed, Sir,
There were Turks there by the score,
And didn't their batteries paste us
As we waded to the shore.

But we landed in spite of it all, Sir,
And the Turks they turned and ran,
And we chased them over the hill, Sir,
British Bull Dogs to a man.
But then, a sad thing happened, Sir,
After facing death again and again,
We were forced to retire some miles, Sir,
For our reinforcements never came.

Then we entrenched ourselves, Sir,
Still feeling stiff and sore,
And we held the line right bravely,
But alas! advanced no more.

Then, water, it was scarce, Sir,
Till we found a Turkish well,
And the snipers they got going
And they made it a little Hell.

By now the casualty lists just for the Royal West Surrey and East Surrey Regiments were filling more and more columns in the Dorking Advertiser. Killed, wounded, missing, gassed – the lists seemed endless. As men came home from leave with stories of unbelievable horror, it is small wonder that joining up had become less and less appealing.

Total British casualties on all fronts up to the 9th December 1915 were announced as 528,227.

With Christmas approaching and memories of the fraternisation that had taken place a year ago, the General Staff issued orders forbidding any contact to be made with the enemy. This was reinforced by instructing the Artillery to maintain a slow gun fire throughout the day – a Christmas present for Fritz.

Much serious discussion had taken place at Headquarters. First of all a change of leadership was needed. The 64-year-old Sir John French was removed from his position and shipped back to England to take up his new post in command of the Home Forces. Officially he was thanked for his invaluable work, given a peerage and assured of a handsome pension at the end of the war, but a scapegoat was needed, so Sir Douglas Haig became Commander-in-Chief.

The Battle of Loos showed that success was just a whisper away and with more careful planning a decisive breakthrough was possible. It was clear that more heavy guns and shells were needed to sufficiently cut the wire, more men were needed to support the initial breakthrough, and careful planning was needed to ensure that advances were consolidated. Getting at Germany through the 'back door' did not work, as was proved at Gallipoli, and the only real chance of success was on the Western Front where all resources could be concentrated.

Thus the seeds for the Battle of the Somme were sown.

Meanwhile back at Newdigate the menfolk, as they gathered in the Six Bells and the Surrey Oaks, reflected upon over a year of warfare. Many of the Newdigate lads with the Queen's had been involved in very fierce fighting but apart from Jack Burberry, over a year ago, they had all got through. It was difficult for those still at home to have a clear picture. Obviously there had been a lot of casualties, but the army had extricated itself brilliantly from the disaster at Gallipoli and would be able to concentrate on the main theatre of war in Flanders. Some of the lads had spoken of exhilarating and exciting times, and some had come back on leave morose and deep in their thoughts. True, the people in the big houses had suffered. They all knew the rector's son, Wilfred Bird, and sympathised deeply for his loss. Mr. Goldberg had lost a son, Mrs. Janson a nephew, Mrs. Bray was still waiting for news about her husband and the Misses Tyler had lost a brother and two nephews, but these were not really 'Newdigate people'. No, the village had got off lightly. Little did those men know, as they sat chatting over their glasses of ale, what the Army Commanders had in mind and of casualties that would be inflicted upon their village over the following months.

Pte. Herbert Harold Hopkins (1891-1981)

The Fuller Family

The Fuller Family outside their home at Kingsland

1916

Lord Derby's report was made public on Tuesday, 4th January 1916. It showed that over a million single men of military age had not attested and 651,160 single men were not accounted for. Under the first Military Services Act of January 1916, the so-called 'Bachelor's Bill', compulsory service was introduced to all single men between 18 and 41. The second Military Services Act of May 1916 included married men too. Many people were unhappy that exemptions had been made for conscientious objectors, who can briefly be defined as those whose religious beliefs forbade them from fighting, such as Quakers or Jehovah Witnesses, and those who were pacifists or political objectors who did not consider the German Government to be their enemy. Life was far from easy though for this group, as they were branded 'conshies', 'anarchists' or 'sickly idealists'. The No-Conscription Fellowship had issued the following proclamation:

Fellow citizens:
Conscription is now law in this country of free traditions. Our hard-won liberties have been violated. Conscription means the desecration of principles that we have long held dear; it involves the subordination of civil liberties to military dictation; it imperils the freedom of individual conscience and establishes in our midst that militarism which menaces all social graces and divides the peoples of all nations.

We re-affirm our determined resistance to all that is established by the Act.

We cannot assist in warfare. War, which to us is wrong. War, which the peoples do not seek, will only be made impossible when men, who so believe, remain steadfast to their convictions. Conscience, it is true, has been recognised in the Act, but it has been placed at the mercy of tribunals. We are prepared to answer for our faith before any tribunal, but we cannot accept any exemption that would compel those who hate war to kill by proxy or set them to tasks which would help in the furtherance of war.

We strongly condemn the monstrous assumption by Parliament that a man is deemed to be bound by an oath that he has never taken and forced under an authority he will never acknowledge to perform acts which outrage his deepest convictions. It is true that the present act applies only to a small section of the community, but a great tradition has been sacrificed. Already there is a clamour for an extension of the act. Admit the principle, and who can stay the march of militarism?

Repeal the Act. That is your only safeguard.

If this be not done, militarism will fasten its iron grip upon our national life and institutions. There will be imposed upon us the very system which statesmen affirm that they set out to overthrow.

What shall it profit the nation if it shall win the war and lose its own soul?

Some conscientious objectors accepted call up to the Non-Combatant Corps (NCC) or the Royal Army Medical Corps (RAMC) as non-combatants but often they faced ridicule and hostility. One paper called the NCC the No Courage Corps. The coming of conscription had however increased the employment of women in all types of industries, munitions, land-work, bus and train work, etc. and this led the way for women's suffrage several years after the war.

Pte. William Capon of Reffolds

Wounded list, 11th January 1916 – Pte. W. Capon, 10397, of the East Surrey Regiment.

News of 'shirkers' back at home had reached the men in the trenches and this letter from Corpl. R.E. Scott has presumably been written for the benefit of his concerned wife. Corpl. Scott had formerly been a postman in Reigate and was connected to the 5th Battalion, Queen's, before being transferred to the 8th City of London Territorials (Post Office Rifles).

We are right in the thick of it and we are simply swimming in mud. It's mud! mud! everywhere! We live in it, eat in it, walk in it and sleep in it. In spite of it all we are happy and cheerful.

I'm sure it would do the people of England good just to see our boys marching to and from the trenches, covered with mud from head to foot. They march past to their rest billets singing a popular chorus, laughing and joking as though they were returning from a big school treat. Of course they grumble sometimes (every good soldier does) but there are no shirkers. There is one thing that damps their spirits a bit, and that is when they get hold of an English paper and read how the single young men of 'Dear old Blighty' are holding back. I can tell you England would be proud of her soldier lads could she but see them here. They may give vent to their feelings in a curse occasionally when discussing the Bosches, but a more sober, level-headed man could not be found than the average Tommy Atkins. The discipline he learned at home in the training camps has stood him in good stead, and now he is out here doing the real thing he is putting the training he received to good purpose. I am sorry to say we have had some casualties, but thank God they are not heavy. We know we can beat the Huns, but we want to see the young men of England ready to back us up if they are needed. So the sooner they come forward and prepare themselves the sooner we shall be able to finish this horrible slaughter of human beings. Our lads out here are quite ready and daily wait for the order to 'Go'. They'll go right enough and show the Bosches that England's New Army is just as full of fight as the contemptible little one was. The Huns have had a taste of that and I can tell you they did not like it. But they've got more to follow.

The German nation, towards the end of 1915, was growing restless. A springtime offensive was planned. General Von Falkenhayn's plan to capture Belfort and Verdun and 'bleed the French white' was accepted. The offensive began on February 19th and Germany came very close to success after the capture of Fort Vaux on the 7th June but could not press home its attack. Fighting continued in this sector until November 1916.

Westley, Purdey and Emma Johns

Hampshire Telegraph & Post.
28th January 1916

Young Man's Suicide
Portsmouth Naval Barracks Tragedy
Diseased Foot & Delusions

The sad death of a young country lad who joined the Navy as a Cook's Mate and ended his life at the Royal Naval Barracks, Portsmouth because he was afraid he would be invalided on account of a bad foot was the subject of an inquest held by Sir Thomas Bramsdon JP at the Portsmouth Coroner's Court on Friday. The deceased was Westley Johns, aged 18, who joined the Navy with his chum named Reginald John Wooltorton in November. They had both been born and brought up at Newdigate, Surrey, where the deceased's father was formerly a gamekeeper, but was now doing labouring work. Deceased was always a cheerful, high spirited lad, but from birth had had a mild form of paralysis in the foot, which at times caused him great pain and caused him to limp. Lately the foot had been bad, and in consequence the deceased had been put on the sick list and was due to go before the doctor for medical survey. This worried him very much and he was also troubled because he had had a letter from his sister saying that his father had been drinking. He was, however, apparently quite well when he turned into his hammock alongside that of his chum on Wednesday night, but the following morning he was found strangled in the lavatory adjoining the dormitory. He had apparently made a slip knot in the cord of the blind, placed the noose around his neck, and thrown himself forward, causing the cord to tighten and strangle him. 1st Class Petty Officer H.L. Lympeny made the discovery and at once released the body and sent for Surgeon Reid RNVR who attributed death to strangulation. Deceased had evidently suffered from a wasting of the muscles of the left leg, and the foot was deformed. In every other respect the deceased was perfectly healthy.

Coroner's Officer Saxey, who searched deceased's effects found the following letter addressed to his mother:-

January 20th

"Dear Mum and Dad,
Thought I had better let you know. Hear I have to be shot so shall never come home no more. I am writing this letter in my hammock about 4 o'clock. Can't let you know anymore, so goodbye from West. Forget me not. Heard this yesterday."

On the envelope were initials which Saxey told the Coroner meant ' Sealed with a long kiss, from West'.

In several other letters deceased had said that his foot had been troubling him so much that he was afraid he would get his discharge from the Navy, which he did not want; and in another he remarked that he was very nearly a cripple.

A verdict of 'Suicide whilst of unsound mind' was returned.

Cook's Mate 2nd Class WESTLEY JOHNS M/16918
H.M.S. Victory, Royal Navy

Westley Johns was born in Harbridge near Ringwood in Hampshire in 1897 and was the son of William and Gertrude Johns. William was born in Newdigate and became a gamekeeper. His work took him to farms in Surrey, Hampshire and Sussex before he returned to Henfold in Newdigate. During this time he had married twice, his first wife, Julia Sarah, having died in 1893, and had nine children. His last two sons, Westley and Purdey, he named after the famous rifles. Westley was a member of Mrs. Janson's carving class and joined the navy, following his brothers, Purdey and Walter. He became a Cook's Mate attached to the Royal Naval Barracks in Portsmouth. On the 20th January 1916 he hanged himself there in 'D' room lavatory, whilst – according to the Coroner, the Hon. Sir T.A. Bramsdon – he was in 'a state of unsound mind'. He was just eighteen years of age. Strangely in 1933 his father, at the age of 71, shot himself and died as he was being taken to hospital.

The Rectory
January 25th, 1916

My dear Friends,
I have not much to say this month except again to express a hope that we shall all try our very utmost to serve God and our Country in the very best way we can. There are a few who make a point of being present at all the Wednesday Evening Services, but the number is small. I wish, at least, all who have friends serving at the Front, or in training, would feel it a privilege to remember them in their intercessions on Wednesdays
Mr. Palmer gave the sandbag makers an excellent tea at the Institute and my daughter gave her children one in the School-room.
With all best wishes,
I am, your sincere friend, H.G. Bird

In early February there was a serious outbreak of measles in the village, particularly amongst the larger families, and the school was closed for a month as over fifty children were absent out of 117 pupils on the books.

The Bishop of Dorking
February 1916

My dear People,
We are coming to another Lent, the second Lent of the Great War – and with all my heart I ask you to join in using it for the good of our Church and Country.
It finds us sadder and more anxious than the first Lent did, with heavier losses and more widespread sorrow. We have made mistakes. We have experienced in Gallipoli and Mesopotania

very humbling buffers. The nation has indeed made a mighty effort – yet we have not succeeded as we hoped: and the questions have been many about the foresight, skill, or energy of our Government, Statesmen and Commanders. But we have been disappointed also with ourselves. There has been much religious feeling, especially at the Front, but nothing like the great stirring for which we hoped at first.

Are we sure that if the war ended we should be nearer putting away drunkenness, with all its countless cruelties and waste of life.

Brethren we must begin again; we must do better: we must not be content with what we are, or what the Church is, or the nation.

You have seen in the newspaper that the leaders of the Church are inviting us all to prepare for a big effort this year called a National Mission of Repentance and Hope.

I desire to be yours in sincere and fatherly care, Edw. Winton

Thus the message and tone of the newsletter had changed with the commission of patriotic appeals and letters from the Front to the introduction of morality inducing articles. The moral condition of the population had become uppermost in the minds of the Church and much importance was given in the following months to the National Mission of Repentance and Hope. The purpose of the mission was to unite the Church and the Nation in one great effort to turn to God. October was the date for the mission and the nation was urged to use the ensuing time for preparation and prayer.

An appeal was made in the newsletter for women to offer their services to fill the places vacated by men, and as living was nearly 42% dearer than before the war, there was an urgent need to cut down on imports.

Dorking Advertiser – March 4th, 1916

<u>*A Battlefield Dirge*</u>

Weep not for me when I am dead,
Let no warm tears o'er me be shed
Think that for country dear I bled
And now I sweetly rest.
Grieve not your hearts that youth should yield
Its life upon the battlefield –
Regard it as a faithful shield
For those it loveth best.

Weep rather that the mind of man,
Evolveth yet no wiser plan,
Since disputations first began
Than the appeal to arms,

> *Grieve that the savage and the brute*
> *Still scatter wide their bitter fruit*
> *While nobler hopes are hushed and mute*
> *In midst of war's alarms.*

EFH, Dorking, 28th February 1916.

On the 11th March the Dorking Advertiser advised that Miss Goldberg of the Red House, Newdigate, had become the Village Registrar for the War Agricultural Service for Women to mobilize women for land work. Thus the great struggle for equality took a giant step forward as women throughout the country took on jobs previously the domain of men only. But not everyone agreed with this. Mrs. A.L. Cox of Blanks Farm, Newdigate wrote to the Advertiser on the 17th April:

I am a farmer's wife well on for fifty, and was born and brought up in Devonshire. I have done everything it is possible for a strong woman to do, both in the farmyard with cattle and on the land. Last Autumn I actually asked to be allowed to plough, to know if a woman could do it. To be candid, I only went four times through a thirteen acre field (my husband driving the horses), and although he said I mastered the plough well, it was enough to prove it is not a woman's work. Woe betide England if the land falls to women to cultivate!

I tried my hand at sheep shearing when I was a girl, for the same reason as I tried ploughing, but farm work from beginning to end is essentially men's work. Women can be and should be a great help to farmers to milk cows, feed calves, pigs and poultry, and very useful, indeed valuable, in the sheepfold with lambs. They can weed corn, hoe, pull and clean roots, help with the light work in hay and harvest field, but they must be countrywomen born and bred, and men must be at both ends of all these things to be a success. Countrywomen should do as they did when I was a girl – bake their own bread, make butter and cheese, cure their own bacon and hams, knit their family's stockings and make all their clothes instead of buying ready-made ones, and rear healthy children to replace the terrible devastation of this world war.

But it will be a great failure to send town women and girls on the land. They should remain in town to replace men called to the colours from shop, office and factory.

Under the Military Services Act, panels were established to examine people's claim for exemption. And each month the findings of the Dorking Urban Tribunal were published:

18.3.1916 – Hubert Wooltorton, gardener and in charge of electric plant at Newdigate. – refused exemption.

Dorking Advertiser – March 18th, 1916

Although now officially reported to have been killed at Suvla Bay, on the 9th August 1915, the family of 2nd Lieut. G.T. Bray, 5th RWSR are not without hope that he may be alive and a prisoner in Turkey. Lt. Bray, who was previously reported wounded and missing, was last seen carrying a wounded man on the slope towards the village of Anafarta, beyond Chocolate Hill. He is the youngest son of his Honour Judge Edward Bray and Mrs. Edward Bray, of 26, Queen's Gate Gardens, London SW, and was educated at Charterhouse. In 1911 he married Joan, elder daughter of the late Mr. and Mrs. Broadwood of Lyne. In the Autumn of 1914 when at Vancouver, British Colombia he enlisted in the 2nd Canadian Contingent and on his return to England received a commission in the 5th RWSR.

On the 15th April the Dorking Advertiser recorded the death of Mr. Richard Fogden following an accident. In November 1904 the Newdigate Parish Magazine had published details of his career as the local postman. From 1862-1891, having walked 14 miles per day and 12 miles every Sunday, he had totalled 145,788 miles. In November 1891 his round was altered and during the weekdays he had to walk 18 miles per day, making a total, up to November 1904, of 81,120 miles. A grand total of 226,908 miles or 9 times round the globe. This of course did not include the four miles there and back in getting to work. Although he had worked for 42 years he had made up his mind to retain his post for a while longer.

Parish Magazine – March 1916

Mrs. Winfield is glad to say that the little concert on March 6th was fairly successful from a monetary point of view, considering the 'times' we are passing through and the absence of the 'young' men who are serving their 'King and County'. It was very nice to see the room so well filled in spite of the snowy weather.

Dorking Advertiser

Military Tribunal – April 1st, 1916
Ebenezer Edwards, wheelwright and hay-rake manufacturer, Trig Street, Newdigate, applied for exemption on the grounds that he was in a certified occupation. He said he had lost his only man in the hay-rake department and it was not possible to replace him. He also assisted, with his brother, to support their mother. She was at the present time very ill, and he produced a medical certificate to that effect. If he went his brother would not be able to carry on the business. The tribunal was of the opinion that from the agricultural point of view the hay-rake department was the more important and they agreed to three months' exemption.

Miss Constance Aston of Sondes Place was appointed as the representative of the Dorking Rural District of the Surrey Committee for Women and Farm Labour and on the 17th April she arranged for a meeting to take place in the Village Institute. It was chaired by the Rev. H.G. Bird, who said that he was very interested in the subject of women's employment. His daughter, Ethel, was appointed as assistant registrar as Miss Goldberg, the officially appointed Village Registrar, was often away.

Miss Aston said that the cultivation of land must be done either by women or small boys but she felt that the former were more suited as it would be a pity to

Joseph Edwards (the brother of Ebenezer) and his wife Nellie and their four children, Philip, Eunice, Amy & George

On the farm

Rakemaker's Cottage on Trig Street – the home of the Edwards Family

take young boys out of school at the age of twelve. Miss Vaughan Williams spoke and said that she had many years' farming and in her opinion women could do anything – milking cows, dairy work, ploughing etc. She asked what those present grew in their gardens as she noticed that vegetables in Newdigate were scarce – she suggested that a village market might be started to sell the garden produce.

The Rectory
April 28th, 1916

My dear Friends,
First let me thank you very heartily for your offering at Easter. It was most kind of you and I value it very much, though what I value more deeply is the fact that a large number made their Communions on Easter Day.

I have spoken already of the National Mission of Repentance and Hope, which the Archbishops and Bishops trust will take place throughout England in the Autumn. So many people in England have given up their religious observances altogether, that we feel very strongly the need of a great revival.

We all of us feel the deepest sympathy for Mrs. Janson and the members of her family, for the terrible loss they have sustained by the death of Mrs. Janson's son, Walter Fitzroy Herron, whilst instructing some men in grenade shooting. A defective grenade exploded and he lost his life instantly, dying in the arms of his Colonel who loved him very dearly. Everyone speaks of his bravery and gentleness, and he won the affection of all – officers, non-commissioned officers and men alike. May God comfort those left behind by the remembrance of his unselfish and devoted life. 'Greater love hath no man than this that a man lay down his life for his friends.'

We are greatly indebted to Mrs. Janson for her gift of two carved Angels for the ends of the Choir Stalls. They have been beautifully done by Wm. Broughton, a member of her carving class who, like so many others from this parish, is training to do his bit for his country.

I am, your sincere friend,

H.G.Bird.

Will all those who have had Parish Blankets this year kindly wash them and return them to the Rectory before the 15th May.

Lieutenant WALTER FITZROY HERRON
4th Dragoon Guards

Walter Fitzroy Herron was born on the 4th February 1872 at Formosa Lodge in Twickenham but grew up in Kensington where he worked as a young man as a clerk at the family wool merchants business. He was educated at Uppingham, a school near Tours in France and Frankfurt-on-Maine. He shared with his brother Kenneth a love of sailing, and had a boat at Cowes and on the Blackwater River. He was also clerk to Gatwick Racecourse and a member of the Vale of the White Horse Hunt.

Walter served in the South African War with the Imperial Yeomanry (Queen's Medal with three clasps), volunteered on the outbreak of the war and was gazetted 2nd Lieutenant in the 4th Dragoon Guards (Royal Irish) on the 23rd September 1914 being promoted to Lieutenant in August 1915. He went to France in March 1915, leading his men at the cavalry charge at Ypres, and also assisted in trench fighting. The war diaries for the regiment take us to the 3rd April 1916 and state that 'Lt. Herron conducted his pioneer class at 8.30 a.m. at Cormont. In the afternoon a sad accident occurred at Inxent through the premature bursting of a rifle grenade. 2/Lieut W.F. Herron was killed instantaneously and Corp. Wheatley and Private Deardon wounded. The C.O., Capt. (Robert William) Oppenheim, Lieut. Farley and several other ranks were quite close when the explosion occurred, but were luckily not touched. 2nd Lieut. Herron had served continuously with the Regiment since April 1915, and during 1916, in the trenches, and in billets had performed the duties of Regimental Bomb Officer and Pioneer Officer untiringly. His loss is universally deplored. In the afternoon of the 6th April the Regiment marched to Etaples for the funeral of the late 2/Lieut. W.F. Herron. The service which took place at 3.00 p.m. was conducted by the Rev. E. Barclay, Chaplain to the 2nd Cavalry Brigade. Eight sergeants of the Regiment acted as coffin bearers, Lt. Herron's servants carried wreaths given by his Mother, Cousin, Officers of the Regiment, Officers of 'B' Squadron and 2nd Troop 'R' Sqdn. The Regimental Trumpeters sounded the

Lieut. Walter Fitzroy Herron

last post at the conclusion of the service'. He was 44 years of age. On the 1st August 1916 the London Gazette confirmed that his brother, Kenneth Chester Herron and his brother-in-law, Dennis William Bradwell had been appointed joint executors of his will and his addresses were given as 123 Pall Mall and 25 St Thomas's Street. He left over £50,000. He is buried at the Etaples Military Cemetery and like his brother he is remembered in a window in the south aisle in Newdigate church.

The Germans pressed home their attack around Verdun on May 23rd. On both Mort Homme and Hill 304 the grey piles of dead and wounded formed barriers some yards in height.

Meanwhile at sea the growing success of the British blockade persuaded Admiral Von Scheer, the new Commander of the German High Seas Fleet, to make a direct challenge against British naval supremacy. The Battle of Jutland on the 31st May was the last great fleet action. Within fifteen minutes of firing the British had suffered the disastrous loss of the Indefatigable and the Queen Mary, both having sunk after a few minutes of concentrated fire.

"There seems to be something wrong with our bloody ships today" complained Admiral Sir David Beattie.

At the end of the action the press heralded a great British naval victory – British casualties amounted to 343 officers and 6104 men killed and on the German side 172 officers and 2414 men were killed. Nevertheless this was the last time that the German High Seas Fleet ventured out en-bloc into the North Sea.

Dorking Advertiser – May 6th, 1916

At St. Peter's in Newdigate on Saturday a very impressive service was held in memory of the late Lieut. Walter Fitzroy Herron, 4th Dragoon Guards, who was accidentally killed while demonstrating the use of the rifle grenade. There was a large attendance of his family, friends, members of the staff of Messrs. G.R. Herron & Sons and most of the employees of Newdigate

Place house and estate, but unfortunately, military duties prevented his brothers, Lieut. G.F. Herron, RNVR and Lieut. K.C. Herron, Essex Yeomanry being present.

The rector, Rev. H.G. Bird, gave a very touching address, pointing out how much Lieut. W.F. Herron had given up for the sake of his country, first serving with the Imperial Yeomanry through the war in South Africa and again throwing up business, sport and all he held dear, at the very commencement of the present war, when he volunteered and was gazetted in the 4th Dragoon Guards in October 1914 and was sent to the Front in March 1915. The Rector also read letters from the Colonel of the 4th Dragoon Guards, stating that 'beyond being greatly loved and respected by both officers and men, his death was a serious loss to the Regiment, as he had always been a most useful officer, had served in every capacity from 2nd Lieutenant to Squadron Commander, was very cool and brave when in action, and had twice been recommended for mention in despatches, though unfortunately the honour had not arrived in time. He also said his own personal grief was very great, as Walter Herron had so endeared himself that he had left a blank which could never be filled, and that though he had died from an accident, he had given his life for his country just as much as though he had fallen in action.'

After other kindly and hopeful words from the Rector the service was brought to a close by the 'Dead March' from 'Saul' being duly rendered on the organ by Miss M. Broughton.

We may add that the late Lieut. W.F. Herron was the son of the late Mr. G.O.M. Herron and Mrs. Janson of Newdigate Place, was educated at Uppingham, and after serving through the war in South Africa was made one of the Managing Directors of the firm of G.R. Herron & Sons, Wool Merchants, London. He was a member of the Conservative Club, the Royal Corinthian Yacht Club and the Quorn Hunt, was a good all-round sportsman and proficient at all games. He was killed on the 3rd April 1916, age 46, but it was not till the 18th April his promotion was gazetted as dating from the 5th August 1915.

(He was in fact 42 and De Ruvigny's Roll of Honour states that he was a member of the Vale of the White Horse Hunt whilst the obituary states the Quorn Hunt.)

F.E. Green, ever mindful of the needs of the poor, wrote to the Dorking Advertiser. Newdigate is one of many parishes to benefit from Henry Smith's Charity whereby a grant of money is issued each year and the trustees are entrusted to distribute the amount to needy villagers. The tradition continues to this day.

Barings Field,
Newdigate
May 11th, 1916

Dear Sirs,

As the high price of the necessities of life are pressing heavily upon old age pensioners, so much so that the purchasing power of 5s has dropped to 3s., I would like to suggest that either the Trustees of Smith's Charity in our village should make an extra grant of food to old age pensioners or that the local Emergency Committee should make a weekly allowance out of the funds at their disposal for the relief of distress.

F. E.Green

Sapper Matthew Cassell, 65561, enlisted in Guildford on the 26th January 1915 and joined the 106th Field Company of the Royal Engineers. He was a plumber, living at Kingsland, Newdigate, and he left behind his wife Alice Caroline and four children. His only medical problem was defective and deficient teeth. He received an injury to his back on the 18th December 1915 and was sent to the 4th North Lincolnshire Hospital and later sent home to recover. He was discharged from the army on the 11th May 1916 as no longer physically fit for duty, suffering from rheumatism to the back and legs.

On the 17th May there was a prize presentation for members of the Rifle Club and of the Institute. A special presentation was made to Mr. John A. Steeds, the headmaster, before he joined the colours. The Rector made the presentation which took the form of a leather case containing £17 in Treasury Notes. Mr. F.E. Green spoke of Mr. Steeds' unremitting labours with the Volunteer Training Corps, the Rifle Club, the Emergency Committee, the Institute and other social activities. He presented Mr. Steeds with a long churchwarden's pipe (he was a churchwarden) which he was asked to smoke as a pipe of peace after victory was assured.

27th May 1916 – Pte. William T. Eade, 5941, Royal West Surrey Regiment, Labour Corps, of Newdigate, appeared on the Casualty List. He lived at Dowces Farm from 1907-18 and was living at Brook Cottage in 1918.

The Dorking Advertiser started carrying half-page advertisements listing people and their last known address who had failed to appear for Military Service. Information from the general public about the whereabouts of these people was requested. There was no hiding place for the 'shirker'.

The Rectory,
May 27th, 1916

My dear Friends,
May I take this opportunity of asking everyone, young or old, to take his part in the work of the National Mission of Repentance and Hope? I ask the prayers of all for a great outpouring of God's Holy Spirit on England.
"Our boys" are fighting for us; over 5,000,000 of them freely volunteered to undertake the hardest of tasks and endure the most severe hardships, in order to defend us at home. Brave good fellows. But let us be equally brave, equally courageous in fighting against sin and the evils of sin.
I am, your affectionate Pastor, H.G. Bird

On the 9th June attendance at the school was down to 58 due to a scarlet fever epidemic, and the school was closed for ten days over the Whitsun holiday period. It was closed again at the end of the month when, in addition to scarlet fever, German measles had also arrived. Measles, whooping cough, diptheria, scarlet fever and German measles could all be fatal and it was considered that isolation was absolutely essential. The school re-opened on the 3rd July but, with attendance down to 43, it was closed again for another week.

The effects and the powers of the Defence of the Realm Act, which virtually put Britain under Martial Law, had to be carefully explained so Mr. Gordon Clark came to the village on the 23rd May and addressed an audience. He explained that people caught spying or interfering with military installations could be court-martialled and that the Government had powers to control all energy supplies, seize land, clear areas of inhabitants and arrest anyone causing alarm or disaffection.

Under the Act, people who considered themselves to be exempt from military service had to present themselves to the Dorking Urban Tribunal and the results were published by the Dorking Advertiser in their issues of the 24th June and 1st July.

Arthur Mark Weller, 35, Cudworth gardener – application for exemption withdrawn
Edward Vine, 39, Village Club, poultry farmer – conditional exemption till 1st January 1917
Henry Voice, 38, Lyne Farm, farm bailiff – conditional exemption till 1st January 1917.
Thos. Voice, Marelands, farm manager, ploughman, stockman – conditional exemption till 1st January 1917.

> *The Rectory*
> *June 26th, 1916*

My dear Friends,
I am anxious to address you again on the great need of preparation for the National Mission which will be so soon upon us. May God grant that it may be greatly blessed in this Parish.
The National Mission is, in the first place, a call to the Church to repent.
We are to repent not because we believe that we were guilty of provoking this war, but because we, together with the other nations that profess to be Christian, have failed to learn how to live together as a Christian family, how to set forth Christ to the peoples who do not know him.
I am, yours affectionately in Christ, H.G. Bird

Will members of the Nursing Association kindly note that Nurse Elderson is now living at Mrs. R. Butcher's, "Goss Croft", opposite "The Knowle", Newdigate.
A charming tea was given by Mrs. Middleton and Miss Seward Hill in the Institute, on June 7th to the members of the Mothers' Union. After tea, the mothers danced, and played musical chairs etc. most vigorously.

The London Gazette is an official newspaper 'published by authority to disseminate and record official, regulatory and legal information'. On the 15th June 1915, as was customary, it published a report sent to the Secretary of State for War from General Sir Douglas Haig GCB, Commander-in-Chief of the British Forces in France.

General Headquarters, 30th April 1916
'I have the honour to forward herewith the names of those under my command whom I wish to bring to notice for gallant and distinguished conduct in the field.'

Amongst a long list is the name of 2nd Lt. W.F. Herron (killed), 4th Dragoon Guards. The parish magazine brought this to the villagers' attention with the following comment:

It is sad to think that he never had the satisfaction to hear of this honour, nor of his promotion from 2nd to 1st lieutenant, though the latter dated from August 1915. We wish to congratulate Mrs. Janson and the members of her family for the distinctions gained by the late Lieut. Walter Fitzroy Herron. Newdigate will always be proud of him.

Saturday 1st July 1916 was the first day of the Battle of the Somme – the expected and much anticipated 'Big Push'. A mighty bombardment of more than a million and a half shells preceded the attack, and floors in London and the South East shook with the vibration from the big guns. When thousands of Allied troops emerged from their trenches to advance towards the enemies' position, they found the ground covered with unexploded shells. As they moved forwards the German machine-gunners, virtually unharmed during the artillery attack, rose from their deep trenches to exact a withering fire at the ponderous allied troops who were walking, not running, towards them with full packs on their backs. The regiments wasted away on an impossible task.

Nearly 20,000 British soldiers died on that first day and nearly 40,000 others were seriously wounded. This was the volunteer army of Kitchener and they had expected a conclusive victory.

Sir Douglas Haig's despatch was published on July 11th. It stated that, after ten days and nights of continuous fighting British troops had completed the 'methodical capture' of the enemy's first system of defence on a front of eight miles. Prisoners exceeded 7,500 and twenty-six field guns had been captured.

Early reports of 'slight losses' and 'some wounded' were negated as newspapers published pages after pages of the dead and missing. Frantic letters to battalions, hospitals and soldier friends were sent in attempts to locate missing friends, relatives and lovers – and to learn more about the exact circumstances, reasons and manner of death.

Newdigate was to lose seven men over the next few months – Stephen Harber, John Kempshall, William Wyatt, George Howson, William Chatfield, William Beadle and Arthur Monk.

The Rectory
July 25th, 1916

My Dear Friends,
We have been passing through a time of great rush I think. So many have been helping in the hay fields, and others have been doing quite useful and important work. In the midst of it all we had a visit from the Pilgrims. Their visit was a very happy one. These ladies are giving up their happy, quiet homes, in order to come and speak to us on the most important subjects connected with our life, but their time in Newdigate was made very happy by your kindness to them.

*Albert Henry Horley with his parents Henry
& Emily*

We are grieved to say some of our dear ones at the front have been wounded. We were first told of Albert Horley, who had been recommended for the D.C.M., who is now in the military hospital at Kendal. Then we heard of one of the Kempshalls, and now we are told that William Hopkins has been wounded and is in hospital at Manchester. I am afraid there are others who are wounded, but not, I hope, seriously. May God be with them and soon restore them to health again.

In great haste, I am, your affectionate Pastor H.G. Bird

The National Mission

The importance of a good start cannot be over-estimated and our Winchester Diocesan Council has certainly realised this, seeing it has now been in active work since the beginning of March.

All the groundwork necessary to commence the great work has been covered, and committees duly appointed and it is now "up" to the Rural Deaneries and their respective parishes to put in the spade work.

The owners of the smallholdings at Cudworth were playing an important role in food production, as can be illustrated by the fact that at the Military Act Tribunal of July 13th the panel stated that John Ernest Aitcheson (36), a smallholder of Cudworth, should be excluded from military service as he was engaged in work of national importance. Similar judgements were passed on Lionel Bedding (36) of Ash Farm, Walter Hawkins (32) of Oulton and Henry Winfield (40) of Brook Farm.

The Battle of the Somme wore on through the month of August giving way to the great battle of Ancre which began in mid September and continued till mid December. The pattern of war was attack, retire, attack, retire – for example four parts of the Hessian Trench had each changed hands four times by the 30th September.... And the slaughter continued.

Private WILLIAM CHARLES CHATFIELD G/2770
1st Battalion, The Queen's
(Royal West Surrey Regiment)

William Charles Chatfield was born in the small village of Nutley on the edge of the Ashdown Forest near Uckfield in 1894 where he grew up with his brother

Alfred and sister Mabel. His father died in 1904 and his mother, Harriett Annie, married William Henry Wheeler in Cuckfield two years later. They set up home in Marshalls Cottages in Maresfield where Henry (as he was known) and his stepson William worked on the local farm whilst Harriett looked after the children and her new daughter Millie. Eventually the family moved to New Barn Cottages in Seale near Farnham, but before that William and his mother came to work for Captain Palmer at Oaklands Park, Partridge Lane, Newdigate, where he became well known and respected throughout the district. William enlisted into the Queen's at Dorking. The battalion

Pte. William Charles Chatfield

was involved in the bitter fighting from the 15th to the 22nd July 1916 around High Wood and the attack on the trench known as the German Switch during which there were 1,697 casualties. Pte. Chatfield was accidentally killed on the 29th July by a bomb which he was about to throw into an enemy trench, and is buried in the Dernacourt Communal Cemetery which at the time was used by the Field Ambulances. His name is also recorded on the memorial in Nutley Parish Church.

Private STEPHEN CHARLES HARBER G/440
7th Battalion, the Queen's
(Royal West Surrey Regiment)

Stephen Harber was born in Banstead in 1887, the son of Charles Henry and Ada Harber. Charles worked on maintaining roads, and he and his wife had eight children. They moved from Banstead to Walton-on-Thames and then to Holmwood before settling at Newdigate in 1911. Stephen was a member of the Newdigate Rifle Club. Before the war he was in the Territorials and was known to be a good shot. During the war the family lived first at Myrtle Cottage and then at The Mascot which had more land.

Trônes Wood was deemed to be tactically vital if the Somme battle was to be successful since, all the while it was in German hands, the main attack northward would be seriously delayed. The orders for the 7th Queen's were to attack the wood from a point on the railway to its north extremity, and to occupy and clear it, consolidating the eastern edge. The Battalion front of attack was 730 yards and Private Stephen Harber and his comrades moved off at 5.30 a.m. on the morning of the 14th July 1916. It became clear that the bombardment of Trônes Wood had been insufficient to neutralise the enemy. When the artillery barrage was lifted the Battalion was immediately met with heavy machine-gun and rifle fire from the west and by a heavy barrage of artillery. The first two lines suffered very heavy casualties in impossible conditions, and it was here that Private Harber fell. His body was not recovered. He is remembered on the

Pte. Stephen Charles Harber

Thiepval Memorial. Two days later his cousin, Lance Corporal Bertie Charlwood, G/2016, was also killed whilst serving in the same regiment.

Private AUBREY HUDSON, 1986
22nd Battalion Royal Fusiliers

The records show that Aubrey Hudson was born in Ifield in Sussex and was resident in the Rusper Road, Newdigate, when he enlisted into the army at Horsham at an unknown date. He was awarded the Victory Medal and the British War Medal. Aubrey Hudson was born on the 30th June 1901 so he would have been just over fifteen years of age when he met his death. He grew up in an old timber framed cottage called Ivy Cottage, which can still be found in Langley Lane in Ifield, with his father (a Yorkshireman called George), his mother (a local woman called Rosa), and his older brother George and younger brother, Walter David. His grandfather farmed 210 acres at Howsham in Yorkshire and in the 1890s his father travelled south to manage the farm in Ifield, before later moving to Home Farm in Newdigate.

According to Reginald Trow (1901-1986), who remembered him, Aubrey was a tall lad and good at boxing; he joined up at a very young age. John Steeds, the headmaster at Newdigate School, had reason to enter his name in the punishment book on five occasions from January until September 1914 for such crimes as 'generally slack, talking and inattention, careless writing and spelling, talking and being idle'. Aubrey joined the 22nd Battalion Royal Fusiliers which

Home Farm

Major R. Barnett Barker

was raised by the Mayor of Kensington in response to Lord Kitchener's appeal in September 1914. The new battalion, 1000 strong, was billeted in Horsham and Roffey for intensive training, so perhaps this was when Aubrey Hudson enlisted. In June 1915 they left Horsham for further training in Clipstone and then to Tidworth on Salisbury Plain, before finally leaving for France on the 16th November 1915 under the popular command of Major R. Barnett Barker (later Brig-Gen R. Barnett Barker D.S.O. and Bar, who was to die on the 25th March 1918 when he was hit by a stray shell at Guedecourt whilst commanding the 99th Infantry Brigade).

The 'History of the 22nd Battalion' takes up the story: 'Christmas was spent on the front line but by May the battalion was in the Vimy sector. With July came the Battle of the Somme but it was not until the 20th July that they went south to Amiens and then marched to Montauban and Delville Wood where they arrived on the 25th. The march had been exhausting and exciting, through the old front lines and into the tortured, littered area of the stinking battle ground: such artillery fire, such debris, such smells, such confusion were all new experiences, and to these were added during the next few days the whirr and plop of tear-shells and gas-shells to add to the general discomfort. At 3.00 a.m. on the 27th C and D Companies moved to some trenches in the valley, and H.Q. to a ditch at the road-side near the bottom of Bernafay Wood, while A and B Companies were organised into carrying parties. (*Aubrey Hudson was with B Company in Delville Wood and the action of that day saw four officers and 26 other ranks killed and 143 wounded.*) The communication trench to the wood, Longueval Alley, was a shambles, full of dead or sleeping men, and the open ground was swept by shell-fire continuously; so the exhaustion of the carrying parties can be neither imagined nor described.'

The devastated Delville Wood on the 20th September 1916 (Ref. Q1156) Reproduced by kind permission of the Imperial War Museum

Aubrey Hudson died on the 28th July 1916 and his body was never found. On the following day the battalion, now consisting of just 18 officers and 400 other ranks, was withdrawn from the front line.

After the war an Old Comrades' Association was formed and the following message was distributed to the next-of-kin of their fallen comrades.

'We, the first General Meeting of the survivors of the 22nd (Kensington) Battalion of the Royal Fusiliers, wish to express to you, the relatives of our comrade who gave his life for our King and Country, the deep and unfailing honour in which we hold his memory. We, who knew something of the daily hazard of life on the Western Front – how one man is taken and the other left, how death may come in an instant or after hours of suffering; we, who are proud of our battalion and of the spirit that animated it throughout its history, wish to place on record at this first opportunity our gratitude to our fallen comrades for the example and the inspiration that they gave us in their lives and by their deaths. And we pray for you, who waited in suspense and at the end heard the grievous tidings from across the sea, that God may comfort you in your loss, and that pride in the record of our battalion may temper the bitterness of your sorrow.'

Aubrey's name is recorded on the Thiepval Memorial and also on a plaque in the vestry at Newdigate church which was hand-carved by William Broughton in memory of the members of Mrs Janson's wood carving class who died during the war. If he joined the regiment when it was billeted in Horsham, then he would have been under 14 years of age at the time of his enlistment.

Private JOHN KEMPSHALL G/6925
7th Battalion, The Queen's
(Royal West Surrey Regiment)

The first record of the Kempshall family in Newdigate was in 1605, when Richard Kempsell and his wife Susan moved to the village from Chipstead and had their five children baptised in the church. John Kempshall was born nearly three hundred years later in 1895 and was one of the twelve children of Henry John and Alice Kempshall. Henry was a waggoner on a farm, and John along with some of his brothers became farm labourers. They all lived in cramped conditions in North Barn Cottages, Newdigate, just north of Lyne House. John Kempshall was posted to the 7th The Queen's, the same regiment as Stephen Harber, and he was killed at the Battle of the Somme during the engagement at Trônes Wood. On the 13th July 1916 the trenches received heavy enemy shelling but nevertheless the battalion assaulted the wood over a 750-yard front. They were met by heavy rifle, machine-gun and shell fire, as the enemy positions had suffered little damage from the earlier bombardment. The men were ordered to withdraw, but John Kempshall was already dead and did not make the comparative safety of

Bedford Trench where a roll call revealed that 13 officers and 216 other ranks had become casualties that day. It took nearly a year before Private Kempshall's death was officially confirmed. Another Newdigate lad from the battalion, Stephen Harber, was killed the following day at the same place. Their bodies were never recovered and both young soldiers are remembered on the Thiepval Memorial. John Kempshall also appears on the Rusper war memorial.

Trônes Wood on the 10th August 1916 (Ref. Q861) Reproduced by kind permission of the Imperial War Museum'

Sapper WILLIAM WYATT, 139570
Royal Engineers

William was the son of William and Fanny Wyatt and was born in 1867. He grew up with his parents and sister, Annie Harriett, at the Abinger Arms where his father combined two occupations, that of the innkeeper and also as a bricklayer. William married Ann Selina Smith in 1887 and like his father worked as a bricklayer. They moved to Brendon Cottage, Kingsland and had fourteen children.

The parents, children and William senior slept head to toe in a tiny cottage. One day William shook his head when he saw young men in the village who had not joined up, so – determined to set an example – he duly enlisted. He was killed on the 14th July 1916 and is buried at the Basra War Cemetery. His wife was left to look after all the surviving children but she must have been a very strong woman as she lived to be 101 and died in 1975.

In August 1916, Lt. Arthur Graeme West from Norfolk obtained a few weeks' leave and visited his friend, Cyril Joad and his new bride, Mary, at Box Hill. Arthur had been desperately unhappy and – after intently listening to his pacifist friend – he resolved to resign and walk away from the war. He wrote a letter to his Commanding Officer but as he was walking towards Westhumble Station, he stopped at the letter-box, hesitated and put the letter back in his pocket. Less than a year later, in April 1917, he was shot by a sniper near Bapaume aged 25. He kept a diary and wrote poetry.

The Night Patrol

Over the top! The wire's thin here, unbarbed
Plain rusty coils, not staked, and low enough:
Full of old tins, though – "When you're
Through, all three,
Aim quarter left for fifty yards or so,
Then straight for that new piece of German wire;
See if it's thick, and listen for a while
For sounds of working; don't run any risks.
About an hour; now, over!"
And we placed
Our hands on the topmost sand-bags, leapt, and stood
A second with curved backs, then crept to the wire,
Wormed ourselves tinkling through, glanced
back, and dropped
The sodden ground was splashed with shallow pools,
And tufts of crackling cornstalks, two years old,
No man had reaped, and patches of spring grass.
Half-seen, as rose and sank the flares, were strewn
With the wrecks of our attack: the bandoliers,
Shell fragments, and the huge whole forms of shells
Shot fruitlessly – and everywhere the dead.
Only the dead were always present – present
As a vile smell of rottenness;
The rustling stubble and the early grass,
The slimy pools – the dead men stank through all,
Pungent and sharp; as bodies loomed before,
And as we passed, they stank: then dulled away
To that vague fœtor, all encompassing,
Infecting earth and air. They lay, all clothed,
Each in some new and piteous attitude
That we well marked to guide us back: as he,
Outside our wire, that lay on his back and crossed
His legs Crusader-wise; I smiled at that,

And thought on Elia and his Temple Church.
From him, at quarter left, lay a small corpse,
Down in a hollow, huddled as in bed,
That one of us put his hand on unawares.
Next was a bunch of half a dozen men
All blown to bits, an archipelago
Of corrupt fragments, vexing to us three,
Who had no light to see by, save the flares.
On such a trail, so lit, for ninety yards
We crawled on belly and elbows, till we saw,
Instead of lumpish dead before our eyes,
The stakes and crosslines of the German wire.
We lay in shelter of the last dead man,
Ourselves and dead, and heard their shovels ring
Turning the earth; then talk and cough at times.
A sentry fired and a machine-gun spat;
They shot a flare above us, when it fell
And spluttered out in the pools of No Man's Land,
We turned and crawled past the remembered dead:
Past him and him, and them and him, until,
For he lay some way apart, we caught the scent
Of the Crusader and slid past his legs,
And through the wire and home, and got our rum.

Private WILLIAM BEADLE, 4125
9th Battalion East Surrey Regiment

William Beadle was baptised in Newdigate in 1888, one of twelve children born to Francis F. (known as Frank) and Ellen (née Sanders) Beadle. Four of William's siblings died in infancy but the rest of the family grew up at Cider Mill Farm where his father Frank was the estate carpenter and engine driver. The Beadles had been wedded to Newdigate for generations. As was common in remote communities, people stayed in the area for centuries and inter-married into other Newdigate families. Ellen's father James farmed 160 acres at Nyes and lived there with his wife and eight children, while young Frank worked as a labourer there – he had left home probably because he was one of a large family and space was very limited in a small cottage. Frank married Ellen in 1876 when she was nineteen, just as previous generations of Beadles had married into other long-established Newdigate families such as the Wellers and Horleys whose names feature elsewhere. William worked as a gardener in Uxbridge and enlisted into the East Surrey Regiment at Harrow-on-the-Hill. The 9th Service Battalion (The

Dead in a captured German trench near Guillemont, August 1916 (Ref. Q4217) Reproduced by kind permission of the Imperial War Museum

Gallants) was raised as part of Kitchener's Army at Kingston-upon-Thames and landed at Boulogne on the 1st September 1915.

On the day of his death, the 16th August 1916, the battalion had just relieved the 8th Queen's Regiment in the trenches south of the Guillemont – Trônes Wood Road. C & D Companies were selected to carry out an attack on a German stronghold but the attack failed. The commanding officer laid out six reasons for the failure, the main one being that the supporting artillery barrage was poor and was not even discernible to the men. The left and right flanks were exposed to rifle and machine-gun fire. 9 officers and 181 other ranks were killed, wounded or missing in that day's fighting.

William Beadle was 28 years of age, and as his body was never found, his name is remembered on the Thiepval Memorial.

The Rectory
August 24th, 1916

My dear Friends,

Our little village has suffered very seriously since I last wrote to you and we very deeply sympathise with those who have lost their dear ones on the front. Sapper William Wyatt leaves behind him a very large family, and we feel acutely for them all. We know, too, how deeply Mr. and Mrs. Harber feel the loss of their son, Stephen, who lost his life in the great attack in Flanders. We grieve also for William Hopkins, who is lying seriously ill in the Albert Edward Hospital in Wigan. William had been seriously wounded, but was progressing well when blood poisoning set in and his leg had to be amputated, though he was terribly weak at the time. We trust he may recover, but his case is very serious. One of our brightest girls, Alice Collinson, is very seriously ill in a hospital in London. May God help all in their troubles.

Mr. Vine, the caretaker of the Village Club, has been called up to join the Forces and during his absence for military service his place will be taken by Mrs. Vine, who has been appointed by the Committee.

With best wishes, I am, yours affectionately in Christ, H.G. Bird

Pte. William Hopkins learning to walk on crutches

Pte. William Hopkins convalescing

Pte.William Hopkins in the light blue uniform issued to injured servicemen

A desire has been expressed by some who are hoping to take part in the preparation for the National Mission that opportunity should be given them for a longer period of quiet and devotion than is afforded by an ordinary Quiet Day. The Women's Committee hope, therefore, to arrange two days (three nights) Retreats in different parts of the Diocese during the Summer months, to which women who wish for deepening of their own spiritual lives may come. Retreat at Highfield Park, Heckford, Winchfield, from September 4th (evening) to September 7th (morning). Cost 12/6. Further information from Miss Danby, Hesparia, Dorking.

The Military Tribunal attracted considerable controversy and on the 30th September the Dorking Advertiser published the following letter from Alfred Dean. The

Tribunal was always going to be open to accusations of favouritism, with people thinking that their occupation justified exemption whilst others did not. Joseph Sanders was granted exemption earlier in the year having been described as Mrs Janson's coachman at Newdigate Place stables.

The Crossways, Newdigate
September 21st, 1916

Dear Sirs,

Will you allow me through the medium of your paper to bring the following before the public. On August 29th I applied at the Dorking Tribunal for conditional exemption on the grounds of being a married man of over forty and passed for garrison duty abroad only, and that out of a staff of five there were now only three left including my father (a man of nearly 70), to carry on the business of a grocer, baker, ironmonger, corn, meal and general country stores merchant. As a food distributor I claimed my services were more valuable in my present occupation than doing garrison duty abroad: Application refused.

Alfred Dean

At the same court a gentleman applied for his coachman, a single man of 36, who is in the same class as myself – garrison duty abroad: Exemption granted till 1st January 1917.

Now, not only do I call this an injustice to myself, but is it fair to the State to have to contribute to the support of my wife when there are single men of his class left? Whilst quite willing to fulfil my obligations to King and Country and recognising the necessity of the gentleman having a coachman, I think that there should be equality of service and sacrifice for all, which in the present case, like a good many more, there is not.

Alfred Wm. Dean (now serving in France)

Dean's Stores with Fred Dean and Mark Weller

The Dorking Advertiser of the 23rd September reported the deaths of two young soldiers connected with Newdigate and the injury to one more.

As reported on the 2nd September, Pte. S.C. Harber was killed in action on July 14th. He was the son of Mr. and Mrs. H. Harber of Laundry Hill. A member of the Newdigate Rifle Club, he was well known in the district. Previous to the outbreak of the War he was in the Territorials and was a good shot. Mr. & Mrs. Harber have two more sons in the fighting line.

Pts. W.C. Chatfield QRWS, who as already reported has been accidentally killed. He was the son of Mr. & Mrs. Chatfield of Oaklands Park, Newdigate.

Pte. James Taylor, 5653 reported wounded.

The Rectory
September 1916

My dear Friends,
The National Mission is still uppermost in the thoughts of many of us and we hope most earnestly that it will result in the raising of the moral and spiritual life of the whole nation.

The War has brought out the great need of a deeper Christian Brotherhood. The Church believes strongly in this and knows no class or distinctions.

I am, your affectionate Pastor, H.G. Bird

Corporal ARTHUR HENRY MONK, 10697
7th Battalion, The Queen's
(Royal West Surrey Regiment)

At the outbreak of the war, the Monk family was running the brewery at Kingsland which had been started in the 1880s by Arthur's grandparents William and Mary. Arthur's uncle Ernest continued the business but his parents George and Kate moved to Hertfordshire where George took a job as coachman at Wellbury House near Offley. Arthur Henry Monk was born there in 1892 and was one of nine children. His mother died in 1901, so George moved back to Newdigate with his three youngest children, Arthur, George and Kate, and moved in with Ernest at the brewery. Arthur worked as a gardener and became a very keen bell-ringer. He was a very popular young man and was one of the first to join up with his friend Jack Burberry. His brother, Albert Ernest, had been a regular with the Royal Garrison Artillery since 1906 and was posted on the 5th August 1914. He was discharged on the 12th October as no longer physically fit for war service as he was suffering from myalgia. In the meantime, Arthur was posted to the 7th Battalion, The Queen's, and after a brief period of

Cpl. Arthur Henry Monk

Panoramic view of the Ancre Valley looking towards Beaucourt, Miraumont, St. Pierre Division, Schwaben Redoubt and Thiepval, October 1916 (Ref. Q1544) Reproduced by kind permission of the Imperial War Museum

training he went to France on the 14th December 1914. He was in the struggles at Neuve Chappelle, Festubert, Loos and at Auber's Ridge, and took part in some of the most desperate battles of the war. He may have witnessed the deaths of his fellow villagers, Stephen Harber and John Kempshall, in July 1916. But still the war carried on and again another attack was planned, this time the 7th was directed to attack the Schwaben Redoubt. There was continuous fighting at close quarters on the 28th and 29th September, and this continued until the 5th October when most of the Schwaben Redoubt was captured. Arthur Monk did not witness this success, as he died on the 30th September as a result of his wounds. He was buried at the Contay British Cemetery, which was the chosen site for burials of casualties from the 49th Casualty Clearing Station.

The first tanks arrived in France in August 1916 and they quickly made an impression upon the troops as this anonymous person wrote in September:

We give our thanks; for the lovely 'Tanks'
To the man who came to invent them
For we got our fun, when the filthy Hun
Found his 'stink' shells couldn't dent them.

They wobbled along, sehr gut, sehr schon*,
And didn't their guns just find them;
They settled those near, all dazed with fear;
Then went for the devils behind them.

To see them go was the finest show
Our Tommies have had for years;
They got their strafe, and they got their laughter
Till their laughter brought them tears.

They swept down trees, with the greatest of ease,
And they played 'Old Nick' beside 'em;
So here's to the man who made these 'Tanks',
And, the jolly fine fellows inside 'em.

* *in the hog-like gutteral language of these barbarians – very nice, very pretty.*

Tanks were brought into the attack on the Somme on the 15th September but these thirty-ton monsters were not, at this stage, reliable. Fourteen out of the fifty tanks brought forward broke down due to mechanical problems.

A reader of the Dorking Advertiser did not agree with Alfred Dean's views and described himself as a 'Looker-on':

As there are generally two sides to a question, I should like to say just a word about this 'wail' of Mr. Dean's. In the first instance, I take it that every case coming before the Tribunal is decided on its own merits, and each individual case no doubt was well debated before decision. Mr Dean does not say that the gentleman who applied for his coachman has had well over twenty of his men join the forces since the war started, and is very short-handed in every direction; he does not tell us that this coachman is also driving the engine for electric light, and also doing lots of odd jobs, in fact, is the only man left in the stables and engine room. If Mr. Dean was as willing to do his bit as he tells us he is, I don't think his remarks would have been in print.

Parish Magazine – October 1916
The members of the choir had a most enjoyable tea given them by the Rector. After the tea, which, needless to say was thoroughly appreciated, the members were invited to take part in various games which had been arranged. Mrs. Janson very kindly came and bought [sic] many presents and prizes with her, which were very keenly competed for by those present. We thank her very much for her kindness.

Dorking Advertiser – October 7th, 1916
A very successful social evening was held at the Institute on Monday. Although the weather proved most unfavourable the room was crowded. During the evening a presentation was made to Miss Broughton, who has recently resigned the post of organist and choir-trainer at St. Peter's Church. The Rector made the presentation, which consisted of a purse containing £17 10s. in notes. The Rector spoke of the excellent way in which Miss Broughton had trained the choir and thanked her for the marked improvement shown. He was extremely sorry that Miss Broughton had thought it her duty to resign, but she had his best wishes for an even more successful career in her new sphere of labour. Miss Broughton, who was received with much cheering, and was taken entirely by surprise, thanked the audience for their exceeding kindness to her and especially for her magnificent present. After partaking of refreshments, dancing, songs etc., were much enjoyed till midnight. Mrs. Lucas, Mrs. Hopkins, Doris, Marjory and Harry Bedding, Messrs. Carpenter, H.G. Winfield, G.J. Butcher, E. Powell and G.C. Headland contributed to

the evening's entertainment. Special notice should be made of little Marjory Bedding's song 'Keep the Home Fires Burning' which brought down the house, and the splendid rendering of 'There's a Land' by Mrs. Lucas.

The Rectory
October 19th, 1916

My dear Friends,

I have great pleasure in printing after these few words a letter from the Rev. David Green, Vicar of Bramley, who is our Messenger. He asks us to pray for him and a blessing on his work. I know many of you have been doing this for some time, and I should be so glad if I could feel there is not a single person in Newdigate who is not doing it. I beg of you therefore, if you have not already done this, to ask that God's blessing may be abundantly poured out upon our Parish at this time. There are three points that we might keep prominently before us in our prayers for ourselves and others. (1) Ask God to show us ourselves – that we may see ourselves as he sees us – that we may see how sinful we are. (2) Ask God to show us Himself, with all His love and beauty and holiness. (3) Pray that we may daily become more and more like God, that our sins may be washed away by the Blood of Jesus and that we may daily advance in grace and holiness. May the Mission have the effect of drawing us all closer to God and closer to each other.

I am, Yours affectionately in our Lord Jesus Christ, H.G. Bird

Bramley Vicarage, Guildford
October 14th, 1916

My Dear Friends,

I am looking forward to my visit to you as the Bishop's Messenger, and am continually praying that God's blessing may rest upon us and that during those few days we may be drawn very close to one another in our Lord and Saviour, Jesus Christ.

My special part is very solemn and responsible and so will be your part, so we must help each other as much as we can, and we must ask the Holy Spirit to help us all.

I know you have been thinking a great deal about my coming, and that you will give me a Christian welcome. If I did not feel quite sure about this I should be afraid to come.

Believe me,

Yours sincerely in our Lord, David Green

The Parish Magazine continued:

The Call of the Mission
The Archbishop of Canterbury has addressed a personal Call to the people of this land, as follows:-

"England is fighting a great war for the cause of truth and honour. The greatest victory will not be won if it is our earthly enemies only who are defeated. Among us at home the forces of sin and ignorance are mighty. You were pledged at your Baptism to fight manfully under Christ's banner against them."

"Through the National Mission of Repentance and Hope, we, in Christ's Name, call upon every English man and woman to strike a blow at Christ's enemies."
"This is the Victory that overcometh the world."

Again another brilliant career has been cut short. England has lost one of her most promising lives and Newdigate one who was sincerely respected and liked by all.

Lieutenant F.W. Goldberg, son of L. Goldberg Esq., was a very clever man and an all-round athlete. He was educated at Charterhouse and University College, Oxford, where he graduated with honours in jurisprudence.

He received a commission in the "Queens" in November, 1915. He was sent to Egypt in May, 1916, and from there to Salonika and the Doiran Front, where he was killed in action on October 3rd.

Lieut. Goldberg, in spite of his achievements, was a man of great modesty and his disposition was charming in its gentleness, child-like simplicity and unselfishness. By rich and poor he will be remembered as one ever ready to sympathise with the sorrows and needs of others.

We also have to announce with much regret the death of Corporal Arthur Monk, who was killed in France on September 3rd. A Memorial Service was held on October 17th. At this service the Rector, who gave the address, spoke of him as one who was revered and respected by all, one of the straightest and nicest young men in the village. Corporal Monk was one of our keenest bell-ringers, and never lost a chance of taking a rope when possible in France as well as in England.

After his training he went to France on Dec. 14th, 1914, and was engaged first in the battle at Neuve Chappelle, then at Festubert, where he lost all his things, then at the terrible struggle at Loos, then at Auber's Ridge, where he was hit fiercely on the head by a German, who broke his rifle in the act. He was insensible for some time and had to rest for a few weeks, and lastly he was engaged at Fluerbury, where he met his death — so he had, poor fellow, seen some of the fiercest of the struggles. His conduct was always very good and he had two promotions — first as Lance Corporal and then as Corporal, and was promised to be promoted to Sergeant. He was one of the very best, and Newdigate will ever be proud of him. He was not a fighting man, but a peace-loving citizen, and took up his profession simply from a sense of duty, and just before going away for the last time after a short leave, he said to his friends, "I am going out to fight for you and your home." May he rest in peace, and may his bright and good life be an example to us all and enable us to do whatever we may be called upon for the honour of our country and the welfare of those near and dear to us at home.

Dorking Advertiser – October 14th, 1916

We record with deep regret that 2nd Lieut. F.W. Goldberg, the Queens RWSR, attached Royal Dublin Fusiliers, was killed in action on October 3rd. The gallant officer who was 34 was the youngest son of Mr. L. Goldberg of the Red House, Newdigate, and of Cadogan Gardens. He was educated at Charterhouse and at University College, Oxford, whence he graduated with honours in jurisprudence. He was subsequently called to the Bar. Since July 1st 1910, he held an appointment on the staff of the Public Trustees.

In June 1915 he joined the Inns of Court Officer Training Corps and in November of that year he received his commission in the Queens. In May 1916 he was sent to Egypt, and from there to another front, where he was attached to the Royal Dublin Fusiliers. His elder brother, H.W. Goldberg, who had a commission in the same regiment, was killed in France in July 1915. Lt. F.W. Goldberg was keen on games, he represented his college at cricket, association football, hockey and lawn tennis and obtained his 'half-blue' for hockey and tennis. Later he got his international cap for hockey. In the lawn tennis world he was well known and for some years took part in the Championships at Wimbledon. He was a prominent member of Redhill Lawn Tennis Club, which has suffered so heavily in the loss of some of its most distinguished players during the war.

Lt. Goldberg was a man of refined literary tastes and a great lover of music. He will be remembered by many as a most loyal friend and by all who knew him as a man of wide sympathies and one who was guided in his conduct by the highest ideals of life.

2nd Lieutenant FREDERICK WILLIAM GOLDBERG
3rd Battalion, The Queens (Royal West Surrey Regiment)
attd. 7th Battalion Royal Dublin Fusiliers

Frederick William Goldberg, who was known as Fritz, was born at Clapton on the 4th April 1882 and like his brother was educated at Charterhouse and University College, Oxford, whence he graduated with honours in jurisprudence.

Although he was not in the Charterhouse eleven he represented University College at cricket. He was called to the bar at Inner Temple in 1904 and during the same year he played hockey for England against Ireland. He was a prominent member of Redhill Lawn Tennis Club, playing right up to the start of the war, and took part in the Championships at Wimbledon. In June 1915 he joined the Inns of Court Officer Training Corps and in the November received his commission in the Queens. He was sent to Egypt in May 1916 and then to another front where he was attached to the Royal Dublin Fusiliers. The combined British Salonika Army under Lieutenant-General G.F. Milne C.B., D.S.O

Lieut. Frederick William Goldberg

and the French Army were combating the Bulgarians who had advanced into Greek Macedonia. On the morning of the 3rd October 1916 preparations were made to capture the village of Jenikoj on the main Serres road. The operation was preceded by an artillery barrage and then an infantry brigade composed of the 6th Dublins and 7th Munsters with the 7th Dublins and 6th Munsters in

View showing the river Struma and South Wood, part of the panorama at Jenikoj (Ref. Q23424)
Reproduced by kind permission of the Imperial War Museum

support – took their objective with few casualties. As they advanced, some 7th Dublins were killed by their own artillery and both Dublin battalions were caught between the allied bombardment and a Bulgarian counter attack. Following this bombardment six or seven enemy battalions advanced with a view to enveloping the held position and succeeded in entering the northern portion of Jenikoj where hard fighting continued all night until fresh reinforcements succeeded in

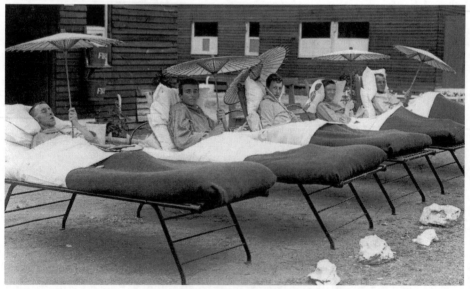

*Injured troops at the Doiran Heights. (Ref.Q2339)*Reproduced by kind permission of the Imperial War Museum

clearing out the enemy. During this operation 385 men were killed, wounded or missing and 128 were from the Royal Dublin Fusiliers. Frederick Goldberg was killed during the fight for Jenikoj on the 3rd October 1916 and is buried at the Struma Military Cemetery, ref. III H2. Like his brother he is also remembered on memorials at Charterhouse, Temple Church and on his parents' gravestone in Newdigate churchyard.

Still the shells kept battering the hopeless Flanders landscape, and still the pattern of attack and retire continued with appalling loss of life. By November it seemed that the Germans had fought their opponents to a standstill.

The rain fell incessantly day and night and the shell holes were filled with water so that men drowned in the gloom of the night. Their boots stuck in the deep slime as they had to work day and night in the shallow linking trenches. At night it grew bleak and cold.

For some news of a bereavement came quickly. For others, such as Joan Bray, hope continued only to be shattered.

Dorking Advertiser – November 4th, 1916

2nd Lieut. G.T. Bray, 2/4th Queens, who had been previously reported wounded and missing at Suvla Bay on 9th August 1915, is now officially reported killed on the date mentioned. He was the youngest son of His Honour Judge Bray and the nephew of Sir Richard Bray, Manor House, Shere. He was thirty years of age.

Military Act Tribunal, Dorking Rural, 4th November 1916

William Monk (20), Kingsland Farm, cowman and stockman – Conditional exemption till 1/1/17 on joining the Volunteers.

The Rectory
November 23rd, 1916

My dear Friends,
The Mission proper has passed but the afterwork, which is far more important, still remains and I am most anxious that the good work commenced may, by God's blessing, have a lasting effect in the Parish.

It will give me great pleasure to do anything in my power for the Parish. Would a men's meeting or a Men's Service, say once a month, be a help?

I am, Your affectionate Pastor, H.G. Bird

The Mission of Repentance and Hope which the Archbishop of Canterbury and his Messengers had hoped would energise the church, and bring lapsed Christians once again into a closer relationship with God, was not considered to have been a success. Too many young lives were being lost and God's part in this was being severely questioned.

Dorking Advertiser – December 2nd, 1916
A rifle match between Newdigate and Capel Section, 10th Batt. Surrey Volunteers Regiment, was shot on Tuesday resulting in a win for Newdigate by four points.
Newdigate Section – Corpl. F.E. Green 99, Pte. J. Edwards 98, Sgt. J.A. Steeds 97, Pte. J. Charman 95, Pte. H.T. Whittingham 94, Pte. W. Monk 93. Reserves – Pte. E. Powell 94, Pte. M. Dean 93, Pte. H. Horley 92.

Parish Newsletter – December 1916
The Rector has received the following letter respecting Aubrey Hudson.

October 18th, 1916

Dear Sir,
In reply to your letter of the 11th inst., I regret to inform you that No. 1986 Aubrey Hudson was missing, believed killed, whilst with a carrying party, when the Battalion was in action on July 27th last. No information as to his admission to a Medical Unit has been received by me, as would almost certainly have been the case had he been admitted to any such Station. It is with regret, therefore, that I am obliged to conclude that he was killed on his way to the front line.
I am, yours faithfully, C.R. Stone, A/Adjutant, 22nd Royal Fusiliers

.... and so Rev Bird would have left his rectory, on that Autumn day, and trudged down the Rusper Road to New House Farm to tell the Hudson family that their son, no more than a boy, was dead. Major Christopher Reynolds Stone DSO, MC, who went into action many times after writing this letter, survived the war and lived at Peppers Farm in Ashurst near Steyning in Sussex.

An excellent Concert was given by friends in the Parish in the School Room on Wednesday, November 8th, the proceeds of which will be used for purchasing some Christmas Comforts for those who are engaged in the War. The room was packed and the receipts amounted to over £13. The concert was started by the members of the Wyatt family. In addition to this Miss Herron, Mrs. Janson, Miss Ferard, Mr. Goldberg, the Rector and the Misses Bird have sent donations so that the total amounts to about £30. May God bless the dear ones at the front.
We have been greatly touched at receiving from one of our soldiers 10/-, his week's wages. He sent it to the Rector as a thanksgiving for recovery from sickness – to be used by him for any good work he chooses.
We are promised a Concert on January 10th on behalf of the Newdigate Working Party. A very large number of useful and warm things have been made by this party which meets on alternative weeks in the Institute, and no soldier or sailor who has left this Parish has been forgotten by them. We hope the Concert will be well patronised, otherwise as will be seen by the Balance Sheet which follows the work will have to be abandoned.

Newdigate Working Party for sending Warm Knitted Garments to our Soldiers and Sailors.

Balance Sheet, 1916.

Receipts	£	s	d	Payments	£	s	d
Grant from Emergency Committee 1915	5	0	0	Wool (P.Robinson) Oct. 31st	3	0	3
Ditto 1916		5	5	0	Flannel (Harrods) Oct. 27th	2	0	0
Donations:-							
Mrs. Palmer		10	0	Wool (P.Robinson) Nov. 28 th	3	10	2 ½
Mrs. Irwine		2	6	Flannel (Harrods) Nov. 28th	2	9	6
Mrs. Hogsflesh		1	0				
Deficit		1	5½				
	£10	19	11		£10	19	11

M.H. Bird – Treasurer

As 1916 drew to a close the Prime Minister, Mr. Asquith, considered his position. His son, Raymond, was killed in September and following a disagreement in which he insisted on sitting as chairman in the newly formed War Committee, he resigned and David Lloyd George was accordingly asked by the King to form a Government.

Still none of the austerity usually associated with wartime existed. Over one million people previously involved in ill-paid, non-productive jobs, were now earning two or three times as much performing war work on farms, munitions factories, etc. Thus the suppliers of luxury goods also prospered.

Trade in general was also booming. The export trade rose in 1916 to a figure which exceeded British exports in any of the years before the war except 1913.

The Rector, ever mindful of the losses suffered by his parishioners, sat in his study and wrote his last letter of 1916.

The Rectory
December 28th, 1916

My Dear Friends,

It is nice to begin these few words with a hearty good wish that the New Year may bring many blessings to you and those near and dear to you. Amidst all the gloom and sorrow which is affecting so many at this time may you be able to look through the cloud of sorrows and see more fully than ever the joys which God will give to those who most truly love him.

I am, your sincere friend, H.G. Bird

Newdigate had suffered sorely in 1916. Many of the lads were in the infantry, and it was the infantry that suffered such appalling losses in the great battles. No fewer than eight village boys had lost their lives and many of their families had other sons in France. Christmas in their simple country cottages was not a joyous occasion in spite of the Rector's words of hope.

1917

On New Year's Day, for a detachment of the King's Royal Rifle Corps work continued as normal. For a period wiring and trench repairs had taken place during the night, but the Germans had realised this and had started shelling during that time, making the operation dangerous. New arrangements were made and they fell in at 6.50 a.m. and worked until 1.30 p.m. on the Taupin and Southern Avenue trenches, which had been knee-deep in water but had finally been pumped out. The Germans could see that fresh earth had been thrown over the top, so they battered the trench during the night and work had to start all over again. Steady, soaking rain filled up the trenches and once again the soldiers were knee-deep in mud. When they returned to their billets, which were often no more than open, rat-infested barns, they had to somehow get dry, feed themselves and sleep until reveille next morning.

Work on the farms continued even though it was New Year's Day, in peace or in war.

New House Farm Diary – January 1st, 1917
Davey at home ill
Burrows to Mr. Lucas's with fifty faggots and then loaded up fifty more on waggon and carting up dung and loaded back with swedes.

    Hogsflesh, Sadler, Shoebridge jnr., Leadbeater and Capon all pulling and trimming swedes.

Vestry Meeting – January 1st, 1917
A letter had been received from the Surrey County War Agricultural Committee respecting purchase of seed potatoes. It was agreed that notices should be affixed at various places in the Parish so as to make the scheme known.

    A discussion arose re the bridge at Horsieland Farm having been washed away by the recent floods. The Clerk would write to agents.

The weather conditions in the trenches were appalling but Sir Hubert Gough, a cavalry officer and now in command of the 5th Army, was determined to press on and a strong attack was delivered on the high ground above the river Ancre, east of Beaumont Hamel. The

British troops were ankle-deep in mud on the firm ground and up to their thighs in slime in other places, but then came the great frost that whitened the battlefields for weeks, hardening the mud and freezing the shell holes.

During the evening of the 17th January an explosion was heard throughout Newdigate, and those who ventured out would have seen a light in the sky towards the north-east. A huge explosion had occurred in a factory at Silvertown in East London which purified TNT. Seventy-three people lost their lives and four hundred were injured. It was estimated that sixty to seventy thousand properties in the surrounding area received damage of some kind. The losses could have been much worse, but the blast took place at the end of the working week and many workers were safely at home.

The Rectory
January 24th, 1917

My dear Friends,

We all long for Peace but it must be an honourable one, and we must be certain to provide against the repetition of a war like the present one. We must have freedom for all Countries and the small states must be protected. Besides this, there must be full restitution and reparation. We must win the war and the full conviction that we shall accomplish this grows every day. As the Bishop says, we must not trust in our bows and arrows but in the power of God. By this I mean we must do our utmost and God will bless our endeavours. Germany has done much but not what she expected. She did not take Paris in two months and she will not land in England, but we must be prepared for the worst. Let us commit our cause to God and do on all occasions with our whole might what He would have us to do.

With every best wish, I am, your affectionate Pastor, H.G. Bird

The Bishop's Letter

January 13th, 1917

The discussions about peace and the American Note have, I think, plainly done good service by compelling us to think and speak more clearly about our principles in the War.

Again, we were always confident that with such and such a fleet we must command the seas. This has been so, nobly, so far – may it be so at the end! But it has hardly been enough observed how an entirely new factor, the submarine or U Boat, has created an anxiety which could not have been anticipated. Illustrations like this help us almost to see, as well as believe, the uncertainty of the best human plans, and our dependence on the Providence which rules the changes, chances and accidents of life.

Yours faithfully in our Lord's service. Edw. Winton

On the 16th January 1917, Arthur Zimmerman, the German Foreign Secretary, sent a telegram to Heinrich von Eckardt, the German Ambassador in Mexico in which he announced that as from the 1st February, Germany would commence unrestricted submarine warfare in order to compel England to make peace. If the United States did not stay neutral then Germany would create an alliance with Mexico and reconquer the lost territory in

Texas, New Mexico and Arizona. The British Admiralty de-coded the message which became known as the Zimmerman Note.

Dorking Advertiser – January 27th, 1917

Military Act Tribunal

Frederick Chandler (35) Hammonds Farm, Newdigate, working farm bailiff, exempted until July 1st.

Henry William Horley (37) Burghurst Cottage, Newdigate, farmer and timber merchant, exempted till July 1st on the ground that it is work of national importance.

Parish Magazine

On February 1st, the Rev. H.G. Bird very kindly gave a treat, inviting the Sunday School children and members of the Newdigate Choir. 4.30 p.m. found us all sitting round to tea where we were gaily waited upon by Miss Herron, Mrs. Janson, Miss M. Bird, Miss Wilson, Miss Ferrard, Mrs. Steeds and above all our most amusing rector.

L/Corpl W. Worsfold was a Reigate lad serving with the 8th Royal Scots Fusiliers. He had been injured for the fourth time in Salonika and returned home. He wrote this verse about his nurses.

I'm only one of many men
In hospital today,
But everyone will bear me out
In what I'm trying to say - - - -
That Tommy's pal when he is down
And not feeling fit to fight
Is the lady dressed in iron grey
With cap of snowy white

From morn till night and night till morn
She tends with simple care
The war-worn warriors from the hills,
Each finding solace there,
And when one's doubled up in pain,
Far through the darkest night,
The lady's there to soothe him,
Dressed in grey with cap of white

The symbols, which one can't mistake,
Are eloquent to all,
Of calm and true devotion
To the work and to the call,
And the arms of British heroes,
While upholding Britain's might,
Are ever at the service of those
Ladies capped in white

And this poor tribute represents
The least that I can do
To show our heartfelt gratitude
To every sister who
Has faced the dangers of the sea and land
Through dark of night
To serve us — those brave ladies
In iron grey and white.

VAD (Voluntary Aid Detachment) nurses were dressed in grey with white caps and pinafores. At first they were not allowed to go to the front line and were looked down upon by more qualified nursing staff, but as shortages increased so they were given more responsibility and were posted to France, Mesopotania, Gallipoli etc. Often they were daughters of the wealthier class and amongst many famous VADs were Agatha Christie, Vera Brittain and Naomi Mitchison. Violet Jessop, another VAD nurse, was rescued from the Titanic when it sank in 1912 and was serving on board her sister ship, the hospital ship Britannic, when she was torpedoed and sunk in 1916.

Due to a very heavy snowstorm in the early morning of the 5th February less than half of the children attended school. Another attempt was made to establish a Drum and Fife Band in the village.

Parish Magazine – March 1917

Newdigate Drum and Fife Band.
I am glad to say that another start has been made with the Village Drum and Fife Band after a very successful meeting on Tuesday, Febr. 20 th. The time is approaching when bands will be wanted. How unfortunate it will be if the Newdigate band is allowed to fail through lack of enthusiasm. Soon we hope to see our brave lads returning from the front to their village homes. What a regrettable thing it will be if we have not a band to receive them and cheer them with old familiar tunes that were their delight in days gone by.
E. Powell – Hon. Sec. and Treasurer.

The demand for more soldiers was not abating and the Military Tribunal in Dorking was kept busy. In response from a plea by Lord French, even exempted men were ordered to join the Volunteers.

Lord French's letter re. Volunteers
I am of the opinion that all men, physically fit, between the ages of 45 and 60 are capable of performing the duties required of a Volunteer and it is with regard to men between these ages that I wanted to ask you to make an appeal to their sense of duty and patriotism at this moment of crisis in the history of the Empire.

Military Act Tribunal:

Arthur Mark Weller (36) Manor Cottages, Cudworth, gardener – temporary exemption till substitution

William Henry Spiller (38) Brooklag Farm, Newdigate, farmer – conditional exemption till October 1st an d to join Volunteers

Charles Rowland (36) Hillside, Newdigate, carter – conditional exemption until April 1st and to join the Volunteers

Harry Still (40) Henfold Cross, Beare Green, agricultural labourer – conditional exemption until July 1st and to join the Volunteers

Harry Groves Winfield (40) Brook Farm, Newdigate, farmer and cowkeeper – conditional exemption until July 1st and to join the Volunteers

Henry Thomas Whittingham (34) Newdigate, working master baker – application withdrawn, rejected by medical board

Leonard Henry Bedding (36) Ash Farm, cowkeeper – conditional exemption till July 1st and to join the Volunteers

Tom Voice (37) Newdigate, farmer – conditional exemption till October 1st and to join the Volunteers.

The continuous attack on allied shipping had started to have a severe effect on food supplies. It was reported in March that the German raider 'Moewe' had alone accounted for 110,000 tons of British shipping. The U-boat campaign against allied shipping was crippling the merchant fleet and by April it was estimated that the food stock in Britain would last just six weeks.

Owing to the need to supply goods in vast quantities and the appalling losses at sea, standard commodities had become very scarce or expensive. Cotton prices had risen four-fold and leather and metal articles had become difficult to obtain. Efforts were made to increase production of food, and the Food Production Department was formed as an offshoot of the Department of Agriculture.

The agricultural industry was placed directly under governmental control, much the same as the shipping and engineering industries. Armed with its powers under the Defence of the Realm Act, the Board of Agriculture determined what additional land should be ploughed and who should plough it. A later order made it legal for the Board to enter and

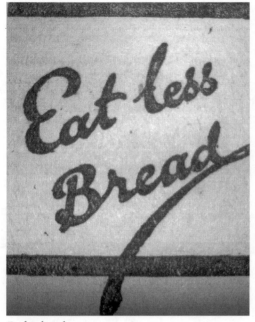

Eat less bread

POTATOES in 1918.

Last year the County of Surrey

(Not including the London area)

Produced 43,000 Tons of Potatoes.

Consumed 82,300 Tons of Potatoes.

DEFICIT **39,300** TONS.

Lord RHONDDA and Mr. PROTHERO appeal to every Man who has a Farm, a Garden, or an Allotment to PLANT MORE POTATOES and

MAKE THE COUNTY SELF-SUPPORTING

Potatoes in 1918

take possession of any land which in their opinion was not being cultivated in a way which would increase the food supply of the country.

The Rector received this letter from Miss Ferard of which he heartily approved.

Ockley Lodge
Feb. 25th, 1917

Dear Mr. Bird,
Since speaking to you on the subject I have been in communication with the National Food Reform Association and with the National Food Economy League, both of which Societies send out ladies whose lectures and demonstrations in food and cooking are very much appreciated by their hearers.

I hope to be able to arrange to get one to come to Newdigate in a few weeks time but I am told there is a great demand for them.

I think that it would be very interesting if we could get up a little competition and exhibition of home-made articles in connection with the lecture. If this could be managed and meets with your approval notices could be sent out later.

Yours very sincerely, Beatrice Ferard

Dorking Advertiser – March 3rd, 1917

The Battle of the Ancre – We hear that seats at the South Street Electric Theatre are being rapidly booked for the early part of next week, when the famous film 'The Battle of the Ancre and Advance of the Tanks' is to be shown. There are exhibitions every afternoon and evening.

Dorking Advertiser – March 24th, 1917

Mr. Pethick Lawrence is standing as the 'Peace by Negotiation' candidate for South Aberdeen

Parish Magazine – April 1917

The Window in memory of the late Lieutenant Walter Fitzroy Herron will be dedicated by Canon Chichester, Vicar of Dorking and Rural Dean, on Wednesday, April 4th at 3.30 p.m.

We are all called upon to do all in our power to help win the War. No one who has a friend at the Front will fail to do this. One of the ways by which we can all help is by using great economy of food, especially in bread, meat and sugar. We must all try to lessen the consumption of these things. We must do it not for our own sakes but for others who are not so well off. 'If one member suffers all the members suffer with it'. We shall do all we can to lessen the suffering of others.

The Magazine is not paying its way. Two courses are open to us, either to increase its price to say 1½d; or to make it smaller. The Editor is always glad to receive any contributions to the Magazine and these should be sent to him on or before the 20th of the month.

A Demonstration Lecture on "Housekeeping and Cooking in War Time and After" will be given at the Newdigate Village Institute by Miss Dorothy Moore, of the National Food Reform Association, on Wednesday, April 18th, at 3.00 p.m. Doors open at 2.30 p.m. Entrance, including tea, 3d. Tickets obtainable until Monday, 16th April, at Mr. Dean's Stores and the Newdigate Post Office. Useful books at 1d. and 2d. will be on sale. The food cooked will be on sale at the end of the lecture. Those wishing to purchase should provide means for carrying their purchases away.

Dorking Advertiser – April 12th, 1917

Fate of a Missing Newdigate Man.

Previously reported missing, Pte. John Kempshall, Queens Royal West Surrey Regiment, is now officially reported to have been killed in action on July 14th 1916. He was the fifth son of Mr. & Mrs. John Kempshall of North Barn Cottages, Newdigate.

Vestry Meeting – April 16th, 1917

The Chairman, having received a petition for allotments would write to Mrs. Watson respecting the field in front of the Old Post Office.

Gardening was an important part of the school year and on the 27th April the School Log records:

Extra gardening lessons have been taken during the afternoon sessions. The garden seeds arrived at the early part of the week and in consequence of their late arrival and hindrances through bad weather, it was absolutely essential that every advantage should be made of a week's fine weather. The attendance has been quite good except in the upper standards, for which, agricultural exemptions are chiefly responsible.

German submarine warfare had now spread to the American coast, so President Wilson called Congress together. On April 2nd he asked the members to declare that a state of war existed between the United States of America and Germany. The U.S.A. entered the war

and the policy of armed neutrality was abandoned. The first contingent of American troops landed in France on the 26th June 1917, although their first engagement was not until May 1918 at Château-Thierry.

Meanwhile on the Western Front the Hindenburg Line was impregnable in spite of Allied attempts. The British made some advances in the Second Battle of Arras, with the Canadians capturing the important Vimy Ridge on April 11th. It was soon reported, however, that the German commander had set up a heavy counter-attack. The Prussian Guardsmen had swept the attackers with machine-gun fire subsequently coming out of their trenches and opening a terrific hand-to-hand combat. Many of the men were up to their thighs in mud, and many thousands lost their lives in the area around Pimple Hill.

Parish Magazine – May 1917

The Rector has received some most interesting letters from old members of the congregation who have joined the Forces. Corporal George Horley gives a most interesting account of his work, etc. He most kindly sent 10/- to be given towards the Church Expenses. Pte. J. Elliott, who is in Mesopotania, received the parcel on Feb 20th, and begs to thank the Newdigate people for their great kindness to him, and wishes all every blessing for the new year. He says 'It was a great treat to him to taste a piece of good old Blighty cake out here in this wild country among the sand and flies, which are a perfect pest.'

The Editor received this letter, dated the 8th February 1917, from Pte. Percy Weller who was also serving in Mesopotania.

Dear Friends of Newdigate,
I feel I must write a few lines to let you know I received the parcel quite safe which you were all so kind to send me. I assure you all it came as a great surprise to me, and I am sure I feel very grateful to you all in thinking of me out in this desolate place. In closing, dear friends, I wish you all a very happy New Year, once again thanking you all for such a nice treat.

I remain, yours respectfully, Percy Weller

Percy Weller as a young man

There was a splendid meeting in the Institute on April 18th to hear a lecture given by Miss Moore on 'Cooking in War Time'. The lecture was most interesting, and no doubt gave most valuable hints to those present, but is far beyond the power of the writer to describe. A few most valuable and earnest words were spoken by the Rev. F.W. Marshall, Rector of Ockley, on the duty of economy and of adhering to the ration scheme. That a most trying time is before us is certain, but how trying we cannot at present tell, but it behoves every one to do his utmost to economise, and especially in bread and flour. We do not grow in England more than enough wheat to last two or three months, so that we depend very largely upon our imports. The wheat crop of the world last year was greatly below the average, and is one great cause of the shortage; moreover, the submarines have made the importation of wheat difficult.

A very pleasing part of the afternoon's arrangement consisted of viewing the various competitions, which were extremely interesting, and showed great taste and ability.

The 24th May was Empire Day and the school celebrated by hoisting the Union Jack. The School Log recorded:

In response to an appeal from the Over-Seas Club, just over a hundred of the children played a most noble part in bringing forward their mites to help to provide Funds for sending tobacco and cigarettes to our men at the Front, and by so doing so were granted the privelege [sic] of writing their names on one of the two Rolls of Honour provided by the above club.

Nearly every child contributed and as a result one pound has been sent to the Honorary Treasurer of the Fund. During the morning suitable lessons were given in all Classes and in response to the circular letter from the Education Committee the subject of 'Food Economy' was introduced specially dealing with the important question of bread and flour.

In the afternoon Empire Day & other patriotic songs were followed by Maypole & Swedish dancing and Sir Roger de Coverley.

The children then saluted the flag and after singing the National Anthem were dismissed.

3rd June 1917 – Military Act Tribunal

Henry Groves Winfield (41) Brook Farm, Newdigate, farmer and cowkeeper, conditional exemption until October 1st.

George Alfred Horley (35) Broad Lane, Newdigate, farm labourer, conditional exemption until October 1st.

The shortage of food was becoming a matter of the utmost urgency and in June 1917 the King issued a Proclamation.

We, being persuaded that the abstention from all unnecessary consumption of grain will furnish the surest and most effectual means of defeating the devices of Our enemies and thereby of bringing the war to a speedy and successful termination, and out of Our resolve to leave nothing undone which can contribute to these ends or to the welfare of Our people in these times of grave stress and anxiety, have thought fit, by and with the advice of Our Privy Council, to issue this Our Royal Proclamation, most earnestly exhorting and charging all those of Our loving subjects the men and women of Our Realm who have the means of procuring articles of food other than wheaten corn, as they tender their own immediate interests, and feel for the wants of others, especially to practise the greatest economy and frugality in the use of every species of grain: And We do for this purpose more particularly exhort and charge all heads of households to reduce the consumption of bread in their respective families by at least one-fourth of the quantity consumed in ordinary times; to abstain from the use of flour in pastry and, moreover, carefully to restrict or wherever possible to abandon the use thereof in all other articles than bread: And We do also, in like manner, exhort and charge all persons who keep horses to abandon the practice of feeding the same on oats or other grain, unless they shall have received from Our Food Controller a licence to feed horses on oats or other grain to be given only in cases where necessary to do so with a view to maintain the breed of horses in the national interest: And we do hereby further charge and enjoin all Ministers of Religion in their respective churches and chapels within Our United Kingdom of Great Britain and Ireland to read, or cause to be read, this Our Proclamation on the Lord's Day, for four successive weeks after the issue thereof.

Given at Our Court at Buckingham Palace, this Second Day of May, in the year of our Lord one thousand nine hundred and seventeen, and in the Seventh year of Our Reign.

GOD SAVE THE KING

The Battle of Messines Ridge was a continuation of the British 1917 offensive. Parts of the French Army had mutinied and the Russians were embroiled in the Revolution which was to take them out of the war. The Messines Ridge was important as its possession allowed Germany a dominating observation position over Ypres. The attack by Sir Hubert Plumer's 2nd British Army had been well rehearsed and planned. After constant bombardment from May 27th to June 6th, the attack was made on June 7th at 3.10 a.m. Following the explosion of nineteen mines, a most intensive artillery bombardment was aimed at the German line. The infantry advanced with the support of forty tanks. It was death to enter the huge craters, which were filled with gas from tons of ammonia; even soldiers who approached the lips of the gigantic holes became dizzy and sick from drifting fumes. Barrels of burning oil were sent tumbling into the enemy trenches breaking in floods of flame into the dug-outs. The operations at Messines came to an end on the 14th June. In his report Sir Douglas Haig said, 'Yesterday's victory was due to causes which always have and always will give success – namely, the utmost skill, valour and determination in the execution of the attack, following on the greatest forethought and thoroughness in preparation for it.'

On July 1st it was reported that 8,686 German prisoners were captured during June. After the success at Messines Ridge, Sir Douglas Haig was free to concentrate on his preparations for what was to be known as the Third Battle of Ypres, July 31st to November 6th 1917.

Dorking Advertiser – June 9th, 1917

A most successful concert, was organised by Mr. and Mrs. Harry Winfield, and held at Newdigate School on Saturday, June 2nd in connection with the Farmers' Red Cross Week at Dorking. There was a most attractive programme. Miss Rosamond Croudace, formerly of Reigate, who had already given great pleasure at a Newdigate concert last year, fascinated the audience in her own inimitable way by her charming recitations and songs. 'The Limitations of Youth', 'Kiddie Stories', 'Mr. Bear', and duets, 'Love Story' and 'Zanzibar' in which she was ably assisted by Mr. Arthur W. Steeds, who also most cleverly gave some splendid recitations, 'If I were King' and 'Yankee Stories.' Miss Marian Herron's violin solos were a source of great enjoyment to all, Lce-Corpl. E.W. Scovell, of the Queen's Westminster Rifles, very kindly came down from Roehampton Camp at much inconvenience, and captivated all who heard him with his lovely voice in the following songs: 'Love's Garden of Roses', 'Jeunesse', 'Every Little While' and 'Boots'. Mr Whitehouse opened the concert with a splendid piano solo, and he also gave a capital musical sketch, and was most good at acting as accompanist throughout the evening. Small Marjorie with her smiling little face, in her Red Cross Nurse's uniform, pleased all with her songs 'Nurses and Soldiers' and 'The Shut-eye Road' accompanied by her sister Doris Bedding. Miss Mildred

Smith also kindly sang. The programme sellers, a Red Cross nurse and three small helpers in white dresses with red ribbons and crosses, lent a touch of reality to the scene, while the stage and rooms looked bright and gay decorated with the flags, flowers and plants so kindly sent by friends. The Chairman, the Rev. H.G. Bird, proposed a vote of thanks to all who were so good in helping in every way. The sum of £11.16s.11d was realised.

Rosamond Croudace (b.1889) married Arthur Steeds (b.1882) in London in 1918 whilst he was serving with the Surrey Yeomanry. They lived their latter years in Hendon. She died in 1969 and he in 1945.

Newdigate Fête in 1917

Dorking Advertiser

For the first time since the war commenced, Newdigate Place on Wednesday in last week, presented a merry scene, and though there was no band or expense incurred in the way of preparation, never have the grounds known a merrier or happier aspect. The long absence from pleasure made everyone in Newdigate determined to enjoy themselves, and enjoy themselves they did, and the superior sales of jumbles (evening dresses, etc., from 3 to 4) at Mrs. Nicholls', and hats at Mrs. Palmer's fascinating stalls made many ladies pay their one shilling instead of 3d entrance fee (tea included). Then at four, came people thick and fast, and the sellers had a busy time. Mrs. Hornsby's fancy articles, which had hung fire at the Newdigate bazaar in 1914, on account of the pouring wet day, sold like wildfire, and her beautiful Champion of England Great Dane dog collected over 10s in pennies in his Red Cross shaped box. Miss Bird's odds and ends, from pictures, books and flower pots down to waste paper, were simply grabbed at, and potatoes in 1lb. bags, fetched fancy prices, while Mrs. Seyd's stall, containing old boots, sweets, garden requisites, and what looked like rubbish, was simply besieged.

Hoop-la, conducted by Mrs. Barris, Mrs. Junis, Mrs. Cornfoot, Miss Herron, and Mr. and Mrs. Shepherd, as usual, attracted old and young all afternoon, and a kitten, a dog and a rabbit sold for £3 4s. 7d. Competition tickets for a valuable picture presented to the Red Cross fund by

Mrs. Janson, and a beautiful dessert service of Worcester china, presented by her brother, Dr Chester, LL.D., CC., of Poyle Park, Tongham (near Guildford), were raffled by their niece, Miss Ida de Wend (1896-1988), a VAD nurse, who also held an interesting show in an Arabian tent brought from Cairo by Mrs. Janson some time ago, but still glowing with Oriental colour. War trophies, shell cases, German helmets, etc., were kindly lent by Col. Nicholls, now occupant of Boothlands, Newdigate, and brought from the front by his son, and many interesting objects were to be seen from the Newdigate Place collection of ancient articles.

The baby show next demanded attention. Mrs. Smith took first prize, her baby (7 months old) weighing 22lbs. 7oz. Mrs. Horley's baby was second. There was only one entry for babies from 10 to 18 months, and none up to 24 months. Then Miss Bird's Girls' Friendly Society, in whom she takes great interest, performed their club and flag drill, dressed in white, with fascinating white muslin caps, trimmed with cherry-coloured ribbons made by Miss Bird herself. The exact precision of the girls' movements gave great credit to both the teacher and the pupils.

Next took place the great event of the day, the Maypole dance, conducted by Mr. Steeds, helped by his wife and Miss Broughton at the piano. After seeing the admirable performance of the sixteen happy and fairy-like girls, with flowing hair and dainty frocks, other village teams competing in the Dorking Maypole show may well tremble in their shoes, for all went without a hitch, though through not being able to get the pole fitments till quite lately the children have had but little time to practise the winding and unwinding of the plaited ribbons. The greatest praise, therefore, must go to Mr. and Mrs. Steeds and the children.

A very small portion of the pageant arranged by Mrs. Janson to represent members of the Newdigate family from Edward 1's reign to George V's then formed up and marched two and two around the lawn, finishing up at the ice cream pavilion, where they were regaled with ices and lemonade free of charge. The costumes were a little weird, owing to their unfinished state. Sir Roger Newdigate had to wear the head-gear of another representative of a totally different date, and as most garments were hurriedly pinned on, as hooks, and eyes, buttons, etc., had not yet been fixed, some anxiety was felt as to how long in Oliver Cromwell's time Newdigate breeches would remain in place, or Charles 1's time lady's upper skirt descends below the under one. Hats of one period were on the heads of another, and so on, but in spite of all, the little procession was effective, and by the time it reaches Dorking will be correctly in order.

The Rector was to have presided over games on the tennis lawn, croquet etc., but everyone was far too interested to tear themselves away from the scene of pleasure, and he was also so occupied with cheering everything, that his duties entirely escaped his memory. But fortunately they were kindly arranged by Mr. Powell of Cudworth, and Mr. Pinnock of Brockham.

The contributors included Mr. Whitehouse (piano), Miss Smith, Baby Bedding (aged five, action songs), Miss Broughton, Mr. Winfield, and Mrs. Curtis, while part of the time Mrs. Pertwee explained the good work done in France by the English Women's Emergency Canteen from Paris, two miles behind the trenches, interlarded by the most amusing soldiers' stories. Then came supper for helpers in the dining room, and dancing for the young people on the tennis lawn, accompanied by Mr. Whitehouse, and arranged by Mr. Whittingham as master of ceremonies.

About ten o'clock a thunderstorm finished the proceedings with great applause, and sent dancers flying homewards; otherwise when the festive day would have terminated goodness *knows as, once again when Newdigate villagers are on the dance, they don't go home till morning if they can help it.*

Mrs. Janson wishes to take this opportunity of thanking all kind helpers, friends for tea, cake, bread, sugar, and milk for the teas, and everyone for their cheerful spirits and the happy faces of the children, and above all for, as usual, the universal response to her small effort and the many demands on their time, trouble and patience. As she is now so busy arranging and making the costumes for the Dorking-Newdigate pageant she hopes she may be forgiven writing to thank friends, farmers, smallholders, and villagers for the many presents of eatables she received for the teas and kind help given. A total of 186 tickets were sold, and the splendid sum of £109 8s. 8d. was realised, the whole proceeds, without any reservation whatever, being given to the Dorking Farmers' Red Cross sale.

In January 1916, Pte. Capon was reported as wounded but by July 1917 he was back with his regiment as can be seen from a postcard sent on the 17th July 1917 and addressed to Pte. W.J. Capon 22558, 6th Queens R.W.S., C. Division, No. 11 Hut, Summerdown Camp, Eastbourne. 'Dear Will, Just a card to let you know Alice is much better and all the rest well. Hope you are feeling better, thanks for cheerful letter will answer it this evening. Love from us all, yours Lily.'

Parish Magazine July 1917

The Newdigate Place Fete and Sale was a great success in every way. Everyone must have enjoyed the afternoon and the financial result was splendid. We are told that Newdigate will be able to send £200 as the result of the Sale and donations received. The following very kindly took charge of the Stalls and did a most roaring sale: Mrs. Nicholls, Mrs. Palmer, Mrs. Hornsby, Mrs. Seyd and Miss Bird. The Hoop-la conducted by Mrs. Barris, Mrs. Junis, Mrs. Cornfoot, Miss Herron, Mr. and Miss Shepherd was greatly patronised. Colonel Nicholls kindly lent many war trophies, shell cases, German helmets, etc. which had been brought back from the war by his son.

The Baby Show attracted much attention and prizes were won by Mrs. Smith and Mrs. Horley. The Girls' Friendly Society gave an exhibition of their club-drill which was excellent, as was the May-pole dance given by the girls from the Schools. Entertainments were given in the Hall of Newdigate Place, arranged by Mrs. Powell. The dance which was greatly looked forward to was alas! stopped by a severe storm at 10 o'clock. We wish to thank most heartily Mrs. Janson and her helpers for the pleasant and most successful afternoon.

Nora Richardson, of 4 Kettles Cottages, took part in the fête, and sent this postcard to her father who was staying at the Vickers Hostel at West Hill in Dartford. Dartford had become a centre for munitions manufacturing, and many workers stayed at the hostel which was formerly the workhouse. During this time they were subjected to a number of bombing raids from

A Gotha bomber

Gothas, (a German bomber with a range of 500 miles and a bomb load of up to 1100 lbs) but, in spite of damage, there were no fatalities. Nora wrote:

Dear Dad,

Mum thought that you would like this card with us girls in our fancy dresses at the fete. We had another one on Wednesday but we had a storm to finish up with as usual.

Lots of love from us all <u>Nora</u> your loving daughter.

Private GEORGE WELLER, G/6934
11th Battalion,
The Queen's (Royal West Surrey Regiment)

George Weller was christened Frederick George in 1885 and was the only son of Frederick and Agnes Weller. As soon as he left school George followed his father and laboured on the local farms, as had his grandfather and great grand-father before him. Like his cousins, Ernest and Percy Weller, he answered the call and joined the army. He was living at Ratfield Cottages, Beare Green, and enlisted with the 11th Battalion the Queen's at Guildford on the 22nd November 1915. His medical examination certificate showed that he was unmarried and was a small but healthy man weighing just under nine and a half stone and under five foot six inches tall. He was described as a carter. The battalion left Aldershot on the 3rd May for Southampton but, owing to fog, embarkation on the *Cesarea,* was delayed. Havre was not reached until the fifth of May 1916. A period of intense training followed and, over the subsequent months the Battalion occupied a number of front-line positions. After a period of inactivity, the Battalion left Alberta Camp in Reninghelst and occupied a position in Old French Trench. At zero hour (3.10 a.m. on the seventh of June 1917) a large mine exploded and the barrage opened with great intensity. The leading wave entered the German trenches without great difficulty. The ground had been very much cut up by shell fire and nearly all the trenches obliterated, so there was difficulty in recognising any particular portion of the enemy lines. Four officers and twenty-nine other ranks were killed that day and five officers and 157 other ranks were wounded. Private George Weller was one of those killed, and is remembered at Ypres on the Menin Gate Memorial which would indicate that the whereabouts of his body were unknown. However his identity disc and one photograph were found and returned to his half-sister, Lilian Evans at 459 Cokeham Cottage, Sompting, near Worthing. His father was already dead and his mother died aged just 55 shortly after her son's death. The Victory Medal and British War Medal were sent to Lilian Evans in July 1921.

The Dorking Advertiser continued printing the results of the latest sitting of the Military Act Tribunal so that it was clear who had a legitimate reason for not joining up.

14.07.1917 – Henry William Horley (38) Burghurst Cottage, Newdigate, farmer etc., conditional exemption until January 12th 1918

Frederick Chandler (35) Hammonds Farm, Newdigate, working farm bailiff, conditional exemption until October 12th

28.07.1917 – Spencer Lucas (40) Kingsland, Newdigate, coal merchant's manager, application refused

Leonard Henry Bedding (37) Ash Farm, Newdigate, cow keeper and dairyman, conditional exemption until January 26th 1918.

25.08.1917 – William Beadle (33) Cidermill Cottage, Newdigate, agricultural carter, to appeal to the Guildford Appeal Tribunal when necessary.

Rifleman BERNARD WHITEHOUSE, 44595
12th Battalion, Royal Irish Rifles

There is only one Bernard Whitehouse listed by the Commonwealth Graves Commission and it has proved to be quite difficult to find any connection with Newdigate. He was born in Greenwich in 1897 and enlisted at Bow, joining the 5th London Regiment (2972). He later transferred to the 12th Battalion, Royal Irish Rifles (12/44595). The 6th June was a tense day for the men in the trenches at Kemmel as they were were given precise instructions concerning the forthcoming attack on the Wytschaete-Messines Ridge. The men were told that souvenir hunting was strictly forbidden and that Germans who showed the slightest sign of resistance had to be killed at once. Prisoners had to be employed taking the wounded back to the lines. Haversacks could not be carried into action, and shaving kit and other small articles had to be left in them and clearly labelled with the man's name and platoon. A small pack on the back was permitted and was to contain a filled water bottle, iron rations, unexpended portions of the day's rations and a waterproof sheet. One man in four, in addition, had to carry solidified alcohol. All officers had to wear rifleman's clothes and equipment but they had to wear their badge of rank on their shoulder and the regimental blue tabs on the back of the collar. They were not permitted to carry sticks. On the 7th June 1917 at 3.10 a.m., just as the first rays of light gilded the Eastern sky, mines were exploded and the artillery struck with a deafening roar. The men went over the top and Pte. Whitehouse was killed when several men were caught by falling debris from a late-exploding mine. The crater today is known as the Pool of Peace. He is buried at the Lone Tree Cemetery along with eight other comrades who died on the same day. The company achieved their objectives and the commanding officer, Lt. Col. W.R. Goodman reported that twenty officers and 507 other ranks had gone into action and losses were slight, two officers and fourteen men killed. He spoke in glowing terms of the bravery of the officers and that many prisoners had been taken and six machine-guns, two large trench mortars, three minenwerfen (mortar) and one flammenwerfen (flame-throwers) had been captured. He also reported that, wherever the wounded men were lying, the man's rifle was stuck with the bayonet in the ground, and this was of great assistance to the stretcher bearers when searching for wounded.

A Mr. Whitehouse played the piano at a concert in Newdigate on the 2nd June, and again at the Newdigate Place Garden Fête on the 6th June, so it is possible that he had an affection for Newdigate as he had been there at the time of his son's death, and so requested that his son's name be put on the memorial. However, further evidence appears in the 1911 census where Bernard Whitehouse, then aged 14 and at school, can be found living at The Waldrons, 6 Gravel Hill, Bexleyheath with his elder brother, mother and father, William Edmund Whitehouse, who was a teacher of music. By 1918, according to the electoral register, William was living at Greenhill (later known as Stoneways) in Partridge Lane, Newdigate so the connection becomes clear.

Frederick Pethick Lawrence, who was a staunch supporter of the Women's Political Movement (Suffragettes) lived with his wife Emmeline at the Dutch House on the main road to Dorking. He was a pacifist and refused to join the forces, although he said he was happy to do work as defined by the Committee of Work of National Importance. F.E. Green of Barings Field offered him a job on his smallholding but the proposal was rejected by the commissioners as not of sufficient national importance. Frederick was made to work for William Batchelor of Wattlehurst Farm in Capel and was paid twenty seven shillings per week. His sister, Caroline Aspland Lawrence, lived at Hatchetts in Newdigate. Her friend Marion Leighfield, who also lived there, had been arrested at Westminster in October 1908 and appeared on a Home Office list of suffragettes arrested between 1906 and 1914.

Private PERCY FREDERICK WELLER, M2/202311
783rd Motor Transport Company,
Army Service Corps

Percy Weller was born in Newdigate in 1883. He was only eight when his father died and twenty-three at the time of his step-father's death. He started his working life as a brickmaker but later worked as a gardener, and lived with his mother at Clerk's Cottages (now Church Cottages). In 1913 he married Nellie Steere and moved to 4 Prospect Cottages in Dunsfold, where they had two children. He enlisted in 1916 and joined the Army Service Corps. These were the unsung heroes who had to maintain the supply chain for the army. His company embarked on the SS Runic II from Devonport on the 25th September 1916 and arrived in Bombay,

via the Suez Canal, on the 30th October having made calls at Valletta and Alexandria. Places which he would only have dreamt about when he was a boy, certainly miles away from the leafy lanes of Newdigate. They then boarded the SS Barletta and sailed to Basra, arriving on the 6th November. In December, they supported the 13th Division at Sheik Sa'ad and reported that the road was very bad and that they had to abandon a van with a broken axle at No. 5 post. By 10th March 1917 they had moved to Baghdad and the city was captured the next day, but the war diaries finish then. Percy Weller died from heatstroke on the 22nd July 1917. Gertrude Bell, a liaison officer to the Arab Bureau, who also knew T.E. Lawrence (Lawrence of Arabia who at this time

Pte. Percy Weller

was orchestrating the Arab Revolt against the Turks), wrote to her father on the 20th July. In temperatures not below 116 deg. F and dripping with sweat she wrote: 'Yesterday I visited one of the big hospitals and went to the ward where they treat the acute heatstroke cases, men with temperatures of 109-110 degrees – the latter don't often live. People here say they haven't had such a burst of heat since 1882.' She later wrote 'It has caused as many casualties as a battle. In the middle of the

SS Runic II

fiercest heat an attack on a small Turkish position on the Euphrates was ordered. It resulted in 60 casualties inflicted by the enemy, 450 by the sun and a retreat to our starting point. No troop could stand such heat – why call upon them to try?' So Mary was left alone at her home in Clerk's Cottage and in just over a year's time another telegram was destined to be delivered to her door with the news of the death of another son, Ernest. Two days after Percy's death, his Commanding Officer, Major John N.G. Gibbons (later Lt. Col. who was awarded the MC), OC. 783 MT (Mechanised Transport) Company, ASC, Mesopotania Expeditionary Force wrote to his widow, Nellie –

'Dear Madame,
With deep regret I have to tell you that your Husband M2/202311 Pte. Weller P.F. died from heatstroke on July 22/1917.

Your Husband joined my company on formation at Bulford and from the start showed me that he meant to serve his King and Country to the best of his ability in that branch of the service to which he was called.

Although not in the firing line his work was just as important and he carried out his duties like a man.

I share with you, your great loss.'

Private Weller is buried at the Baghdad (North Gate) War Cemetery which is situated in a very sensitive area of the Waziriah Area of the Al-Russafa district. In 2006 the New York Times reported that the grass in some places reached up to the chest and the chiselled faces of some of the tombstones are too worn to read. He is also remembered on the Dunsfold War Memorial and on the grave of his wife at Dunsfold. He never saw his daughter, Joan.

Pte. Percy Weller in 1917

Joan and Victor Weller – the children he left behind

Lieutenant WALTER EDWARD WORSDALE COTTLE
Grenadier Guards attd.
Guards Machine Gun Company

Walter Cottle was born in Dulwich on the 31st January 1895 and his sister Aileen followed three years later. They were the only children of Walter H. and Agnes

Cottle. He was educated at Dulwich College. The family together with their servants moved first to Kenley and then to Leigham Park Road in Streatham. Agnes died in 1913; Walter Snr. married Cicely Selby in 1915 and shortly after moved to Melton Hall in Newdigate. Both father and son worked for the Lloyds Register and undertook sea voyages together on ocean liners in the years just prior to the war.

When war broke out Walter Jnr. was rejected as medically unfit. He therefore took up work for the Royal Automobile Club, driving his own car for many months in the service of Lord Salisbury's Division at Chelmsford. The open-air life did him good and he eventually passed the doctor and joined the Artists' Rifles (28th Battalion London Regiment) in January 1916. His Officer Training Corps training at Dulwich, together with the

Party of German prisoners carrying a British stretcher case over difficult ground at Pilckem Ridge on the day Lieut. Cottle died. (Ref. Q5731) Reproduced by kind permission of the Imperial War Museum

Melton Hall, the home of the Cottle Family

knowledge he had picked up during the manoeuvres in the Eastern Division, made him very proficient, so that in less than a month he was sent to the Guards and gazetted 2nd Lieutenant, being amongst the first to go to Grantham for training in the Machine Gun Guards. After about twelve months in England he went to France, being promoted Lieutenant in September 1916, and attached to the 1st Guards Brigade, Machine Gun Company. He was present at the battle of Pilckem Ridge, north of Ypres, and fell on the 31st July 1917. His name is remembered on the Ypres (Menin Gate) Memorial, and the Crawley and Ifield War Memorials.

Source – Dulwich College Roll of Honour

On the 18th August 1917 the Dorking Advertiser reported that Capt. (Acting Major) F.E. Bray, Royal West Surrey Regiment was mentioned in despatches from Mesopotania. He commanded 'C' and 'D' Companies of the 1st/5th The Queen's in support of the 39th Garhwalis and the 90th Punjabis in their attack on the Aziziyeh Ridge and between them they captured three Turkish guns and took many prisoners. Francis Edmond Bray was a cousin of Lt. Gerard T. Bray and rose to the rank of Lieut. Colonel in the 4th Battalion R.W.S Territorials. He was awarded the MC He died on the 8th May 1950.

On the 5th August, a day observed as a special day of intercession for the war, in the course of his sermon, the Rector made the remark that the war was a colossal sign from God, and he urged the people of Newdigate, rich and poor alike, to give the spiritual side preference over the material. He had not written a letter for the parish magazine since January 1917, so the editor published the following letter from the Bishop. Perhaps the Rector had simply run out of words of encouragement.

The Bishop's Letter
August 1917

My dear People,

The third anniversaries are with us, and still there is War: war more intense, more devouring, more appalling than ever. And still our gallant fellows stick, and serve, and fight, under the most intolerable strain. And from among them come the stories of individual heroism, that of the airman who plunges into the centre of a whole squadron of enemy planes; that of a private who swims back over the Yser under enemy fire to bring the end of a rope by which comrades who cannot swim and are between enemy and the water may have a chance to get across and save their lives. These are just outstanding examples of what is done and men are ready to do, by hundreds and thousands.

God be praised; and manhood be honoured for such things.

But the fruits of war are not all good. Even from the front they tell us sometimes pathetically how hard it is for men not to become hard and coarse and reckless, or to let faith in the goodness of God give way: and though at the front the old generosity towards the enemy in the main still remains, at home we have to keep sharply on our guard against the poisons of hatred and revenge. It is easy to forget that these are worse than any injuries which the Germans can do us; and then we punish ourselves more than him if we denounce 'Huns' and practice Hunnishness. We can trust our Government to hit back – the harder the better – but by honest fighting ways and blows at strategic points. But let us remember we are Christians and if we must fight at duty's call, let us leave vengeance to God. Above all, let us not justify ourselves by treating the Old Testament as if it were the New, and quoting things and words which might be right for God's half-taught children in rough old days, as if they were also right to us, who have been brought out of twilight into the glorious light that shone on the world in Christ.

Your faithful Servant and Bishop Edw. Winton

A major offensive was launched on the 31st July 1917, striking from Ypres to the Belgian coast. All through the night of the 31st it rained steadily, and for four days afterwards the downpour was continuous.

Sir Douglas Haig wrote:
'The low-lying, clayey soil, torn by shells and sodden with rain, turned to a succession of vast muddy pools. The valleys of the choked and overflowing streams were speedily transformed into long stretches of bog, impassable except by a few, well defined tracks, which became marks for the enemy's artillery. To leave these tracks was to risk death by drowning and in the course of subsequent fighting on several occasions both men and pack animals were lost in this way.'

Thus the scene was set for the next four months – the time it took to advance four miles to the Passchendaele Ridge and the time it took to sustain over 300,000 casualties.

On the 12th September it was reported that there had been two cases of diptheria in children living in the Rusper Road and as a consequence the Medical Officer of Health instructed that all children from the Rusper Road should be sent home from school.

Vestry Meeting – September 17th 1917

A letter was read from the Surrey Agricultural Committee concerning the destruction by house sparrows of corn crops. The Clerk was instructed to affix notices asking farmers to take active steps to destroy these pests.

The Bishop's Letter
October 1917

My dear People,

There is a matter – and a very difficult one – upon which I think that some words from me to my people may not be unwelcome and are perhaps a duty.

The weather has been in all our thoughts. In two ways fine weather has been of more importance than at any time in living memory; first, for harvesting our home food supply at a time of dearth; secondly, for an effective offensive in Flanders in the crisis of the greatest of wars. And at this moment we have had an almost unprecedented August (beginning, just as our move started, with torrential rain for four days) and a broken September. We go back to last August when torrential rains reducing the country to 'liquid mud' checked as with a bridle our advance on the Somme.

How are we to think? 'Why is God always against us?' said a General abroad. 'The weather has turned Boche' is another saying evidently not of a moralizing parson!

There is an instinct in most people to see some kind of 'providence' in these things. Is it a sound instinct, or a superstition?

I suppose under the Old Testament there would have been no hesitation; pestilence, dearth, calamity were all ascribed to God and to his chastening Hand.

But in the Old Testament itself the question is in the book of Job sharply raised. Admitting that it is often true that calamity is chastisement, the universal truth of this is unchallenged. And Job, who challenges it, is markedly blessed. But what of the New Testament? and what would Our Lord teach?

In passages often quoted, about the Galileans whose blood mingles with the sacrifices (human cruelty), those upon the tower in Siloam fell (physical 'accident'), and the man born blind (natural infirmity), He rebukes easy and confident interpretations (as that the victim or 'his parents' were specially sinful). But it is to be observed that He does not say that 'these things are purely accidental' and leave it there. His words in the first two cases seem, indeed, half to suggest that the victims were sinners, though 'not above all' the others. In the blind man's case He even indicates an object 'that the glory of God may be made manifest in Him' which resulted, and may have been intended.

So when they happen we shall not let our hearts be hardened by taking them sullenly as the work of cruel fate; but they shall draw us nearer to the God in whose hands are all our ways.

Yours very sincerely in fatherly regard, Edw. Winton

Mrs. Janson visited the school on the 19th September and presented a charming brooch to each of the maypole dancers in recognition of the creditable performance the girls gave at the Dorking Red Cross Competition.

Parish Magazine – November 1917

We deeply sympathise with Mrs. Gadd in the great loss she has sustained by the death of her son Pte. Percy Weller. It would indeed be difficult to find a straighter and nicer young man than Percy and he will be greatly missed by all his numerous friends.

Pte. Percy Weller, A.S.C., who has died at Basra from heatstroke was the youngest son of Mrs. M.A. Gadd, of Newdigate, where he was a member of the Choir and also Conductor of the bellringers. He had been in the Army about twelve months and before he joined up he worked at Dunsfold where his wife and two infants are now living. Pte. Weller, who was 34 years of age, has another brother in France.

Mrs. M.A. Gadd and family wish to return thanks to all kind friends for their sincere sympathy in their very sad bereavement.

The Rectory
October 24th, 1917

My dear Friends,
I have not written a letter in the magazine lately but as some have expressed a wish that I should do so, I, of course, fall in with their wish.

I am receiving so many letters respecting the duty of advocating the strictest economy in our living that I feel I must refer to it. Let us do our very best. What we can each one save can be used by others or be reserved for the more serious times that we are threatened with. We must think of others ('If one member suffer all the members suffer with it') and not live for self only but especially for others. Sir A. Yapp, in the National Food Journal, says 'Waste of all kinds must be stopped. One cannot emphasize too often or too strongly that there is urgent need for economy in the use of breadstuffs, bacon, ham, meat, tea, sugar and dairy produce. It is regarded as an economic fact that the fall of prices encourages increased consumption. This must no longer be the case.' I must not quote more but what I am anxious to impress upon myself and all of us is, that what we save ourselves can be used by others who are not so well off or be reserved till the stress is greater than it is even today. Let us do our best and so possess a clean conscience.

My younger daughter will not be able to collect for the S.P.G. as she is fully engaged in voluntary work in one of the large Hospitals for soldiers in London. Will some one kindly undertake this work. There is not much to be done, but it requires one to keep the Society going.

With every best wish
I am, yours very sincerely, H.G. Bird

We are greatly indebted to Mrs. Janson for her great kindness in taking such an interest and trouble in having the heating apparatus attended to. It has been a very troublesome affair but we think the mischief has been discovered and removed and we trust the difficulty of having good fires is now a thing of the past. At any rate the stove goes much better at present.

On November 8th the extreme wing of the Petrograd Soviet under the leadership of Lenin announced that it had deposed the provisional government of M. Kerensky and a proclamation was made for immediate peace. By the 17th Lenin was in complete control of Moscow and on December 15th an armistice was signed with Germany at Brest Litovsk.

The editor of the Dorking Advertiser was in sombre mood –

November 10th, 1917
The present situation is serious. To deny it is not optimism but folly. It is worse. It is to invite disintegration when every man and woman needs to have their faces like flint. We cannot afford to have Russia madly quarrelling with the foe knocking at its door. We cannot afford to regard the state of Italy with any spirit but the gravest of concern. In everybody's heart must burn that 'pour la patrie'. The strain of the war tells on us. Privation, financial loss, inconveniences, beset us like many thorns in the flesh, and if we think only of ourselves they become unbearable. We spend our days and weaken our powers of resistance by continuously asking why should these things be, and blaming Governments because they will not, like old Nehemiah, cease their God-given task, and come down to debate with us. But to every loyal son and daughter of the Empire comes that insistent cry, 'For the Country'. Once feel all that cry means and how little are the things we are called upon to bear. Suppose that many of the luxuries of life have to be given up and that even in necessaries we are rationed, what is this in comparison with the hardships, the sufferings of our brothers, our husbands, our lovers, are daily enduring to keep the old flag flying.

On November 15th it was announced in Parliament that since the beginning of the war the British Armies had captured on all fronts about 166,000 prisoners and over 800 guns. Territory conquered in all theatres was about 128 square miles.

The Rectory
November 21st, 1917

My dear Friends,
We are passing through times of great anxiety and cannot but be saddened by the losses sustained in Italy and the disaffection and disappointment in Russia. We can only hope and pray that all will be well in the end and that those set backs will work for our ultimate good. All I can say is that I hope and trust we all intend to do our very best. We will put our trust in God and then all will be right.
The losses of life we have already sustained from the war and the fear of still more before the end comes, causes us to think much of these dear ones who have laid down their lives for us and we are constantly asking ourselves such questions as: Where are they? What are they doing? Do they take an interest in our welfare? What do they know about us and so on. I

hope therefore to take some of these questions for our consideration on the Sunday Morning Services in Advent.

I have just heard from an old friend of mine, the Rev. E. Gordon Savile, the Secretary of the Church of England Men's Society, that one of our lads on service abroad has joined the War Roll, which consists of men who have signed a Pledge of Allegiance to our Lord Jesus Christ, and have promised to fight His battles and to bring victory to His Kingdom. This gives me the greatest pleasure and I trust there will be others who will follow his manly and Godly example.

With every best wish, believe me,

Yours affectionately in our Lord. H.G. Bird

Dorking Advertiser

A Newdigate Hero

Pte. Cecil Thomas Hills, who has died of wounds in Palestine, was the youngest son of Mr. & Mrs. A. Hills, of Buckhurst Lodge, Wadhurst, and late of High Trees, Newdigate. He was 24 years of age and on the 3rd November 1914 he joined the Australian Light Horse. He went to the Dardenelles, where he was wounded. Mr. & Mrs. Hills have two other sons serving – one has been wounded in France and the other is lying ill in a Malta hospital.

Lance Corporal CECIL THOMAS HILLS, 316
12th Australian Light Horse

Cecil Thomas Hills was born at Copdock in Suffolk in 1892. His parents were Arthur and Emma Hills and he grew up, along with his seven brothers and sisters, on a farm where his father worked. The family moved south, and Arthur became

the farm bailiff at High Trees Farm in Newdigate. Shortly afterwards, in 1912, Cecil emigrated by himself to Australia. His records show that he was 5' 8½" tall and weighed 190lbs, with fair complexion, grey eyes and black hair. He took a job as a station hand at Dunvagen in Dieungra, New South Wales. On the 11th February 1915 he travelled to Liverpool in New South Wales and enlisted with the Australian Light Horse. His regiment embarked from Sydney on HMAT A29 Suevic on the 13th June and they landed at Gallipoli on the 29th August, barely six months after he had enlisted. The weather gradually turned as winter set in, and on the 27th November

Pte. Cecil Thomas Hills

the bitterest blizzard for forty years swept across the Dardanelles. It was so cold that at Helles sentries were found frozen to death. The very next day he was wounded in the thigh and hand by gunfire and it must have been some relief to him when he was transferred to the hospital ship Karapara and taken to Malta. In February 1916 he was transferred to Alexandria and a period of training and courses ensued. On the 17th October 1917 he was promoted to Lance Corporal and later that month he was with the 12th Australian Light Horse in Palestine. On the 31st October he participated, as part of 'C' Squadron, in the famous (and last ever) cavalry charge at Beersheba where he received a serious wound in the thigh and groin which punctured his pelvis. He was taken to the 35th Casualty Clearing Station at El Imara but died of his wounds on the 3rd November 1917.

On the 18th March 1918 a parcel arrived at High Trees Farm with all his personal effects. His parents had a memorial card made – *In loving memory of our dear son, Cecil Thomas Hills, 12th Australian Light Horse, who died of wounds received in Palestine, November 3rd 1917, aged 25 years.*

He is buried at the Beersheba War Cemetery.

Lance Corporal Cecil T Hills mounted on his horse

The Hills family outside High Trees Farm where Mr Hills snr. was farm bailiff

Branches of the Rowland family had been in Newdigate for many years but, although Henry and Mary (née Weller) were married at Newdigate in 1874, they had moved around the area returning to the village in later life.

Sgt. Edward Percy Rowland MM and Bar

Rowlands Drapery Store

Dorking Advertiser – November 24th, 1917

Honours for a Newdigate Lad – Sergeant E. Rowland

Newdigate is specially proud of one of her lads, Sergt. Edward Rowland, youngest son of Mr. & Mrs. Henry Rowland, of Church Cottages, who has done some good work during the past two years while serving with the Queens Royal West Surrey in France. During an attack in July 1916 he put a German machine gun out of action and took some prisoners, for which he was awarded the Military Medal.

Then again, on October 14th, 1917, there was a certain part of the line where they wanted to give 'Fritz' a good hiding (to use his own words) and they were successful.

He was in charge of a bombing section which did some good work. He bombed several of the enemy dugouts and was one of the last to return to our lines – for this work he was again recommended and was awarded a bar to his medal.

Mr. & Mrs. H. Rowland have also three other sons in the Army, Lce. Corporal Henry Rowland, oldest son, who went through the Boer War and Corpl. Mark Rowland, RAMC, both serving in France. The other son is Staff Sergeant Major Frederick Rowland, who has been serving with the QRWS regiment for the past fourteen years but was unfit for service with the Expeditionary Force and is now an instructor in the School of Cookery at Camberwell.

Dorking Advertiser – December 1st, 1917

The Workers' Union – The first trade union meeting in the village was held at the Village Club on Saturday, November 24th, under the auspices of the Workers' Unions. Mr. B. Banks, of the National Union of Railwaymen, presided and made earnest appeals to farm workers to organize so as to be able to get their full and just share of the better rate of wages. He pointed out that it was the duty of all men and women to endeavour to make the conditions of life better for the rising generation, and to see that our soldiers and sailors came back to better conditions than those that existed prior to the war – Mr. George Dallas of the Workers' Union explained the recently passed Corn Protection Act, and showed how the farm labourers could, by organization and by helping each other, benefit by it. He compared the wages of the farm labourer in Scotland with the farm labourer in this district, pointing out that in Scotland the average wage was 38 to 40s per week, in spite of the land being less fertile and the climate much worse than here – Mr. F.E. Green, of Newdigate, pointed out some very startling facts in relation to boy labour and low wages in this neighbourhood. The Rev. H.G. Bird welcomed the advent of such a Society as the Workers' Union, and wished the branch about to be formed every prosperity. A branch of the Workers' Union will be opened on Friday, 30th November at the Village Club.

The Institute at Newdigate

Parish Magazine – January 1918

An excellent Concert was held in the Village School on Dec. 5th in aid of the Newdigate Nursing Association. It was excellent from every point of view. We owe all those who came, at no small amount of trouble and inconvenience to themselves, for our entertainment and amusement, our very best thanks. Our thanks are also due to all those who helped in so many different ways to make the concert a success. The room was crowded and the sum of £17. 1s. 4d. was realised.

We feel sure that everyone in the village will accord Nurse [Elderson] their sympathy in the great loss of her only son. Nurse has worked among us a great many years and has always given us of her best, so that everyone will, we feel sure, do all they can to lighten her way by that silent help and sympathy she is herself always ready to give.

Nurse Elderson certainly needed help and sympathy from the village. Born Emma Georgina A. F. Morgan in Hammersmith in 1868, she married a schoolmaster,

Arthur Charles Elderson (1863-1943) in 1886 and after the birth of her son, Arthur Richard George (1888-1917) they settled down in Fyfield in Essex where Arthur took an appointment as schoolmaster at the Endowed School. Their daughter, Dorothy Marion, was born in 1891. Shortly afterwards, the couple separated and Emma came to live at the Rectory in Newdigate, where she worked as the village nurse whilst her daughter lodged with the Hopkins family at Gaterounds. Her son lived with her parents in Chiswick. Arthur Jnr. was an engineer and joined the Territorials, London Division, in 1909 for a four-year engagement. In 1915 he married Laura Ulrich, a tailor's daughter, at St Augustine's in Fulham, the same church as his parents, and he died two years later at Kensington in 1917, aged 30.

The Newdigate and District Miniature Rifle Club
The object of the N. & D.M.R.C. is to encourage rifle shooting among its members by bringing the means to their own doors. The Club's primary interest is in Miniature rifle shooting but regards this not as an end in itself but is looking directly to long range or service rifle shooting.

The underlying purpose of the Club's work is PATRIOTIC, and although the meetings and competitions are all conducted under the usual conditions of civilian sports, the object sought is to train every able-bodied man in one of the first essentials of good citizenship, and to enable him to take part effectively in the defence of his country if and when called upon to do so.

Members are not required to hold any particular views on the subject of Universal Military Service. All that is asked of them is that they should 'LEARN TO SHOOT' and bear in mind the motto 'LOOK FORWARD'.

The Newdigate people woke up on the morning of the 16th December to find the whole area covered in deep snow. Travelling was very difficult and some of the roads, where the snow had drifted, were practically impassable. Forty children turned up at school, the majority of whom were unfit to remain after trudging through the snow up to their knees, and one of the teachers who had walked two miles was wet through. Next day only six children turned up.

Vestry Meeting – December 28th, 1917
A letter was read from the County War Agricultural Committee respecting allotments. Stating that it was resolved to enter upon and take possession of about one acre of land belonging to Mrs. Carpenter.

By the end of 1917 the population was feeling the effects of the war. The early years of prosperity had gone as queues formed outside shops for foodstuffs. The air attacks on London, which had caused many hundreds of deaths, had spread their own brand of terror.

The romantic vision of the war poets had changed into ghastly realism. Wilfred Owen had just completed the first draft of his bitter Dulce Et Decorum Est (It is sweet and meet to die for one's country) and Siegried Sassoon wrote,

The place was rotten with dead, green clumsy logs,
High booted, sprawled and gorvelled along the saps
And trunks, face downwards in the sucking mud
Wallowed like sand-bags loosely filled.

The Rectory
Christmas Eve, 1917

My Dear Friends,

I am glad to have this opportunity of wishing you all from my heart every blessing for Christmas and the New Year. Amidst all the sufferings, anxieties and losses, it cannot be as bright as usual, but may we learn to look beyond the cloud and see Jesus and His love. It seems as if the war must go on for some time yet. Let us all do our bit to shorten it. The Clergy are asked to bring before all the vast importance of economy in the use of food. The suffering is likely to be greater in the future and the next 100 days may be a great trial to England in more ways than one. Let us do our best and have our consciences clear.

I am your sincere friend, H.G. Bird.

1918

As the queues outside shops were lengthening, sugar rationing was introduced in January in London and the Home Counties, and this was extended in April to meat, bacon, butter, cheeses etc. The queues then began to disappear as an orderly system of food distribution was developed.

Prospects in early 1918 looked bleak following the terrible losses at the Third Battle of Ypres, the armistice between Russia and Germany and the defeat of the Italians at Caporetto. Thoughts turned, in hope, to the successes in Mesopotamia and the surrender of Jerusalem in early December, but still the situation on the Western Front looked ominous and a strange silence fell over the battlefields – the lull before the storm.

The Rector received the following letter from Corporal George Horley who sang in the choir and was one of the bell ringers at St. Peter's.

Corp. George Horley and colleagues

George Horley

My dear Rector and Friends,

It is now ten weeks since I left dear old England to come out to British East Africa. The voyage was a long one of six weeks and I hope it will be a very long time before I have another war-time voyage. We were very much overcrowded and the food was not as it should have been. Well, we had a nice few days at Cape Town, and that was a blessing to us to have a good meal or so. The people could not have treated us better, they were all so very kind. As we marched through the town they gave us sweets, fancy pastry and fags, and then most of us got invitations out to tea and supper. We were all very sorry when we had to leave. We were on the water another ten days before we arrived at Dar-Es-Salaam. We had to walk about a mile to Sea View Camp and we had to just sleep anywhere, but the next night we had tents to go to. We did not get a lot to do there as it was so very hot. In the early morning we had a stroll down to the sea for a bathe, then at 9.30 we had O.C. Parade. After this our time was our own, and generally we would go after the cocoa nuts and other fruit, but it was not quite ripe, so we got stopped at this. After this they called for volunteers to go up country three hundred miles to a wild place called Dodoma. After a very rough ride in the cattle truck on the railway we marched to our destination, where I am still. It is not so hot here, but it is not so convenient as Dar-Es-Salaam. Since we have been here I have managed to get a few luxuries, such as a few tins of fruit and milk. In our mess we do not get a lot of food but we manage famously, and hence we are going strong. What keeps us going is the fact that we all believe that each day that passes is a day nearer victory and a day less when I return to you all.

I suppose you all at Newdigate wonder what kind of life we lead. Well, it is not exactly hard compared with what the other poor fellows had to go through before we arrived, or are going through in France, but it is one which tells a great deal on one's nerves. Here we are out in the wilds, wondering if any of our enemy, the lions, wild dogs, snakes, scorpions, or many other different things are getting hungry. We hear the roars and growls near and never knowing when we are safe from them, it is a little trying. Our minds are never completely at rest, but we never get down hearted. We can get a fowl from our black friends after a most amusing talk for 4d. in English money, quarter rupee out here.

Well, I will tell you a little about Christian life now. On the boat we had no Chaplain, so we commenced a little Service each night. At the commencement there were only four of us, but it grew and over 100 were at the last meetings. The Major, being a good Christian man, did all he could to encourage the work and he took the Sunday Services. I shall never forget these meetings, they were a blessing and comfort to all. We all knew what a great danger we were in and we had to keep our life belts on for several days. On reaching Camp (Dar-Es-Salaam) I made it my duty to see the Chaplain, and the night before I had to come away we had a talk about the C.E.M.S and had arranged to have some meetings of this branch. When I got to Dodoma I saw the Chaplain the first night we arrived (it being Sunday). I asked him if he could arrange for meetings in the week. So I am pleased to say at 6.40 p.m. each night we hold a Service in his tent (4.25 p.m. English time) as we are 2 hrs. 25-mins. in front. I am glad to say my first Communion Service since I left dear old Newdigate was on Advent Sunday. I am very glad to think we can have these services, as no one knows what a blessing and comfort it is to us being so far from our loved ones, and we realize it is harder for them all at home. The Chaplain is as usual the hardest worked man here, he has a long distance to visit and he is a jolly good fine man and knows exactly how to speak to the soldiers.

I hope this little note from Dodoma will find you all well, with my very best wishes for the New Year, from

Yours sincerely, Corpl. Horley, G.R. 154258

May God continue to bless you in your good work

Dodoma was founded during German colonial rule in East Africa and by the time George Horley arrived it was under British control.

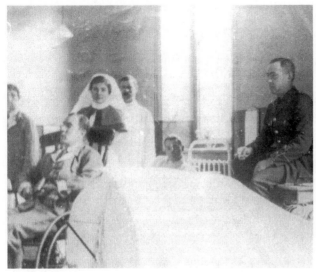

Corp. Horley, far left.

Corp. George Richard Horley and his wife, Louisa

The Dorking Advertiser published this sad little verse:

> *I am the flag in the window,*
> *I am born of the Red, White and Blue,*
> *And the stars that you count in my bosom*
> *Are the sons I have taken for you,*
> *I tell of a home that is lonely*
> *I speak of a vacant chair,*
> *And a mother's heart that is longing*
> *For news of her boy 'over there'*
>
> *Just pause in the day's busy hustle*
> *Don't pass me with only a glance,*
> *Say a prayer for the boys in the home camps*
> *And the ones who are somewhere in France.*

Dorking Advertiser – January 5th, 1918

10th Battalion – Surrey Volunteer Regiment
Owners of two-seater light cars who have laid up their vehicles and would be willing to lend them for service to the 10th Battalion are asked to communicate with C.S. Gordon Clark, Fetcham Lodge, Leatherhead.

Parish Magazine – February 1918

Surrey Prisoners of War Fund
An exhilarating entertainment was given in the Schools on Saturday, January 5th, in aid of the above fund. Some 16 members of a successful London Comedy Company were brought

Officer Prisoners of War – This photograph was taken in a German prisoner-of-war camp. A group at Clausthal Camp: Lieut. Helder, 2nd Lieut. Wingfield, Lieut. Sanders, Lieut. Chance, Lieut. Money, 2nd Lieut. Lloyd-Malloy, all of the RFC. (Reproduced by kind permission of the National Newspaper Archives)

FE2b two seat pusher bi-plane – Lieut. Jas. Sanders was an observer in this class of aeroplane

down by Mr. P.W. Thompson and gave their services. The repertoire was brilliant and highly appreciated by a large audience. The result of the collection by the lady artistes and by Mrs. P.W. Thompson, (whose idea the good work was), was the sum of £28 odd, which has been handed over by Mr. P.W. Thompson who kindly defrayed all expenses. Our warm thanks are due to Mrs. P.W. Thompson who organized and ensured the success of the effort.

The portrait of a former member of the Choir appeared in the Daily Mail on Thursday, January 16th, showing him as a prisoner of war in a camp in Germany. The paper commented 'Lieut. Jas. Sanders R.F.C. is at present in an officers' P.O.W. Camp at Clausthal. His friends must be gratified to see he is sound and looking well.' One of the officers in the picture, Lieut. Chance, became Sir William Hugh Stobart Chance CBE and served with the Worcester Regiment. He wrote about life in Clausthal.

"We duly arrived in the evening and spent the night in the waiting rooms. Next morning we trudged about a mile up hill and arrived at the "Kurhaus zu Pfauenteichen", (The Peacock Lake Hotel), a wooden building converted into a Lager and surrounded by a high wire fence and with wooden barrack huts built at the rear of the hotel. Already there were other P.O.W.'s in residence, mainly those captured in the early months of the War. The senior British officer was Lt. Colonel Bond of the K.O.Y.L.I. and Captain Freddy Bell of the Gordon Highlanders was Camp Adjutant. Others were Captain Skaife of the Royal Welsh Fusiliers, after the War to become Brigadier and Colonel of his regiment. Then there were two brothers by name Boger – one an Infantry Lt. Colonel and the other a Royal Engineer and a pilot R.F.C. There was a very tall and smart Captain Sanderson from my brother's Regiment, the 4th Dragoon Guards.

The Camp was commanded by a Captain Niemeyer – usually referred to as "Mad Harry". He had been a commercial traveller in America and spoke so-called English with a strong mid-western accent. Purple in the face, usually dressed in a long field-grey overcoat with field boots, sword and spurs, he and his twin brother "Milwaukee Bill" – the Commandant of the Holzminden Lager – had been appointed by General von Hänisch who was not enamoured of the British – having been given the Hanover Command after his Corps had had a rough time early on in the War. A committee under the chairmanship of Mr Justice Younger set up to report on the treatment of British P.O.W.'s, reported in 1918 that General von Hänisch was "an unreasonable and cruel man with a violent temper. He took every opportunity of curtailing anything which could make the prisoner's life less irksome. He will march surrounded by his staff and shriek with rage at the British officers, calling them dogs and pig-dogs, as did his Inspector-General Pavlovski." On visiting the Clausthal Camp before we arrived, he had exclaimed very slowly and clearly, "I am hoping every day to receive the order to send some of these people to be put up behind our lines to be shot by British shells."

Of the brothers Niemeyer, the report comments, "Neither of these men could or would speak the truth". There were generally two junior German officers – usually recovering from wounds or on sick leave – an Interpreter N.C.O. and the Reserve soldiers of the Landwehr, who guarded the Camp and provided sentries.

The Kurhaus stood above a lake – the Pfauenteich or Peacock Lake – surrounded by plantations of fir trees, and in the distance one could see the Brockenberg – the mountain famous in German myths and allegories. Some of our officers were housed in the hotel, but I was in a small attic with Money and Ordish and the rest of our party in three hutments adjoining the Hotel. Our British orderlies were housed in huts outside our compound and there were cells for those committed to "Stuben arrest". The huts had rooms each holding six officers and were so small that beds were arranged in pairs – one above the other according to German barrack practice. There was only room for a few chairs and two small tables, and no space for our belongings. Each room had a stove and during the winter months we could generally buy logs. But the un-insulated huts were icy, so overcoats and sweaters were essential. When we arrived and until a room in the Hotel was converted into an anteroom, the only communal accommodation was the hotel dining room, adjoined by its kitchen and canteen. In the summer we were allowed to construct a tennis court and to have a squash court built by a local contractor at our expense. We were able to take exercise in the area in which the courts were located. In the winter of 1917-1918, the tennis court was flooded and used for skating. There was also a small golf putting course which we laid out. A favourite sport, particularly among the senior officers, was "bee ferreting" as there were lots of field mice on the golf course. A captured bumble-bee was introduced into a hole and persuaded to act as a ferret by a stream of smoke blown from a pipe. It was amusing to see ancient Colonels competing with each other on bended knees and puffing away into the holes, having laid bets on who would first cause a mouse to bolt!

The Camp was surrounded by a high wire fence, inside of which was a barbed-wire fence – crossed at the peril of one's life from the trigger-happy guards who patrolled round the perimeter. Outside the Camp was the Guard Room, Kommandantur and the block of cells which had to be enlarged owing to the number of officers who fell foul of the commandant. "'Drei Tage Stubenarrest" was the penalty for incurring his displeasure. The Germans had little sense of humour and were unmercifully ragged. "Mad Harry's" flow of invectives was met with laughter, making his complexion even more purple than usual. "You go right avay – forty meters ago. I send you to little arrest 'ouse". A sentry was summoned and the offender marched off to the cells. In April I wrote to my sister to say that there was plenty of snow – "We get a fall nearly every night". Keeping warm had been a problem and with a diet lacking in vitamins, small cuts turned septic. Most of us went about with bandaged fingers. There was a stage in the Dining Room and officers interested in acting ran a very successful Dramatic Society, putting on several plays. Parcels followed us from Osnabruck, but because it was discovered that some tins contained compasses and other escaping kit, all tins were opened in the Tin Room and their contents tipped out.

On the Fourth of June, 1917, the Old Etonian officers celebrated the occasion with a dinner to which nine of us sat down and drank the toast "Floreat Etona". Those present were Colonel R.G. Bolton (Scots Guards), Major Morrison Bell (Scots Guards), C.K. Hutchison (Coldstream Guards), Captain O.B. Sanderson (4th Dragoon Guards), Jocelyn Lucas (Warwicks Regiment), M. Brocas Burrows (5th Dragoon Guards), C.E. Scarisbrick (The Royal Scots), J.H. McEwen (Cameron Highlanders) and myself. The menu consisted of turtle soup, salmon mayonnaise, curry and rice, cold tongue, fruit salad and coffee.

There were various Camp activities – gambling, drinking, studying and escaping. Two Naval officers made themselves imitation German uniforms – dyed greatcoats, blackened flying boots to resemble German field boots, with spurs made of wire and silver paper, and wooden swords. They made up to represent the Commandant and his Leutnant, with escaping kit hidden under the former's greatcoat to simulate the Commandant's large tummy. One evening they walked out of a side door, passed in front of the kurhaus up to the gate, where the sentry on duty saluted and let them out! Not long afterwards the real Commandant and his Leutnant left their office and walked to the gate to the consternation of the sentry. Unfortunately the escapers did not get far and were captured and brought back to serve a term in the cells. We were allowed to make small vegetable gardens on a plot close to the wire fence and one evening two officers hid among the cabbages at night, cut the wire and escaped. What happened to them, I cannot remember.

The real big escape plot was the making of a tunnel. The floors of the huts were some feet off the ground and the space below them was boarded off. A hole was made in the floor and using bed boards to revet its sides, a shaft was dug which went down several feet. Digging took place during daylight hours and at the end of the day's work, a cover was placed over the shaft and covered with earth. From the bottom of the shaft, a tunnel was dug in the direction of the perimeter fence. This was lined with bed boards and air for the diggers was provided by a bellows with attached tubing. The earth removed had to be disposed of and this was done by filling small sacks hung inside trousers which could be opened up and the contents spread on the ground under the other huts. Work on the tunnel had progressed to the point where it was under the wire fence. One of the orderlies – an Irish Corporal – gave the game away and the tunnel was discovered. "Mad Harry" went wild with excitement – the compound was full of armed Landwehr and we were confined to barracks for some days. Potential escapers had been busy preparing escaping kits, contriving civilian clothes, making maps and with the help of a German Under Officer who was bribed with gifts of food and soap, producing railway passes and other forged documents. A tunnel at our sister camp at Holzminden proved much more successful and many officers escaped, some of them getting over the frontier into neutral Holland, including Jock Tullis who had been with us at Osnabruck. The same Under Officer used to give us advance notice of prospective searches so it was possible to hide away items of escaping kit, hidden largely behind the boards with which the huts were lined and using secret panels whose positions were cleverly disguised.

During the summer we were allowed a number of walks on parole, but as the result of a "strafe" ordered by General von Hänisch, they were discontinued, a pity as the surrounding countryside was attractive. At the end of August, I wrote, "We had a racquets tournament but I did not get very far, being knocked out in the second round. Directly the weather gets better, they are going to have a foursome golf tournament but for the last few days it has poured with rain and the greens have been flooded. It is miserable being confined to our huts all day after being able to enjoy the open air for so long".

At last, in August orders came for those of us captured in the autumn of 1916 to move to Holland. We gave away various treasures accumulated over the past months, packed our bags and marched to the station and took a train for Aachen, where we were housed in a Technical High School building. Sanders, Molloy, Helder, Wingfield and Money came with me. The guards said, "Tomorrow you will be in Holland", but time passed and nothing happened. The Dutch frontier was only a few kilometres distant and we were allowed several walks "on parole" in charge of a German Lieutenant. Many of us were struck down by an attack of influenza which was raging at the time. We lay in bed suffering from high temperatures with only some weak gruel to sustain us. When we recovered we were so run down that we could hardly climb the stairs – in fact we crawled up on hands and knees, having searched the rubbish bins for crusts. The Germans, particularly in the towns, were getting very short of food. Having consumed the tins we had brought with us for the train journey, we were back on vegetable soup and "Kriegsbrot". After six weeks of waiting we had to sustain a severe shock – being informed that the exchange to Holland had broken down owing to the sinking of a British hospital ship on its way to pick up German prisoners from England. We were to be shipped back to a P.O.W. camp on the Baltic. So, packed tight in 4th class carriages, we wended our way by train via Berlin and after several nights, when it was difficult to get any sleep, duly arrived at Stralsund. Our new camp had been occupied by Russians and was on an island called Dänholm, separated from the city by a narrow stretch of water and crossed by small ferry boats. The island in peacetime had housed a garrison H.Q. and was provided with several blocks of barracks and other buildings. We messed in a hall some way from the barrack rooms in which we were housed. Sanitary provision was medieval and consisted of a circular structure, on the first floor of which was a circle of inclined "seats" and underneath the "shit cart" which was drawn out periodically to have its contents tipped. The Baltic winds blew strongly up the apertures which were only partly sealed by their seated occupants! When we arrived, there were about four hundred newly captured British prisoners, mainly taken in the German spring offensive. We – the old hands – had to teach them the various tricks and devices we had learned during our two years of captivity. Food was in very short supply but supplemented by a hoard of potatoes stored in cellars under our ground floor rooms. It did not take long for one of our experts to make a key and open up the door to the potato store. After a time some food parcels began to turn up – if I remember rightly, emanating from Holland and Switzerland.

(The war finally came to an end and the prisoners were repatriated)

We had not long to wait before we were sent off on a train which fetched up at Warnemunde, from where there was a ferry to Denmark. After crossing to Jutland – the mainland – we were housed in a camp, warmly greeted by the Danes who had managed to keep out of the War. The warmth of their welcome astonished and delighted us and at every stoppage the population, many of them wearing gala dress, provided refreshments. We were allowed to take walks without supervision and appreciated the luxury of sleeping between clean sheets. After a stay of about ten days, we went by train to the port of Aarhus, and embarked on a very smelly small steamer. The North Sea was rough. We were crammed tight in what cabins were available and most of us suffered from mal-de-mer – made worse by a diet of very greasy Irish stew! After a stormy crossing, we arrived at Leith, the port of Edinburgh, where we were greeted by local dockers who enquired, "Where have you been spending the War?" R.F.C. officers were sent to Scarborough where we were interviewed and after telling our various stories covering experiences of becoming prisoners-of-war, we were allowed to go off on leave.

What happened to my fellow officers in Room 68? Sanders went to South Africa and returned to farm in the East Midlands. Helder, who had intended to join the Church, became a dentist. Wingfield became a chartered accountant, working in London. Money rejoined his Regiment for a time and then went barn storming in New Zealand, ending his military career as Adjutant of a R.A.F. Reserve Squadron. All others have died except Tom Molloy who rejoined his Regiment – the Dorsets – ending up as a Colonel and for some years has lived in Malta."

More heavy snow fell on the 14th January and to compound the misery scarlet fever had again returned to the homes on the Rusper Road, requiring the school to close for two weeks.

Dorking Advertiser – January 19th, 1918
Oddfellows' Smoking Concert
One of the most successful 'smokers' ever held at Park Gate was that of Wednesday evening, in the assembly room of the Surrey Oaks, under the auspices of Victoria Lodge of the Independent Order of Oddfellows, M.U. The object was to raise funds to wipe off the deficit on the management fund, and it is gratifying to report that there was a crowded attendance. Much disappointment was felt at the absence of Capt. R. Elliott Palmer, who was prevented from taking the chair, but

the gallant Captain very generously sent two guineas towards the fund. Mr. John Horley fulfilled the duties of chairman admirably, and a capital programme was contributed to by Mrs. W.B. Turner, Miss Stella Turner, Miss M.E.A. King, Messrs. Carpenter, A. Gumbrell, W. Hooker, F. Worsfold, L. Harkett, G. Butcher, F. Dean, Widdons and Winfield. Mr. Whitehouse was an excellent accompanist, and by his contributions in other ways largely added to the enjoyment of the evening. During the evening, Mr. A. Gumbrell, the Provincial Corresponding Secretary, spoke on the work of the Victoria Lodge and the Manchester Unity and was followed by the I.P.P.G.M. W.B. Turner. No charge was made for admission, but a collection was made and realised 33s. 5½d which with Capt. Palmer's donation, may be considered highly gratifying.

The Surrey Oaks

The Rectory
January 21st, 1918

My dear Friends,
Before I write to you again we shall have entered upon the solemn season of Lent, which is very early this year. May it be kept very holily by us all. Surely the world-wide war ought to make us most thoughtful and bring us all nearer to God.

We are grieved to hear of the sad loss on Friday, 11th of Alfred Edwin Dean, the nephew of Mr. Dean, and we sympathize very deeply with him and all the members of his family.

With every best wish,
I am, yours very sincerely, H.G. Bird

Sgt. Alfred Edwin Dean (1892-1918) was born in Bundaberg in Queensland and served with the 25th Battalion of the Australian Imperial Force (Queensland). He was the son of Arthur A. and Mary Jane Dean who emigrated to Australia in 1880. Arthur was the brother of the Newdigate shopkeeper, Alfred Dean. Sgt. Dean survived the

mud and slaughter of Passchendaele but died on the 11th January 1918 and is buried at the Underhill Farm Cemetery. Underhill Farm was used as a dressing station and the cemetery is close to the farm on the north west edge of Ploegsteert Wood in the Ypres Salient. A few days after Sgt. Dean was buried, the area fell to the Germans and was not re-taken until September 1918.

Parish Magazine – February 1918

The Rector has received some most kind letters from those at the Front, who have greatly enjoyed their Christmas parcels.

On February 18th the armistice between Russia and Germany ended and war resumed. By the 28th however, Lenin, Trotsky and the Russian Delegation renewed negotiations for peace which were finalized at the Treaty of Brest-Litovsk on March 3rd. This resulted in the loss of one quarter of the total area of European Russia, including Poland, Estonia, Latvia, Lithuania, the Ukraine, Finland and Transcaucasia. The Ukraine became an important granary for the Central powers, which had been facing severe food shortages due to the allied blockade. Most importantly, more German troops became free for the planned great offensive.

The Bishop's Letter
March 1918

My dear People,
It is not a time, as it seems to me, for saying much. It is the critical stage of the war. We hold our breath in suspense. We are awaiting the most colossal onslaught ever delivered. Can we under God withstand it, as our soldiers quietly and firmly believe? Can we at home hold on steadily without weakness and division among ourselves?

I find, for myself, no better guidance than that of President Wilson. His utterances seem to be a touch stone for enfeebling pacifism, and for a mere bluffing militarism, the two great dangers of the true and strong patriotism which we need. With unfaltering determination to use his country's power for the righteous cause, he watches quietly and steadily for any signs among our enemies of disposition for a peace which shall be real. I am glad to believe that our statesmen are at one with him. But he gives out his meaning with telling power.

I hope that you will study the matter of the League of Nations, of which the House of Bishops in the recent Convocation unanimously affirmed approval.

If Lent 1918 teaches us these two things of simple dependence and of corporate prayer, then it may bring us more blessing than happier times.

God defend the right! and give us peace in His time. Edw. Winton

Miss L. Seward-Hill wishes to thank all her kind friends in Newdigate and elsewhere for their very kind and liberal donations to Miss Gladys Storey's Bovril Fund for the brave men in the Trenches. £12. 14s. was the amount collected, for which Miss Gladys Storey sends most grateful thanks and best wishes to all.

Mr. H.B. Burrows reported that in 1917 the magazine account showed a deficit of £8.15s.6d. which has to be advanced from the general fund. The sale of magazines amounted to £5.16s.10d. and the income from advertisements amounted to £2.12s.6d.

Coal and Clothing Club
Possibly all Parishioners do not know how the Coal and Clothing Clubs are supported. Five shillings are added to all subscribers to the Club who are Parishioners. This is granted by the Committee of Smith's Charity and this year amounted to £9. No doubt the committee is acting quite justly, but we are sorry to say that in accordance with the Trust they are unable to add this to subscribers who live at the Henfold Cottages which are in Capel Parish. The Rector very kindly says that he is willing to receive payments from any residing there and he thinks possibly Capel would add the bonus to those living in the Parish.

It is possible that we may not be able to add more than 5/- as bonus to contributors to the Clothing Club which is taken from the General Parochial Fund as by death we have lost three subscribers to that fund so that its funds are not likely to be quite so large in the future. The Rector is desirous of doing his very best for all members and will make himself responsible for adding at least 5/- to all subscribers.

Dorking Advertiser – March 16th, 1918
Military Appeals at the County Appeal Tribunal at Guildford.
W.W. Hawkins (33) Newdigate, engaged in intensive farming (taken in camera), one month final.

March 23rd, 1918
War Agricultural Committee – Dorking Rural
Mr. A. Hills, Coombers Farm, Newdigate, appointed supervisor

April 20th, 1918
Military Appeals – Dorking Rural
Walter John Carpenter (41) Newdigate, general supply stores, conditional till July 1st
Henry Thomas Whittingham (34) Newdigate, baker, conditional till July 1st.

On March 21st Germany launched, as the Bishop had predicted, a huge attack on the Western Front. An hour and a half before daybreak the German artillery opened a bombardment of great violence. Some places twenty-eight miles behind the line were struck by high velocity shells. After the warm weather of early spring, the rain rose from the ground in a dense mist – more than fifty miles of the British front from Monchy to Tergnier were flooded with poison gas which in the foggy air clung to the ground. With visibility at times less than fifty yards, the ghostly German attacks achieved their greatest successes since 1915. The Allied Army fell back in retreat, abandoning the territory so expensively gained in the previous autumn.

Ludendorf, the German commander, claimed to have taken – between the Vimy Ridge and the Ailette River – 95,000 prisoners from March 21st to April 25th 1918. He failed,

however, to sever the railway communications link between the French and the British lines at Amiens.

March 25th and diphtheria had returned to the village. The school was closed for two weeks which included the Easter holiday. Upon their return one child was excluded as he was verminous!

Parliament opened a new session on April 9th. 100,000 fit men were released from munition work and 50,000 were withdrawn from the coal industry. A new bill raised the age for military service to fifty for every able-bodied man.

Sir Hubert Gough, the British Commander, was dismissed following the great retreat. He later wrote in defence of his troops: 'Hold up your heads high with pride. History will proclaim the greatness of what you did. It can be said of no other troops that they did more to win the war. You are the remnants of a gallant band of brothers, buffeted by adversity and grievously maligned, yet your spirit is too fine to be damped by such misfortune.

You are the men on whom Britain is based.'

Vestry Meeting – March 25th, 1918

Letter received from the District Council respecting land for allotments. The Council thought that sufficient land had been provided. It also called for the destruction of rats but steps had already been taken.

The Rectory
April 17th, 1918

My Dear Friends,

I wish to take this opportunity of thanking you most heartily for your great kindness in giving me your offerings at Easter. They were very much larger than they have ever been since I have been at Newdigate and I wish to thank you very much for your kindness.

I do hope and pray that the war may have the one effect of drawing us all more closely to our dear Lord. The Easter Services were very bright and well attended.

The War is causing us great anxiety just now but I trust we all feel it must and will be quite right in the end, and that God will give us the victory.

With every best wish,

I am, yours very sincerely, H.G. Bird

Miss Herron very kindly sends us the following account of the Women's Work on the Land:
The women in Newdigate who had been working on the land during the war and had earned an armlet (i.e. 30 days or 240 hours) were invited by the Dorking District Committee of the Women's Branch of the Board of Agriculture, to tea at St. Martin's Church Room, Dorking, on Saturday, 6th April and afterwards to a meeting at the Public Hall, where Miss Baker, the County Representative, presented Stripes to those who had earned them. Fourteen women from Newdigate were able to go.

The Dorking District includes Dorking, Westcott, Mickleham, Abinger, Wotton, Forest Green, Ockley, Capel and Newdigate.

The following Newdigate women received Stripes:

Miss A. Widdows (3 Stripes) has looked after chickens at Boothlands every day during the last eighteen months and one year before rearing and looking after turkeys.

Mrs. Wheeler (2 Stripes) has milked and looked after cows at Capt. Palmer's every day during the last year.

Mrs. Davey (2 Stripes) has done general farm work at Tanhurst for over six months in 1916 and also in 1917.

Mrs. Harber (2 Stripes) worked in Mr. Dodd's garden for six months in 1916 and nine months in 1917.

Mrs. Smith (1 Stripe) did general farm work at High Trees for six months in 1917.

Miss Clemmans (2 Stripes) has been a worker in the Land Army for one year.

Miss Baker was very anxious for more women, if possible, to come and work on the land, even if only for a few hours occasionally. Also she pointed out that many more are wanted for the Land Army, as all the soldiers now working on the land are to be recalled to the colours, and women must take their place if we are to have enough food.

Lieutenant KENNETH CHESTER HERRON
82nd Squadron, Royal Air Force

Kenneth Chester Herron was the youngest son of George O.M. Herron and Ellen (later Janson) and was born at Harbord House in Richmond on the 6th March 1881. Like his older brother Walter he grew up at 14 De Vere Gardens in Kensington and worked as a clerk at the family wool merchants' business at 25, St. Thomas's Street (just opposite Barts Hospital). In the 1890s the family built and moved to Newdigate Place and Kenneth owned the lower half, park and land. He was educated at Bradfield College, a school near Tours in France, and at Leipzig in Germany. He was fond of yachting and sailing. On the 31st July 1907 he married Alice Kate Smith, whose father, an oil merchant, had died less than four weeks previously. He and his wife were living at Wickham Place, Wickham Bishops near Witham in Essex with their three children when he obtained a commission in the Yeomanry in January 1915 and went to France in July 1916. In August 1917 he transferred to the Royal Flying Corps. Earlier that year, in what became known as 'Bloody April', the RFC lost seventy-five aircraft in action in one week. The average life expectancy of a pilot in France during this time was two months. Some aircrew were arriving with as little as seventeen and a half hours flying time under their belt. By the end of April, the RFC had lost a total of 150 aircraft and 316 crew. The 82nd Squadron had been formed at Doncaster in January 1917 and served as an army co-operation unit on the Western

Front, flying Armstrong Whitworth FK8 reconnaissance/bomber aircraft. It was a massive aircraft by the standards of the day – large, ungainly and sturdy. Although it had an excellent platform from which to drop bombs, it was not very agile, but it was fitted with a Vickers gun on the cowling and a Lewis gun in the rear on a ring mount for the observer/gunner. The squadron transferred from its base in Waddingon to St. Omer in France, where the machines were equipped with wireless and other important equipment. Under the command of Major J.B. Solomon, they moved to Argonvillers and in March 1918 started a 'new career' with two to three bombing raids each day. Between the 28th March and the 10th July they dropped 3227 twenty-five-pound bombs and 264 one-hundred-and-twelve pound bombs, which was a record. Life was very difficult for these flyers. The squadron diary in March 1918 describes how Capt. R.T. Fagan, whilst returning from a patrol, was attacked by six Albatross D5 aircraft. None of the British scouts were in the vicinity but Capt. Fagan was successful in fighting his way through and in addition brought down one of the enemy aircraft.

On the 24th April 1918, whilst flying low over enemy lines at Villers-Bretonneux, observing the world's first battle between two tank forces, Lt. Herron was hit by a rifle bullet and died almost immediately. His pilot was uninjured and flew the aircraft back safely. On that day two other officers also lost their lives, 2nd Lt. L.K.W. Barrett and 2nd Lt. C.A. Procter. In his will, Lt. Herron left an estate

Lieut. Kenneth Chester Herron

to the value of £75,574. He is buried at the Vignacourt British Cemetery and a window to his memory can be seen in the south aisle of Newdigate church. There is also a memorial to him at St. Bartholomew's Church in Wickham Bishops. The Essex Herald recorded his death in their issue of the 7th May 1918.

82nd Squadron Royal Air Force

82nd Squadron Christmas Card – 1917

An Armstrong Whitworth Fk8 – Lt. Kenneth Chester Herron was an observer in this type of aeroplane when he was killed.

Dorking Advertiser – Saturday May 11th, 1918

Pte. Ben Taylor killed.

The Newdigate and Leigh readers will regret to hear that Pte. Ben Taylor, of the Queen's R.W.S. Regt., the eldest son of Mr. & Mrs. Taylor of Broad Lane, Newdigate was killed in action last month. Pte. Taylor, who was only seventeen years of age when he enlisted in June 1915, was fighting in France in the following year and was wounded in April. He was in hospital in England for a time and recovering rejoined his battalion. In April 1917, he was again in hospital, having broken his leg in a trench which fell in. In January last he returned to France, and was in the thick of the fighting in March and April, until he made the supreme sacrifice. Born at Newdigate, young Taylor on leaving school took up farm work in the district, and was very popular with all who were in any way acquainted with him. His brother-in-law, Pte.

Farrington, whose home is 30 South Albert Road, Reigate is in France. On Sunday there was a memorial service at the Newdigate Mission Hall, at which Pastor Herridge officiated, and paid tribute to the memory of Pte. Taylor, and spoke of the high esteem in which his parents were held in the village.

Lieut. Herron killed.

Lieut, Kenneth Chester Herron, Yeomanry, attached Royal Air Force, who was killed in action on April 24th 1918, was born March 6th 1881, the youngest son of the late George O.M. Herron and Mrs. Janson of Newdigate Place. Educated at Mr. G.F. Burgess' School, Epsom, Bradfield College, near Tours in France and Leipzig in Germany, he received a commission in the Essex Yeomanry in January 1915 and went to the Front in July 1916. He was transferred to the Royal Flying Corps as an observer (owing to his age) last August and was hit by a rifle bullet while flying low over the German lines at Villers-Bretonneux, and died almost immediately. His pilot was uninjured and flew back to the nearest British ambulance so he did not fall into the hands of the enemy.

His Flight Commander, 82nd Squadron writes: 'The squadron has had a good many casualties since the present battle started but without exaggeration the loss of Herron is the greatest we experienced. His brother officers in 'A' flight liked and respected him as a man and as an officer who always carried out the work allotted to him well and cheerfully, and was an example to the younger men and we all feel we have lost a good friend and a good soldier from our midst. He is buried at Vignacourt, British Cemetery near Amiens.' Lt. Kenneth Herron has left a young widow and three little children. Besides Wickham Place, he owned the lower half of Newdigate Place, park and land. He was good at all kinds of sports and particularly fond of yachting and hunting. His half brother, Capt. Douglas Herron, was killed in the South African War and his brother Walter F. Herron, 4th Dragoon Guards, in this war, April 1916.

Dorking Advertiser – May 18th, 1918
Miltary Act Tribunal – Dorking Rural Area

Temporarily exempted, conditional on their remaining employed on the land and holding the Surrey War Agricultural voucher till October 1st:
Henry Winfield, Brook Farm, Newdigate
Thomas Frederick Voice, Swires Farm, Beare Green
Harry Voice, Swires Farm, Beare Green

The Rectory
May 28th, 1918

My dear Friends,
I think many of you are aware that the Bishop has asked me to help at Capel during the absence of the vicar, the Rev. C.F. Carver, who is likely to be called up soon to act as a Chaplain in France.

The Bishop in his directions says 'I think that men of military age up to 45, and to 50 prospectively, shall offer themselves to me for national service. They may, if they wish, indicate the kind which they would prefer.'

Private BEN TAYLOR, G/6060
1st Battalion, The Queen's
(Royal West Surrey Regiment)

Ben Taylor was born in 1898 and lived his entire life in Broad Lane. He was one of eight children born to Joseph and Emily Taylor. The Taylor family had been established in Newdigate for many years. From being a carter on a farm, Ben enlisted in June 1915 and was wounded in April 1916 and was hospitalised in England. After his recovery he rejoined his regiment. The great German offensive in Flanders began on the 9th April 1918 and the battalion, under the command of Lt.Col. M. Kemp-Welch DSO, MC, received orders that it had to be ready to move in two hours. The order duly came and they entrained at Aubigny at 3.15 a.m. on the 11th April, arriving at their destination at 2.00 p.m. The men — together with cookers, water carts and mess carts were then bussed to a position south of Meteren. Fighting orders were prepared and ammunition made up to 220 rounds per man. When the enemy launched a heavy attack, they created gaps in the line and exploited this advantage by rapidly pushing through light machine guns. The Queen's were overwhelmed and fell back. It was during this retreat, on the 14th April, that Ben Taylor fell. 387 officers and men from the battalion were either killed or wounded during this operation. Pte. Taylor was buried at the Canadian Cemetery No. 2, Neuville-St. Vaast, north of Arras.

Pte. Ben Taylor

The number of Services held, and of sermons preached, may be considerably curtailed. The Rev. F. Marshall, Rector of Ockley, has also promised to give some help. Mr. Marshall and I will do our very best, first for our own Parishes and also for Capel, but I suppose it must mean that some services will have to be given up.

In asking for your prayers, help and sympathy,

I am, yours most sincerely, H.G. Bird

The Red Cross Week at Newdigate was a great success, and this was mainly due to the great enthusiasm put into the work by Mrs. Winfield, the result, we feel sure, will be quite excellent for a little country Parish. Probably we shall reach nearly £150 altogether. It will be magnificent if we do.

The Battle of the Aisne from May 27th to June 18th saw the German front reach to a point just forty miles from Paris. But the impetus was slowing down.

Dorking Advertiser – June 8th, 1918

Letter read to the Miltary Act Tribunal from Sir A. Geddis:

'At the present critical stage of the war even greater efforts and sacrifice than those already made are necessary on the part of all classes of the community. The demand for men in the higher medical grades or categories is insistent and must be met at once if the national forces are to be maintained in adequate strength —- I rely upon you to keep steadily before the Tribunal at which you appear that no fit man of fighting age shall now receive exemption on occupational grounds unless he is engaged in work directly important to the preparation of war, and also no general paramount necessity than an increased flow of fit men shall be obtained without delay.'

Dorking Advertiser – June 22nd, 1918

Military Act Tribunal

Walter John Carpenter (41) Grade 2, Kingsland, Newdigate, baker, adjourned until considered by Food Distribution Committee

June 29th, 1918

Henry Thomas Whittingham (35) Grade 3, Newdigate, baker, conditional until October 1st.

From June 1917 to the end of the war, two million American troops were transported across three thousand miles of sea. The arrival of such a vast army posed many problems for the allies. Ports had to be rebuilt or extended and the French railway, already hard pressed supplying the French and British troops, had to be dramatically modified. Rail fares in Britain had risen by 50% and vast tracks of line were uplifted and shipped to France.

But fresh help and hope had arrived to assist the fatigued and weary British and French troops and this was just the lift that the allies required. On the night of the 8/9th June 1918 the Americans faced their first artillery bombardment when the entire valley they were occupying was drenched with gas. Casualties were high.

On July 15th the Germans launched their last offensive – the Champagne-Marne Offensive – their last, due to utter exhaustion and the menace of political revolution looming at home. One hundred thousand Germans withered under the unexpectedly hostile shell and machine-gun fire of the French.

The Rectory
June 26th, 1918

My Dear Friends,

There is not a great deal for me to say this month, but first I must congratulate you on the magnificent result achieved for the Red Cross – £140. 8s. is a splendid sum to send up from our small Parish. It was also splendid to send £20.11s.4d to the London Association for the Blind. I have now received an application from from Lord Ashcombe and others respecting the Dorking War Weapons Week. It appears that the sale of National War Bonds and War Saving Certificates have for the last few weeks been considerably below the average. It has therefore been suggested that a War Weapons Week should be organised throughout the Country. Any area contributing £2. 19s. od per head of the population will have the privilege of naming a weapon such as an Aeroplane or a Gun. I am sure we shall do what we can, though we have of late been very severely taxed. We are asked to invest in War Loans between July 8th and 13th in Dorking.

The Schools were examined in Religious Knowledge on June 7th but we have not received the reports.

Let us hope that the magnificent work done by the Italians may continue and that we in the West gain the same advantage.

I am, your sincere friend, H.G. Bird

The Magazine

The Magazine returns for the first five months of this year show a serious deficit. This is undoubtably due to the increased cost of printing etc. Two courses are open to us. We may either increase the cost of the Magazine to twopence or exclude 'The Sign' and limit the issue to Parochial news only, or give up the Magazine for a time. We desire to act in conformity with the wishes of the parishioners and we shall be glad if they will express their opinion on the matter.

The Sign was an illustrated religious magazine which was included with the parish magazine. For the sake of one penny there were no more issues of the parish magazine printed until 1922. The thoughts of the Rector, as the armistice approached, will never be known – and our history is the poorer for it.

Private ROY FREDERICK GOLDSACK, L/11236
6th Battalion, The Queen's
(Royal West Surrey Regiment)

Roy Goldsack was born in Marylebone in 1898. His mother, Ethel E. Goldsack, a domestic parlour maid, was one of the nine children of Frederick George Goldsack, a tailor from Dover who had moved to Reigate. Roy lived with his grandparents in Reigate and then moved in with his uncle George Frederick Trow and his aunt, Margaret Louisa Trow (née Goldsack) who, before her marriage, had been in service with the Herron family at 14 de Vere Gardens, Kensington. They lived at Reffolds and Roy went to school at Newdigate. He was one of the first in Newdigate to join up. In

Pte. Roy Frederick Goldsack

May 1915 his regiment landed at Boulogne, but when on leave he told his friends that he was convinced he was going to die because as a sniper he felt very exposed. When it was time for him to return to Aldershot, he was reluctant to leave Newdigate and it took a lot of persuasion to get him onto the train at Holmwood. The 6th Battalion had taken part in the Battles of Loos and the Somme, so it is not hard to imagine the misery and dread in young Roy's mind as the trees and fields of the Surrey Hills slipped by and he re-joined his comrades.

As a result of the great German offensive of March 1918, the battalion was in constant action. By June they were back at Aveluy Wood and occupying ground that had been fought over three months ago. An operation was planned to gain the remaining high ground of the Bouzincourt Spur. Zero hour was 9.35 p.m. on June 30th and the advance was to be made under a creeping barrage, the 6th Queen's attacking on the right and the 6th Royal West Kent on the left. Stokes mortars opened the barrage at zero less one minute. Artillery barrage opened at zero and the enemy barrage started ten minutes later. About midnight the situation was obscure, but for Roy Goldsack the torment had ended as he fell just as darkness was setting in that mid-summer's evening. He is buried at the Dernacourt Communal Cemetery Extension, just south west of Albert.

After severe fighting on the Piave, by June 22nd the Austrian offensive was at a standstill and the Italian commander, General Diaz reported that the Austrian army had been heavily defeated and was being pursued across the river. At home the ordinary Austrians had been suffering from severe food shortages and Vienna had become a cauldron of unrest. Thousands of Czecho-Slovaks and Yugo-Slavs who had previously been part of the Austro-Hungarian army surrendered and fought alongside Italian troops as they saw their national aspirations most likely to be answered from that quarter.

Dorking Advertiser – July 27th, 1918

Military Act Tribunal
Walter John Carpenter, 41, Grade 2, Newdigate, baker, conditional exemption to January 1st.
Volunteer
Albert Hoskins, 49, Grade 1, Newdigate, gardener, refused – not to be called up for 28 days.

In France the Allies mounted their counter-stroke at the Second Battle of the Marne. There were four days of rain which screened the final preparation, then the rain ceased and on the morning of the great assault, August 8th, a thick summer fog blanketed the battlefield and acted as a shield for the attackers. The British 4th Army and the French 1st Army attacked on a 20 mile front from the Avre river at Bianches to the neighbourhood of Morlancourt. The French progressed on the whole front between the Avre and Oise and the British advanced their line north of the Somme.

Dorking Advertiser – August 17th, 1918

A Sailor's Death

News has been received at Newdigate of the death of Alfred E. V. Wooltorton, aged 19, of H.M.S. Garth, who died in hospital in Edinburgh on the 21st July. He was a very promising lad both at school, at the rifle club, where he was awarded prizes, and at business with Mr. A. Dean, of Newdigate. At the age of 17 he volunteered to fight for his country and on the 3rd July he was cheerfully writing home to say he hoped to be with his parents in August. He was very popular both at Newdigate and with his mess mates on board ship. His father, Mr. George Wooltorton, is well known in Newdigate, being secretary of the Slate Club and of the Workers' Unions and both Mr. & Mrs. Wooltorton have received letters of sympathy from Mr. & Miss Goldberg, Mr. & Mrs. Carpenter, Mr. & Mrs. F.E. Green, Mr. Robert Rusbridge and many others.

Cook's Mate ALFRED EDWARD VICTOR WOOLTORTON, M/22723 HMS 'Garth' Royal Navy

Alfred Wooltorton was born in 1898 and grew up in the village of Raveningham in Norfolk where his father, George, worked as a gardener. The family moved

to Newdigate in the 1907 and lived at Hatchetts Cottage. George worked on the local farm as a hay binder and stockfeeder and Alfred worked as a baker's boy in one of the local bakeries. The extra money was needed as there were now eight children to feed. His older brother, Reginald (M/16919), had joined the navy in 1915 so Alfred followed suit in the following year. He spent from September 1916 to August 1917 at HMS Pembroke, the shore establishment in Chatham, which suffered a tragedy when the drill hall was hit, shortly after he had left, on the 3rd September 1917 by bombs from Gotha aircraft. Over one hundred and thirty sailors were killed. Another tragedy hit the Establishment when, during the Spanish Influenza epidemic of 1918 two hundred and

Two brothers join the Navy – Alfred Edward Victor & Reginald John Wooltorton

forty two sailors died. Alfred was appointed Cook's Mate on board the Hunt Class minesweeper, HMS Garth. (The Commonwealth Graves Commission states that the Garth was a trawler but that was not the case). Days were spent sweeping the west coast of Scotland from Aberdeen to Leith. Illness had struck the ship; on July 12th, 1918 Able Seaman Joseph M.R. Milet died and Alfred succumbed two days later from scarlet fever in the City Hospital in Edinburgh. They are both buried in unmarked graves in the Seafield Cemetery in Edinburgh, but their names are commemorated on a special memorial dedicated to those whose names had not been recorded on a headstone. Alfred's younger sister, Mabel Ethel L. Whiffen (née Wooltorton) lived her entire life in the village until she died in 2004 aged 94.

Alfred Wooltorton as a baker's boy for Dean's Stores

Alfred Wooltorton with his pigeons

Hunt Class Minesweeper similar to HMS Garth (Reproduced by kind permission of the National Maritime Museum)

Dorking Advertiser – August 31st, 1918

Military Act Tribunal

Application has been made on behalf of the Duke of Norfolk for exemption in the case of William Pratt (47) Grade 2, of Park Gate, Newdigate, employed as woodman on the Duke's Newdigate estate – it was stated that a war agricultural certificate had been applied for and the application was adjourned pending its production.

Walter W. Dudley (46) Grade 2, poultry farmer, Cudworth, Newdigate, in support of his claim for total exemption, said he had at present 500 birds. He went in for egg production and since last October he had produced 20,000. This season he expected to double his stock and the majority of the birds would be laying in the autumn and winter. All the cockerels were marketed as soon as fit. This season he expected to have on the market seven to eight hundred pounds worth of chicken meat – Two months exemption.

On the 12th September the school had received permission to take the children blackberrying as part of the National Preservation of Food Scheme.

Dorking Advertiser – September 14th, 1918

Wedding at Newdigate, Thursday September 5th

Staff-Sergeant George Nicholson, Captain of the Canadian Army Medical Corps., and Constance Miriam Long, of Redhill, third daughter of Professor James Long and sister of Mrs. Harry Winfield. The bride was given away by Mr. Harold Long B.Sc., as although her father was present he was not well enough to undertake that duty. The bridegroom came over from Vancouver in 1914 and was one of the first of the Canadian contingent who saw a good deal of active service. Whilst carrying in wounded he was captured and underwent some terrible experiences in Germany for eight and a half months. The bride and bridegroom honeymooned at Seaview on the Isle of Wight.

Professor James John Long was born in Holbeach, Lincolnshire in 1846 and became a successful farmer. He was managing director of the Cudworth Smallholdings Association and in 1910 requested a full timber valuation on the whole Cudworth Estate from Messrs. Crows. By 1924 he owned Cudworth Poultry Farm (now Oaklea) and 30 acres of land. He was co-author of a technical book entitled The Dairy of the Farm which was published in 1885. He had a large family. Constance was born in 1873 and her sister Muriel Estelle (Mrs. Winfield) was born in 1871. As a young girl she was an artist specializing in black and white pictures.

Dorking Advertiser – 28th September, 1918

Major E.P. Nicholls RFA, son of Colonel W. Nicholls VD, son-in-law of Captain and Mrs. R. Elliott Palmer of Oaklands Park, has been awarded the DSO for conspicuous gallantry and devotion to duty while commanding his battery during an enemy attack. Under most difficult circumstances he fought off the enemy all day and in the evening withdrew his battery with the loss of only one gun, which had been destroyed by gunfire. He showed great ability in command.

Dorking Advertiser – October 5th, 1918

Women on the Land

The best evidence possible that the Women's Land Army is proving enormously useful is offered by two facts – 1) that the demand for their labour at present greatly exceeds the supply and 2) that the farmers employing women are practically unconditional in their praises.

These last two months have brought so much personal tragedy to Newdigate. We heard of the deaths of Ben Burrows and George Howson and now we have received news of the death of Mr. John Innes.

Death of a Charlwood Man

Section Leader John Alfred Innes, of the Greenings, Charlwood who died at a field hospital in France after an operation for appendicitis on September 9th, aged 37 years, was the third son of the late James Innes of Roffey Park, Horsham, and 4 Audley Square, London W. After leaving Winchester he went through Messrs. Armstrong's works at Newcastle and subsequently became a partner in Messrs. P. Wigham Richardson & Co. In October 1914 he joined a Red Cross Motor Ambulance Convoy BEF, serving with it at the First and Second Battles of Ypres, was mentioned in Lord French's dispatches and held the 1914 Star. He was afterwards sent to join a convoy attached to the French Army and was present at the Battle of Verdun, and subsequent battles, being awarded the Croix de Guerre and two silver stars. He was recently gassed. His wife, Audrey received this letter at her home, The Greenings, from the British Red Cross Society Headquarters at Army Post Office 3 in France:

Sept. 11th 1918

Dear Mrs. Innes

I find it extremely difficult to know how to sufficiently express my heartfelt sympathy in the terrible loss you have sustained. It came as a complete shock to us: as we only knew he was ill and had not fully recovered from being gassed recently, and the news of his having appendicitis and of his death reached us simultaneously. Personally it is a staggering blow as we were such great friends and I had much the highest regard for him of all the personnel of our convoy working with the French Army. He was so absolutely devoted to the one object of succouring the wounded: time after time taking such personal risks in doing so under fire that the wonder is he was not killed long ago. In all his work he was so absolutely self-effacing and unassuming, so that you would never know from himself of his constant acts of almost unexampled bravery, which the others told me of but never himself. He has truly laid down his life on behalf of the great cause of liberty and I trust it may be some consolation to yourself and his family to feel that a nobler and braver spirit never breathed. If there is, as we trust a hereafter, he shall not be wanting in his reward, for of the talents that god gave him, he spared none in the most divine work that human hands can do on this earth, that of helping the wounded in their agony.

I could say more but it is better not, as already tears are dimming the paper and God Himself will grant you that solace which no human aid can render, however willing.

Yours in inexpressible sympathy,

Saxon Davies.

The headquarters of the British Red Cross Society in July 1914 was in Victoria Street in London and consisted of three rooms occupied by a secretary, two clerks and a boy. They did not own a single ambulance and could not provide a bed. They joined forces with the Order of St. John Ambulance and formed a Joint War Committee. John Innes served with the Motor Ambulance Unit No. 2.

Audrey Julia Innes (née Broadwood)

John Alfred Innes with his two girls

John Innes's original grave

Volunteer JOHN ALFRED INNES (Croix de Guerre)
British Red Cross Society

John Alfred Innes was born in Mayfair in 1881. He was the third son of James and Agnes Innes of Roffey Park in Sussex, who were great benefactors to this new suburb of Horsham. He was educated at a prep school in Southborough near Tonbridge, and then went on to Winchester College. He trained as a mechanical engineer with Armstrongs at Elswick and then became a partner at P.Wigham Richardson & Co, a company which amalgamated with Swan Hunter and built, amongst other ships, the Mauretania which was the largest ever vessel to be launched on the Tyne. In 1908 he married Audrey Julia Broadwood at a society wedding at Charlwood. The reception at Lyne House was attended by the aristocracy of the county and ended with a firework display with his initials J.A.I. brightly illuminated. Afterwards he and his wife went on a motoring honeymoon to Devon and Cornwall. They settled at The Greenings in Charlwood and had two daughters, Joan Helen (b.1909) and Margaret (b.1911) and a son, John N. Innes (b.1914). The Greenings is a large house and the family had a live-in staff of six servants.

In October 1914, John Innes took his car to France and joined a Red Cross Motor Ambulance Convoy serving with it at the first and second battles of Ypres.

He was mentioned in Lord French's despatches and held the 1914 Star. A year later Mr Innes became section leader in a convoy attached to the French army, and was present during the battle of Verdun and subsequent battles. He was awarded the Croix de Guerre and two silver stars.

In September 1918 he was taken to a field hospital suffering from appendicitis and, in spite of the best possible care, he died on the 9th September. He was afforded a full military funeral and Dr. Gauthier from the 77th Division gave the address and this is the translation from the French language:

Matters of urgency make it impossible for General Serrigny (*Chief of Staff 1914-1917 – He was very close to Pétain who said 'Serrigny is my imagination'*), Officer Commanding the 77th Division, to be here himself. He asks me to apologise to you for his inability to accompany to his last resting place Lieutenant Innes, second-in-command of the No. 16 British Medical Section, and he has deputed Captain De L'Horme, one of his Staff Officers, to represent him. The General asks me, in the name of the officers, NCOs and ranks of this division, to speak the soldier's farewell to a comrade at Lieutenant Innes' graveside.

Dear friends of the British Medical Section, during the first four years of the war the Great Reaper was kind to you. When your Commanding Officer, Lieutenant Hindle, first came to the 77th Infantry Division, he listed the battles in which you have taken part, told me of the risks you had run, and was thankful that not one of his men had been lost. Alas! During the last six weeks the hand of Death has struck several times. On the 24th July 1918, in the course of the Battle of the Marne, two of your comrades, Blatch and Clark, were taken from us, killed by the same shell. And they were believed to be amongst the safest in your Section, by virtue of the largely sedentary nature of their occupation.

John Alfred Innes

Today it is Lieutenant Innes who has gone from us, after a short and painful illness. For four years he withstood the fatigue of war without one day's sickness, and he was even fortunate enough to escape injury. He was in excellent health, his constitution was sound. One would have thought him capable of withstanding the onslaught of a dangerous and insidious illness, but one which is recognisable by its symptoms and amenable to treatment. Moreover, he was in the hands of a surgeon who is at the top of his profession, both in his degree of learning and in his ability. But despite all these factors in Lieutenant Innes' favour, it proved impossible to save him. A wealthy man, adored husband and father, he died on foreign soil in a hospital room, devotedly and assiduously tended, it is true, but far away from his own family. Only a short while ago he was making long term plans for the future; today he lies in his coffin. This should serve as a reminder to us all that we are not masters of the morrow, that we should not waste our lives in trivial occupations, but that we should use them to perfect ourselves, and that we should always do our duty.

May Lieutenant Innes remain an example to us all!

He was a man upon whom fortune had smiled. He had a wife to whom he was devoted, and who was devoted to him. He was the father of three young children who needed him, and this might have led him to avoid the risks of war. But his noble country, stirred by feelings of social justice, renounced her splendid isolation, and he himself sacrificed his contented life with his family. He was a modest man, quite without personal ambition, but he felt that he had to do his duty.

From the early stages of the war he worked without one day's respite in the transport sections of the medical corps. He followed the British Army through the first and second battles of Ypres and the battle of Neuve Chapelle, and was then transferred to a section attached to the French Army. In February and March 1916, during the German Army's onslaught on Verdun, he performed feats of ingenuity and endurance to spirit away our wounded from the enemy's fire.

In October 1916 he was present again at Verdun during the attack on the fort at Douamont. He was mentioned in the 33rd I.D. dispatches. In March 1917 he again displayed great courage during the Champagne attack on the slopes at Mont-Cornillet.

In June 1918, during the fierce fighting around Ferte-Milon, he overcame immense difficulties and saved as many of our wounded as possible from capture by the Germans. On this occasion he and his whole section were mentioned in the 26th I.D. dispatches.

In July 1918 he took part in the Battle of the Marne where, under constant heavy shelling and on broken roads, his section evacuated 2,400 wounded and was mentioned in the 77th I.D. dispatches in such terms that the General asked for this section to be permanently attached to it.

In all his actions, Innes displayed a total disregard for danger, but he did not have the satisfaction of dying on the field of battle.

Nonetheless he died bravely and piously, like a good soldier, and he was a credit to his country, immortal England.

The French Army, which adopted him and loved him like a brother, mourns his death and will remain forever indebted to him. We feel for his family in their grief, and I shall be sending them the heartfelt condolences of us all.

Lieutenant Innes, I scatter on your mortal remains a handful of the French soil you helped to defend.

Au revoir!'

As Dr. Gautier said, John Alfred Innes was a wealthy man. He left over £50,000 in his will. He is remembered at the Terlincthun British Cemetery at Wimille as well as the war memorial at Charlwood.

Rifleman GEORGE CHARLES HOWSON, R/17362
16th Battalion, King's Royal Rifle Corps

George Howson was born in Shepperton, Middlesex in 1897. He lived with his parents, Charles and Dorcas, and younger brother Alfred Joseph. Charles was a railway plate-layer and then became a farm labourer at Shepperton before moving to New House Farm Cottages in Newdigate. George was working as a cowman at Crossways, Upper Gatton when he travelled to Guildford to enlist on the 30th November 1915. The medical officer noted that he was of slight build, being only 5'4½" tall and weighing 108 lbs, and that he had a curvature of the spine that would improve with drilling.

British soldiers resting on a felled tree in a road near Le Cateau on the 25th October 1918 (Ref. Q3317)
Reproduced by kind permission of the Imperial War Museum

His regiment embarked from Folkestone on the 14th April 1916 and assembled at Etaples before moving to the Front. Life was very tough for the infantry throughout this period. They were in constant action and conditions in the trenches were uncomfortable in the extreme. On the 27th October, George Howson was wounded in the back and shoulder and nearly a year later on the 20th September 1917 he was buried by a shell but returned to duty five days later. The wet conditions in the trenches affected him badly and he suffered from sore throats and bronchitis and was hospitalised in Boulogne. On the 11th October the 16th Battalion was amongst the Brigades holding the line of the River Selle, whilst the enemy's front line was the Le Cateau-Solesmes railway, which was strongly wired and about five hundred yards from the river. There was high ground about 1,500 yards east of the railway and the Brigade was ordered to make an attack across the river to gain the high ground. Next day at 05.00 hours the Battalion attacked with 'the greatest of dash' against very heavy machine gun fire, and it was here that Rifleman Howson was hit. This time, this brave man succumbed to his wounds and died. He had just passed his 21st birthday.

His name is recorded on the Vis-en-Artois Memorial as his body was never recovered or identified.

Lance Corporal BENJAMIN BURROWS MM, 43461
1st Battalion, Middlesex Regiment

Benjamin Burrows was born in Newdigate in 1884, the eldest child of Henry and Elizabeth Burrows. The Burrows family had always worked on the land or the roads and lived in meagre accommodation with their large families. Benjamin's grandfather, also called Benjamin, had at least eleven children so life was a constant struggle. In order to find work, Henry and his growing family moved around the area. By 1901 the family was unable to pay its way and a pregnant Elizabeth and her five youngest children had been transported away from Newdigate to the Dorking Union Workhouse.

The three eldest children had managed to get work and lodgings; Benjamin and Mary were working at a coal merchants' at Holmwood and Henry Jnr. was working on the farm at Sturtwood. The family was re-united when Henry Snr. found work as a farm labourer in Leigh. He moved to Herons Head Green with his wife and nine children, three further children having been born since 1901.

Benjamin Burrows enlisted with the 1st Battalion Middlesex Regiment which was popularly known as the Die Hards with whom he gained the Military Medal. They were involved in the final advance in Picardy which was where he met his

Oak Tree Cottages in Broad Lane, the home of the Burrows family

death on the 23rd October 1918. By this time the family was living at 1 Oak Tree Cottage in Broad Lane, Newdigate.

In the attack the 98th Brigade of the 1st Middlesex were to lead the assault by capturing the village of Forest, enveloping it on both sides. 'C' Company was to be on the right, 'A' on the left, 'B' Company to 'mop up' Forest, and 'D' in support. The 4th King's were then to pass through the Middlesex and capture the second and third objectives; this was the second phase. In the 3rd phase the 2nd Argyll and Sutherland Highlanders were to advance through the 4th King's and capture the fourth objective, the 1st Middlesex meanwhile moving up to support the Highlanders. The 100th Brigade was then to advance through the 98th and capture the final objective near Englefontaine.

Zero hour for the attack of the Middlesex had been fixed for 2.00 a.m.

The advance began punctually on time, but nothing was heard until 2.45 a.m. when a message was received by Battalion Headquarters from Captain Fate, commanding 'B' Company. This said 'On outskirts of Forest. Everything going splendidly. Enemy retiring. Very few casualties.' An hour later 'A' Company was in Forest, having suffered rather heavy casualties; the remaining companies had already passed the village and had captured their objectives in time. 'B' Company estimated that 200 prisoners had been captured in Forest.

Benjamin Burrows died in the attack and was buried close to where he fell at the Englefontaine British Cemetery.

Dorking Advertiser

For our Blind Heroes

A successful concert was held at the School House, Newdigate, on Saturday evening in aid of St. Dunstan's Hostel for Blinded Soldiers and Sailors. So good a cause would disarm judgment, but the local talent has nothing to fear. The arrangements were capably engineered by Mr. George Butcher and Mr. Harold Barrows (church organist) as a crowded audience testified. Mr. Barrows gave a brilliant rendering of two piano solos, and also acted as accompanist, and Mr. Butcher was loudly applauded when he sang 'Paper Bag Cookery', a subject dear to feminine hearts, and later 'Billy Johnson's Ball.' Mr. E. Richards, a real humorist of the Corney Grain type, was an entertainment in himself, providing songs, anecdotes, and monologue. Among many first-class numbers, mention must be made of Mr. E. Forster, a youthful cornet soloist of much promise. Messrs. Carpenter and Winfield sang popular melodies, and Mesdames Hopkins and Austin gave a spirited duologue. Among the audience, the Rector, the Rev. H.G. Bird, bore testimony to the clerical sense of humour, and thoroughly enjoyed the fun. The concert realised a sum of £20 on which result Newdigate is to be warmly congratulated. The programmes were sold by Mrs. George Shearman, so long associated with Sir Arthur Pearson's City of London Fund for the Children of Blinded Soldiers.

Peace was in the air and the editor of the Dorking Advertiser was writing about the 'fluttering of the wings of the peace-angel'.

We are nearing the old Advent season, which the carnage and barbarities of the war have seemed to put among those old myths that are so beautiful we wish they had been true. But for four long years the only advent to startle us in our dreams has been the whirr of death-dealing Zepps or Gothas. Can it be possible that now we may hear the fluttering of the wings of the peace-angel, and that this Advent season will prove of a surety that the spirit of the Child is mightier than big battalions, and that ideas are stronger than strategists.

Lieut. David Green, 1/5th Suffolks, son of Mr. F.E. Green, Baringsfield, Newdigate has been awarded the Military Cross.

Dorking Advertiser

Memorial Service

A memorial service was recently held at St. Peter's Church, Newdigate, in memory of Ernest Weller, who was killed in action on November 4th. The organist, Mr. H. Barrows, played 'O Rest in the Lord' and the usual service for the fallen was followed; the hymns 165 and 537 and Psalm xxiii. were sung. The Rector in a few well chosen words, spoke of the sacrifice of these lads who had given their lives with the hope of reunion. The 'Dead March' in 'Saul' was played at the close of the service. Mrs. Gadd, Church Cottages, has lost two sons in the war – Ernest and Percy Weller.

Private ERNEST WELLER, G/11989
2nd Battalion, Royal Sussex Regiment

Ernest Weller was born in Holmwood in 1876 but when he was very young his parents Mark and Mary Ann moved to Workhouse Green in Newdigate. Mark was a drayman but died in 1891 aged 37 and two years later his wife married Mark Gadd and they moved to Hatchetts Farm where he worked until his death in 1906 at the age of 57. Ernest worked as a post boy but then became a groom and before the war he took a position as groom at Stanhill in Charlwood. He never married. On the 4th November 1918, the Germans were in retreat and Ernest's regiment, the 2nd Battalion, Royal Sussex, were participating in the Battle of the Sambre-Oise Canal. They had to cross an area of fields bordered with high hedges and then cross the canal near the lock house. The position was heavily defended and it was here that Lieutenant Colonel Dudley G. Johnson led the assault which resulted in him being awarded the Victoria Cross for great valour, coolness and intrepidity. No such honours for Ernest Weller as he fell that day, just a week before the armistice. In the National Probate Calendar under the Index of Administrations he left effects totalling £140 to his mother. He is buried at Le Rejet-de-Beaulieu Communal Cemetery. One week later the bells rang across the country celebrating the end of the war. No such rejoicing for Mrs Gadd and there was grief at another home in Shrewsbury. On the day that Ernest Weller died, and at the same spot, another brave soldier was killed – the famous war poet, Lieut. Wilfred Owen MC.

On November 11th at 11.00 a.m. the Armistice silenced the great guns and the war had come to an end. Three quarters of a million British soldiers had given their lives. Thirty-two came from Newdigate.

The editor of the Dorking Advertiser wrote about the Spirit of the Future.
How long we have lived in these four years. So long in their intensity that it is only when we are able for a moment to put away the present and recall the old questions that stirred us in peace times, the old pleasures and hopes and grumblings, that we realise how altered everything is. This war has absorbed our energies and centred our thoughts. Even to talk of anything else has bored us. We have breathed it as an atmosphere, worked for it as a life purpose, sacrificed for it as a religion, and if called to give our best love have felt as if we were giving them to God. It has been unlike all other wars in the world's history ....

At school the time-table was not followed in the afternoon as news had been received that the armistice was signed. Special war lessons were given, the flag was saluted, and patriotic songs were sung.

At Newhouse Farm worked continued as normal –
'*November 11th 1918 – Burrows and Tugwell ploughed in the field opposite all day*
   Sadler and both boys getting home swedes and getting oats home, collecting pokes up and fetching home ready to take to Rusper.
   J. Leadbeater threshing at Mr Voice's all day

Peace was declared.

11 am – November 11th, 1918
by Bertha M. Broadwood

Whom have we British fought? The Devil incarnate.
First tempter, then forceful driver of a slave, -
A would-be tyrant over kingdoms, Church and state, -
A maniac; manacled 'gainst mercy's sign to save!
How have we fought? – Beside our foes of but ten decades past,
Starting mere thousands! Despised of many-millioned enemy
Who dreamt of crushing Britain's power, then France at last-
After some forty years of 'peaceful' pushing treachery-
With all his devil-master's will to spoil and damn,
Through abuse of Heaven – born laws of science and of art,
Regardless of honour's faith towards God, or man,
Fiendishly confident to cowe, or kill man, body, soul, and heart.

But God our hope, wearied by braggart's blasphemies.
Has justified His word, as each free nation now rejoicing sees.

The Aftermath

So the war finally came to an end. There are no records to describe what happened in Newdigate to celebrate the ending of hostilities, or indeed if there were any celebrations at all. Did the Rector's Drum and Fife Band play to welcome the conquering heroes home? Did the bells ring out a rejoicing peel across the parish? Probably not. Certainly there was no grand parade for all the returning boys from the Queen's. They came back to their country homes in dribs and drabs, some never to talk about their experiences again. Some came back bearing their wounds and scars and tried to make a fresh start. The wives and mothers tried desperately to understand what their menfolk had gone through – they had changed, they were different. Just about every home in the village had been affected by the war. The people who would have been running the estates at Newdigate Place, the Red House and High Trees were all dead, and pictures of young men in army uniform hung on the walls, of many country homes and cottages.

In 1917, Herbert Asquith had turned his attention to peace. Mindful of the treaty that ended the Franco-Prussian War and how resentment simmered over the decades, he was cautioning that peace should come with honour and that it would be unwise to seek massive reparations. At the Treaty of Versailles, however, revenge was in the air and a few years later whilst working for the League of Nations, Vera Brittain (author, pacifist and former VAD nurse) predicted, upon seeing the plight of the German population, that the seeds for another European conflict had been sown. France and England's lust for oil negated T.E. Lawrence's promises to the leaders of the Arab Revolt and he left the conference in disgust and sought anonymity in the guise of Aircraftsman T.E. Shaw, living at Clouds Hill in remote Dorset. The seeds of resentment had indeed been sown. In 1939 the villagers of Newdigate found themselves embroiled in another war ... and in due course another panel had to be inscribed on the war memorial.

Private GEORGE HENRY ACKLAND, 32610
14th Battalion Royal Warwickshire Regiment

Pte. George Henry Ackland

George Henry Ackland was the youngest of the five children of Thomas and Mary Ackland, the others being Walter (b.1869), Mary J. (b.1870), Amelia Anne (b.1875) and Frances Sarah (b.1879). The family worked on the land in the Blackdown Hills on the Somerset and Devon borders. Thomas worked as an agricultural labourer in Hemyock. He later managed a brickworks in the same area but in 1889, the year of George's birth, Thomas made the bold decision to move with his family to Brooklag Farm at Newdigate. Here

Thomas and Mary, both in their early forties, set up a laundry with help from two of their daughters, Mary and Amelia. The three girls married, and Thomas and Mary continued laundering at Brooklag Farm.

The 1911 census shows that George was serving with the 2nd Dragoon Guards, Queen's Bays but on the 18th May 1912 George emigrated to Australia on board the SS Armadale and was described as a farmhand. He joined his sister Mary-Jane and her eight children. Her husband, Harry Bailey, had prepared a home in Australia the previous year. George married Mary-Jane Morley, a nurse from Fremantle. In 1915 their son George Henry was born. George senior came back to serve his country and originally joined the Royal Sussex Regiment (2016) before transferring to the much depleted 14th Battalion Royal Warwickshire Regiment. On the 31st July 1915 he sent a telegram from Aldershot to Steve and Lil Ackland apologising for the fact that he could not attend their wedding – he embarked for France on the 4th August.

Pte. George Henry Ackland

At noon on the 12th April 1918 orders were received for the 14th battalion to advance upon and capture Merville. The battalion had only recently been reinforced by new recruits fresh from England. The advance was made through Tannay-Le Foret and eastwards towards Merville but when they arrived at Le Corbie, orders were received for them to dig in on a line south east of the forest. Whilst waiting the colonel was wounded by shrapnel, and the next day the battalion suffered heavy casualties as a result of a German attack. About this time Private Ackland was seriously gassed and was sent home. He died in his old bedroom at Brooklag Farm on the 8th February 1919 from acute capillary bronchitis as a result of gassing. Frances' husband, William Spiller, was present when he died and Dr. Wakefield certified the death. He was 29 years old and is buried in Newdigate churchyard. In 1920 his wife and young son came back to England, presumably to introduce George junior to his English relatives, returning to Australia in 1923. She married twice more and died in Australia in 1968. Almost certainly George never saw his son.

It has proved to be very difficult to establish what happened to the returning Newdigate men. 60% of all the service records were destroyed in an air raid in September 1940 and many of these so called 'burnt records' are badly damaged. The Dorking Advertiser concentrated on the future and the Parish Magazine had been discontinued several months before the Armistice. Thus the information is sparse, but the following information has been gleaned from various sources.

The Rector's other son, who had been in an institution, died in 1919. The Revd. Bird left Newdigate in 1921 and retired to Wotton-under-Edge where he died in 1925. His funeral took place at his spiritual home in Hillingdon and the Misses Goldberg represented Newdigate at his funeral.

For some, homecoming was painful. George Ackland had left his family in Australia, but after being gassed he went to his parent's home at Brooklag Farm where he suffered sorely, finally succumbing in February 1919. His family said that he died from Spanish influenza.

Capt. Evelyn Henry Tschudi Broadwood (1889-1975) was born into the famous Broadwood family who for generations had manufactured pianos. Old account books show that they had made pianos for such composers as Beethoven, Chopin and Listz. Captain Broadwood grew up at Lyne House which is on the border of Newdigate parish. His parents were James Henry Tschudi and Margaret Broadwood (née Fuller-Maitland). He was already in the army at the outbreak of the war and remained after being wounded, winning the MC and being mentioned twice in despatches. For some time he was at Cambridge, returning to the company as a director in 1918. In 1931 he became chairman. He never married and his war wound troubled him in later life. Much involved in local matters, he was a councillor for the Dorking District Council and Surrey County Council. He had a life-long interest in history and preservation and was a member of the Surrey Archeological Society and the Society for the Protection of Ancient Buildings. In 1957 he became High Sheriff of Surrey. One of his last duties in Newdigate should have been to open a photographic exhibition to commemorate the 800th anniversary of St Peter's Church in 1975, but he died just prior to the event. By this time Lyne House was in a poor state but it has now been totally refurbished and divided up into apartments.

Captain Broadwood's sister, Joan Bray (1886-1972) never remarried and a memorial to her and her husband, Gerard T. Bray, can be seen in Rusper church. Her sister, Audrey (1886-1972) married Charles Hodsoll at St. George's, Hanover Square and moved to Pleystowe in nearby Capel. In September 1936 she and her husband sailed on the brand new Queen Mary just a couple of months after her maiden voyage.

Leopold Goldberg, the father of Herbert and Frederick was left a shattered man after the war. He rarely returned to Newdigate. On one occasion, in May 1923, the Rector let his house to Mr. Goldberg who at the time was described as 'an old friend and benefactor of the Parish'. He died a year later in Chelsea at the age of 83 and is buried in Newdigate Churchyard. The Times described him as 'a man of great intellectual refinement, he was many sided in his tastes and sympathies, retaining to the last his acute brain and clarity of judgment. He was a lifelong student and lover of Shakespeare. By his death another link with the Victorian past is broken, and his loss will be deplored by a large circle of friends who have lost a wise counsellor and a staunch friend.' His son-in-law, Francis Shorland Ball, never fully recovered his health after the war and died from throat cancer in 1952 at his home, 'Littlewood' in Lelant, Cornwall. His wife Ada died in 1968 aged 90. The two Misses Goldberg also moved to Lelant. Maud died in 1945 aged 74 and Lizzie in 1964 aged 91. Lizzie occasionally came back to the village to tend the family grave. The Red House Estate was sold and broken up, and the house itself was demolished after the Second World War as it had been used by Canadian troops and left in a poor state. A new Red House was built on the site using some of the material from the original house.

Once peacetime had come, Mrs. Janson hurled herself into parish affairs. She became one of the main instigators pressing for a war memorial to commemorate the young men who did not return from the war. A meeting was held on the 11th March 1920 to discuss the erection of a memorial:

The War Memorial shortly after erection

It was proposed by Mrs. Janson, seconded by Col. Nicholls and carried unanimously, 'that a faculty be procured for the erection of a war memorial cross in the churchyard of St Peter's, Newdigate, and that the cross be as per design already sent to advisory committee of the diocese of Winchester and be made of Portland stone by Messrs. Gilliam & Sons, Dorking at an estimated cost of £180 of which the sum of £160 has already been collected and the remainder guaranteed. The inscription round the edge of the cornice of the octagon base to be 'To the Glory of God and in grateful memory of our gallant Newdigate men who fell in the Great War, 1914-1919'. In Church text, letters 1½ inches, the 33 names to be alphabetically arranged and engraved on the three frontal panels of the base and capital letters 1 inch, other letters ¾ inch. A Fleur-de-Lys (the Newdigate crest) to be carved round the capital of the column which supports the cross and wreath of laurel leaves to be carved and placed over the centre of the cross where the arms meet.'

The work was duly carried out and 32 (not 33) names, with their ranks, were carved on the three frontals. The memorial was dedicated by the Lord Bishop of Guildford at three o'clock in the afternoon of Monday, 25th October 1920. After the Second World War the carved names were covered by engraved plates which list the men without ranks, and an additional plate bearing the names of the ten fallen men of the second war was added. The dates 1939-1945 were added on the last remaining empty section of the octagon.

It is not known how or by what criteria the names were selected.

In the vestry of the church there is a small wooden memorial carved to commemorate those who had died from the wood carving class. It was carved by William Broughton and included two spelling mistakes. It reads as follows:

Newdigate Carving Class
In Praise and Honour
of
Norman Andrews
William Beadle
John Burberry
Roy Goldsack
Aubery Hudson
Wesley John
Arthur Monk
Walter Skinner
Percy Weller
Alfred Wooltorton
In Memoriam

Two names, those of Norman Andrews and Walter Skinner, do not appear on the Newdigate war memorial.

Norman Frank Andrews was born on the Isle of Wight in 1898 and, shortly after his birth, his parents moved to Surrey where his father, Frank, was a farm bailiff at Russ Hill Farm, living with his wife Annie at Russ Hill Cottages, situated between Charlwood and Newdigate. Norman is named as one of the carvers who worked on the altar in the Cudworth Chapel. He was a gunner with 'D' Battery, 52nd Brigade of the Royal Field Artillery and he was killed in France on the 5th September 1918 during the great allied push, in what is now known as the Second Battle of Arras.

His friend, Lance Corporal Walter Skinner, was also born in 1898. It was hardly surprising that he should have attended the carving class as both his father and grandfather were carpenters in Charlwood. He grew up at Mores Cottage in Charlwood

Wood Carving Class

with his five brothers and sisters. He and Norman Andrews would probably have walked to the class together through the fields and lanes. He was killed in France on the 14th April 1918 whilst serving with 'A' Company, 1st Battalion of The Queen's (Royal West Surrey Regiment). The German assault was at its height and positions that had taken years to achieve were lost in fierce fighting in just a few days. He was just nineteen years of age and died when events were looking very grim for the allies. Both men's names appear on the Charlwood war memorial.

It is still possible to identify the handicraft of some of the men, as the carvers of the motifs on the pew ends in the church are recorded. Percy Weller carved the fish of St Peter, the dove of the Holy Ghost and a lily of Mary, Arthur Monk did a fleur-de-lys and the anchor and shield of St. Nicholas. Raymond Potter, who was seriously wounded at Gallipoli, carved the Christ monogram.

The carving class continued until 1928 under the tuition of Mrs Janson and Joe Sanders.

As already related, Mrs.Janson was formerly Mrs. Herron. The family firm, G.O.M. Herron & Sons, wool merchants, was run for a short while by George Frederick Herron (1864-1941), who survived the war. He was followed by Kenneth Vernon Chester Herron (1908-2003), the son of Lt. Kenneth Chester Herron, who, foreseeing the decline of the business due to cheap imports, sold it and bought a fruit farm in Spain. His last few years were spent in sheltered accommodation at Stamford-le-Vale in Oxfordshire. Nearly all the family archives have been lost. Mrs. Janson died in 1941 and her daughter, Lilian, the following year. Like the Red House, Newdigate Place had been taken over by the Canadian army and the house was left in a desolate state. It was sold in 1954 and demolished shortly afterwards. After the war Mrs. Janson erected a stained glass window

The Herron Window

in the south aisle in memory of her two sons, Kenneth and Walter. A window depicting Christ in the carpenter's shop can be seen in the north aisle which commemorates Mrs. Janson and was installed after her death.

Miss Ferard and Miss Wilson, who hosted the fête in July 1914, left Ockley Lodge in July 1926 and gave up farming. They sold everything privately including 'two cows, fowls, a chaff cutter, pig troughs, churn butter worker, separator, beehives, honey extractor, a quantity of broken bricks, also some carpets, beds, chairs, tables and pictures.'

Alfred Dean continued running the village shop until his death in 1925 when his son Billy took over. The shop continued as a village store under different ownerships right up until the twenty-first century.

Newdigate used to have a number of small, single-storey houses, which many thought were built immediately after the war as 'homes fit for heroes'. Although under the Housing Act of 1919, local councils were required to produce schemes to provide council housing, in reality the first were not actually built in Newdigate until 1927 and these were built privately. William Hopkins, who had his leg amputated

Amputee, William Hopkins riding a bicycle

as a result of injuries, moved into one of these houses, called Ourcot, which was on the site of what is now Casa Mia. He found work, learned to ride a bike and raised his family there. It is estimated that over one and a half million servicemen were wounded. It was not an uncommon sight therefore to see limbless people, as over forty thousand suffered injuries resulting in amputation.

William Hopkins and his son Harold outside Ourcot. The bungalow Casa Mia now stands on this spot.

We will never know how many Newdigate people suffered from shell shock, a term first published in the Lancet in 1915. Often, they were thought of as malingerers or 'sissies' and in the early days of the war the serious cases were considered insane and put into lunatic asylums. As medical knowledge increased, and it was understood that the patients had suffered dire mental traumas, so attitudes changed. It was considered essential that wounded men should find work as it would uphold their manliness and to this end the King's National Roll Scheme was instigated. This was a voluntary scheme which stated that every company with over ten employees should take on at least five percent of their workforce from disabled ex-servicemen, this proved quite successful as over 89,000 found employment but it was nowhere enough and it became a common sight to see ex-servicemen begging or eking out a meagre existence selling matches on the street.

Gradually the lads started returning to the village.

James Frederick Elliott (1889-1972) had gone to Newdigate church to say goodbye to everyone before leaving for France. He survived the war and in 1919 he walked into that same church, hand in hand with his bride Emily Lloyd. They subsequently had four children and lived at Fairyland (later called Dean Cottage).

Private Ernest Trow, G6933 (1886-1965) joined the Royal West Surrey Regiment in November 1915 and was seriously injured whilst serving with the 3rd Battalion. He was discharged permanently from the army on the 22nd August 1917 and lived with his family at Rose Villa.

Cpl. Sydney Rupert Bourne, L/8402 1st Battalion Royal West Surrey Regiment, was born at Epsom in 1896 and enlisted 12th August 1914. He was severely wounded at the Dardenelles, but survived the war and married Laura M. Birch at Dorking in 1922.

Pte. John Henry Grainger was a Yorkshireman who worked as a carter and lived at Ivy House in Partridge Lane. He enlisted on the 29th November 1915 to the 3rd Suffolk Regiment and during bayonet training he jumped into a trench, sprained his ankle, and had to be hospitalised for over three weeks. He was transferred to the 3rd Battalion of the South Staffordshire Regiment and was reported missing in August 1918 during the final push for victory. He became a prisoner of war and was not repatriated until the 13th December when, upon his return to England, he was immediately admitted to King's Cross Hospital for a few days. So he did not get to see his wife Ellen, whom he had married in Dorking in 1916, until Christmas time, 1918. He was a member of the Ancient Order of Druids.

Bertie Hills, 68660, (1886-1935) served as a gunner with the 481 Siege Battery of the Royal Garrison Artillery. He was a tall man, over six feet (which was unusual in those days), and was a groom at High Trees. He was seriously wounded on the 19th August 1917 when he received gunshot wounds to the face, arm, left hand, left wrist, right leg and abdomen, and was admitted to 3 Sty. Hospital in Rouen. Three days later he returned to England on board the 'Duchess of Connaught' and was taken to the Military Hospital in Taplow, Buckinghamshire. He eventually returned to his wife, Harriet, whom he had married in May 1916, and then made attempts to obtain a pension. He received a letter from the Ministry of Pensions, Burton Court, King's Road, London SW3 dated the 15th October 1919:

'I am directed by the Ministry of Pensions to inform you of the under-mentioned decision in the case of a man whose discharge documents have been recently received with the view to having the claim to pensions considered ...REJECTED.'

This man had lost his brother Cecil, was suffering sorely from wounds received during the war, but, less than one year after the armistice, was described simply as 'a man whose discharge documents have been received' and his claim for a modest pension simply 'rejected'.

Pioneer Samuel J. Savidge, 259464, joined the Royal Field Artillery as a gunner in 1916. Before joining up he was a hairdresser and a keen motorcyclist, living on the Coldharbour Lane in Brixton. He later became a despatch rider for 'L' Signal Battalion in the Royal Engineers and was transferred to the reserves on demobilization on the 27th February 1920. He decided to start a completely new life and, together with his mother, he moved to Newdigate and lived in a converted Woolwich Arsenal hut in Hogspudding Lane, on the site of what is now a modern bungalow called Lansdown, where he started a poultry farm. He lived there until his death in 1986 at the age of 93. He always 'held a

Pioneer Samuel J Savidge on the right

Certificate of Transfer to Reserve on Demobilization for Samuel Savidge

candle' for Maudie Hopkins who later lived at Homelea but – as he had to look after his mother and she her brother, Edgar – they just remained friends. In death, though, they are together as they are buried in adjacent graves in Newdigate churchyard.

Kathleen Tyler, the widow of Major Alfred H. Tyler RE, moved with her children from Salisbury to 'St. Martins', Cuthbert Road, Westgate-on-Sea, Kent. In 1920 she applied for the clasp for her husband's 1914 Star. She also presented a brass cross and candlesticks to her local church, inscribed to the memory of her husband, which are still used every week to celebrate Holy Communion.

The two little daughters of Leonard H. Bedding (1880-1955), who charmed the villagers during the war with their singing, both lived long lives. Doris Gertrude (1904-1991) married William L. Roodcock in 1929 and Marjorie Maud (1809-2005) married Alfred H. Burdett in 1934.

Capt. Bertram William Lothian ('Nick') Nicholson had a distinguished naval career and retired in 1922. In 1925 he went to Kenya and became the successful headmaster of the Prince of Wales School in Nairobi where he loved to use naval vocabulary and customs. He returned to active service during the Second World War and retired to Tiphams in Ockley where he died in 1958. His wife Evelyn, whom he married in 1915, died six years later and they are both buried at Okewood Hill.

Lieut. Colonel Herbert French bought Cudworth Manor on the 19th July 1919. He served with the Royal Army Medical Corps during the war and practised as a consulting physician. Opposite the manor is a large, six bay barn, traditionally known as the King

The King John Barn

John Barn. Colonel French fitted it out and started manufacturing chutney, sauces and cider in order to create work for ex-servicemen. He built up a good trade and sold his products through leading London stores.

Before the war, Harry Davey (1883-1969) came down from Essex and was a carter at New House Farm where he lived with his wife and three children. On January 11th 1917 he helped to cart a load of hay from the lower barn at Woodlands until dinner time and then the farmer took him to the Dorking Tribunal where it was deemed that he was no longer exempt, no doubt much to the chagrin of the farmer who wrote 'Davey was summoned to Guildford to join the colours.' He served with the 25th Battalion Tank Corps and was allocated number 112546. He was hospitalised towards the end of the war but the armistice did not signal joy for him as he had just received news that his middle son, Percy Reginald, had died of influenza and pneumonia on the 1st November 1918 aged just nine. His first day back on the farm was the 5th February 1919 when the farmer recorded 'Davey started work harness cleaning all day'. The next day he, together with Burrows and Tugwell, 'fetched home oat straw from Woodlands and stacked it in the grain pits and shed'. The last mention of his name in the farm records was the 10th February 1919. In that same month he wrote to his Lieutenant-Colonel I/C of the Tank Corps asking whether he was entitled to the British War and Victory Medals as he had been out fighting in France. The curt reply came back – 'In reply to your letter of recent date, re medals. If, as you state, you served in France during the recent war then you are entitled to the British War Medal and Victory Medal. These decorations, however, will not be ready for issue for some considerable time.' He did receive his medals in due course.

Luke Gadd (1892-1962)

Alfred James Gadd and Luke Gadd

The School Class of 1919

Harry Davey was not the only soldier anxious to obtain his medals. Pte. James Weller, F27782, served with the Army Service Corps and he enlisted the help of Mr. F.C. Stace of Dulce Domum, Broad Lane, who was the Secretary of the local branch of the British Legion, to try to obtain his medals.

Pte. Luke Gadd (1893-1962), TS 8639, of Lucy's Cottage, Newdigate joined the Army Service Corps as a saddler in July 1915 at the age of 22. He did not return until late in 1919 but was probably the first Newdigate boot repairer to be able to tell his family that he had visited such exotic places as Damascus and Port Said.

Similarly, Pte. Arthur Crowder (1883-1963) who was the local butcher, served in Mesopotania and in 1918 found his regiment, the 545th Co. ASC in Bombay. He finally returned in August 1919 and went to live in Croydon with his wife.

John Albert Steeds was headmaster of the school and enlisted in the Royal West Kent Regiment on the 15th May 1918. After discharge he returned to the school on the 25th February 1919 but by the July he had left the area and taken a new position at Ash. He died in 1939.

Spanish influenza, which caused more deaths throughout Europe than the war, did not appear to have had the same devastating effect upon the people of Newdigate. There were only seven burials in St Peter's in 1919 and, apart from George Ackland, whose death was exacerbated by gassing, they were all elderly people. On the 4th November 1918 only nine children were present at school owing to unspecified illnesses and sickness, and the school was closed until Armistice Day. Young Percy Davey, who died on the 1st November 1918, was probably the only Newdigate child to die from the Spanish flu.

Life in school continued just as before, apart from a brief interlude of excitement when an aircraft descended in a field near the school on the 3rd December 1918 and some of the classes were granted leave to go and inspect it.

Gavrilo Princip, the Bosnian patriot who precipitated the original crisis which led to the war, died saying that he believed it would have started anyway even if he had not committed the fateful assassination. He had been imprisoned in Terezin with five guards, one with a fixed bayonet, constantly in attendance. By 1916 he was suffering severely from tuberculosis which had destroyed his elbow joint. His arm was amputated and his entire upper torso covered with bandages. He died on the 28th April 1918 just three months short of his twenty-fourth birthday.

Field Marshal Sir Douglas Haig KT., GCB., OM., GCVO., KCIE., ADC. (1861-1928) returned from the war a hero. It was he who issued the 'backs against the wall' statement during the German offensive of 1918 and it was he who orchestrated the final push to victory. He was involved in the formation of the Royal British Legion and was instrumental in the setting up of the Haig Fund, known today as the poppy appeal. His tour of his native Scotland was a tremendous success, he was feted wherever he went and was made Freeman of a number of cities. When he died in 1928 there was a great outpouring of sadness, and his body was carried to Westminster Abbey on the same gun carriage that had carried the Unknown Warrior and indeed carried the gun that fired the first shot of the war. He was buried at Dryburgh Abbey, his grave marked by a standard

Commonwealth War Graves Commission white headstone. But history has not been kind to him and David Lloyd George was particularly scathing in his biography using the term 'lions led by donkeys'. The film 'Oh What a Lovely War' reflected the general feeling as time passed by. However, revisionist historians are once again painting a different side to this much-maligned leader.

Menin Gate

	LESLIE J.	PRATT P. K.
	LEWIS H.F.	RICH J.A.
...ON T.F.	LEWIS T.	ROBINSON A.G.
A.	LEWIS W.	ROBINSON C.
	LINDOW A.	ROBINSON W. P.
SAPPER	LOADER H.J.	SHIPLEY H.
ALLAN W. E.	LYON G.T.	SIBLEY R.
BABBAGE W. H.P.	McCABE J.	SPRING H.S.
BARBER E.	McCLENNON W.	SWAINSON J.
BARE C.L.	MACDONALD A.	WILLIAMS G..M.M.
BARKER W. E.	McDONALD J..	WINCHESTER J.H.
BARNDEN S.E.	McGIBBON R.	WOOD A.P.
	McINTOSH W.R.	

GRENADIER GUARDS

MAJOR	SECOND LIEUT.	SERJEANT
COLBY L.R.V.	WALTER S.	EDEN E.C.
		HURLEY H.L.
CAPTAIN	COY. SJT MAJOR	MARSHALL I.
RENNIE G.	GARRARD E.J.	PARKER F. C..M.M.
	LITTLETON S.	SANDAY S.
LIEUTENANT		THOMAS W. J.
ANTROBUS E.	COY. QMR. SERJT.	WALTERS A.
COTTLE W. E. W.	RICHARDSON G.L.	WILLIAMS H..M. M.
DOUGLAS-PENNANT	THOMPSON E.J.	
HON. A. G. S.		LANCE SERJEANT
BLACKWOOD	SERJEANT	BINGHAM J.W.
LORD BASIL	AKERS G.F.	DAVIES H.R.
MILLER F. W. J. MacD.	BREWER A.	HEARN R.C.
WEBSTER C. V. G.A.	DIGBY J.H..	MARSHALL F. J.
		WHITEHOUSE T. A.

Detail from the Menin Gate showing the inscription to Lieut. W.E.W. Cottle

Thiepval

Sylvia McPhee laying a wreath on the grave of her great uncle, Ernest Weller, 2010

Sir Fabian Ware was commanding a British Red Cross Unit in France and, as the death toll kept on rising, he noted that there was no organisation to record the final resting places of the casualties. So his unit started registering all the graves they found, and this eventually led to the setting up of the Commonwealth War Graves Commission. There was much soul-searching as to the design of the memorials. Once a decision had been made banning the repatriation of bodies, three of the most eminent architects of the time, Sir Edwin Lutyens, Sir Herbert Baker and Sir Reginald Blomfield, were commissioned to design memorials and cemeteries. A secular design was chosen for the headstones which reflected the equality of man, and great communal memorials were erected for those whose bodies could not be traced. The largest is at Thiepval which carries the names of over 72,000 dead from the Battle of the Somme. The Menin Gate records many of those missing in the Ypres Salient – *Ad Majorem Dei Gloriam* (To the greater glory of God). In 1923 over four thousand headstones a week were being shipped from Britain to France, and the work was not finally completed until 1938.

David Lloyd George commissioned Lutyens to build a Cenotaph in Whitehall, which was made from wood and plaster and erected in time for the Allied Victory Parade in 1919. This was immediately replaced by a new memorial, made from Portland stone, and erected during the following year. The name 'cenotaph' comes from the Greek 'kenos' meaning empty and 'taphos' meaning tomb.

The remains of several unknown bodies were recovered from the major battlefields on the Western Front, namely the Somme, Ypres, Loos, Arras, Neuve Chapelle and

Cambrai. They were covered in Union flags and placed in the chapel of Ste. Pol near Arras. Brigadier General L.J. Wyatt closed his eyes and placed his hand on one of the bodies. It was lifted into a coffin, which in turn was placed into a casket made from trees from Hampton Court, and was conveyed to Westminster Abbey. The Unknown Warrior was laid to rest on the 11th November 1920. The guests of honour were a group of about one hundred women who had not only lost their husbands but also all their sons.

Over the years memories faded and the people were forgotten. The following are the final direct reminiscences from villagers.

(Walter) John Carpenter (1905-1992) went to school at Newdigate and gained a scholarship to Dorking Grammar School. He was too young to serve in the war but had a successful business career. He lived at Shirley, near Croydon, but kept Kingsland Cottage in Newdigate where he and his wife loved to spend weekends in the country. His father's bake-house was removed to the Weald & Downland Museum at Singleton for eventual reconstruction and these are his thoughts which were recorded in the Autumn of 1984.

'War was officially declared at 11.00 p.m. on August 4th 1914. At 2.00 a.m. the following morning my father was baking in the bake-house next to Deans Stores. There was a tap on the door and the policeman, Tom Boult, announced that war had been declared. My father knocked on Alfred Dean's window with his peel (the tool used for removing bread from the oven) and the three of them sat up all night reminiscing and forecasting the result of the war. Alfred Dean was keen on politics.

Tom Boult lived in a semi-detached house (Hillside) on the right over Laundry Hill.

A recruiting meeting was held on the field where the school now stands. Three or four senior boys volunteered, the boys of fourteen in those days looked old enough to join the army. Roy Goldsack and Aubrey Hudson joined then.

Ninety five percent of the work was agricultural and only the professional people travelled away from the village. The war seemed very distant and life carried on as usual. There was no pressure placed on people to join up in the early days of the war.

I do not remember the Rector having a wife. He had a son, Wilfred, who played cricket for the Gentlemen versus the Players as wicket keeper. One daughter we hardly saw but the other daughter, Ethel, did war work and said she could 'ride a plough along with the next'.

Captain Gibbs was a retired naval officer called up for the reserves. A typical naval man, tanned, square head and shoulders and about five foot nine inches tall. He often wore Scouts uniform.

The Misses Ferard and Wilson were elderly spinsters in their early sixties.

I met Lieut. Broadwood coming off the Boulogne ferry in the late twenties. It had been choppy and he looked very green from sea-sickness.

John Steeds joined up later in the war, probably when the conscription age was made higher. He had a bullet pass right through his thigh!

William George Wyatt was the eldest of twelve or fourteen children who lived with their parents and grandparents at the cottage in Kingsland. The children slept in the attic top to toe and their father joined up and was killed.

I remember a few other people. George Horley was a postman and a fast bowler and another good cricketer was Bob Rowland who was a quick left arm bowler and was unplayable on his day.

Westley Johns joined the navy very young and my father taught Alfred Wooltorton how to bake. The Potters lived in cottages on the right-hand bend just after Broomells and Raymond Potter was red-haired and fond of the girls. I remember that Sidney John Burberry lived in the cottage overlooking the Brocus half way up Laundry Hill. Arthur West was a postman and he was cycling from Beare Green with his basket of mail when a Zeppelin, the only one I knew of, flew low overhead (possibly looking at the brickyard as a possible target). Arthur dived into the ditch and received scratches and bumps. This was probably about 1916. Arthur used to sing comic songs at smoking concerts at the Institute.

I was allowed to beat the big drum of the Pipe and Fife Band going up to Kingsland. Mr. Headland was a small man with a big moustache and very definite ideas about the band. I think it soon discontinued. Mrs. Winfield lived on the left-hand side of Cudworth Lane before the Manor (Brook Farm) and her husband was the local milkman with a horse and cart. He used to dish the milk out to customers straight from the churn. Mr. Winfield was Chairman of the Parish Council and Chairman of the Football Club without knowing anything about football, but he was a good bloke with a deep voice who sang sea-shanties at the smoking concerts.

Fresh butter was short at the time of the first Christmas of the war and you had to be well in with the local farmer.

Leopold Goldberg was either Consul General or Commercial Attaché to the German Embassy. My mother worked at the Red House up to the war end and he used to say with his broad Prussian accent, "Throw up ze blinds, open ze windows, let ze air in."

Being a German he must have had a difficult time owing to the anti-German feeling which was prominent at the time. All the local activities emanated from either Newdigate Place, The Red House, Melton Hall or Ockley Lodge.

Mrs. Elliott Palmer, of Oaklands Park, was an American I think.

The Rev. Bird would not allow entertainment at the Institute during Lent but bridge parties were allowed at the Rectory!

I, together with my brother, belonged to the choir. One evening during the sermon one of the boys broke wind. After the service Rev. Bird demanded to know who the culprit was. Nobody owned up. It became late and the snow was falling. Parents gathered at the church door to find out what had happened to their children, some of whom were only seven. The culprit was not found but the feuding continued until my parents said that we should leave the choir. Mrs. Middleton of Fairholme was on our side and allowed us to sit next to her during church services. Mrs. Middleton's seat was just behind Mrs. Janson and Miss Herron. Miss Herron turned round to me and my brother and said "Get out". Mrs. Middleton put her hand on my knee and said "Stay there". With that Miss Herron got up and left.'

About the same time Reg Trow (1901-1986) was living at George Horley Place, Newdigate, and he remembered his early boyhood.

'When the war started it didn't mean too much to me or my twin brother, but my older brothers were aware and when their papers came they didn't hesitate to join up.

Mr. Jones of Cudworth (Bath House) had a contract with the Government to supply hay for the horses at war. Me and my father cut the hay all round the farms for Mr. Jones and he paid us.

Roy Goldsack came to stay with us. I think he was a relative of Edie Munn's mother. He joined up and when he came back on leave he seemed permanently terrified. He was a sniper. When the time came to go back we had to bodily carry him to Holmwood Station. He was sobbing and crying all the way. "You know as well as I do that I won't be coming back – perched on a tree for two or three hours looking for an enemy soldier – but you don't know who is looking for you and will get you from behind. That's how I shall get my end." That was the last time I saw him.

I went to school with Aubrey Hudson. He lived in a brick built farm cottage in Dukes Drive. He was a good boxer.

I worked in the garden of Major John Innes who lived at Greenings. He was the brother-in-law of Lieut. Broadwood and was in the French Medical Corps. His wife had ginger hair. He came home on leave, a very smart man and a nice bloke. He had a generator for electricity and showed me how to fix it.

William Wyatt lived in Kingsland and had about twelve children. Eight slept in the garret in three double beds. One day he was talking to Bill Monk who lived opposite. "You should be ashamed of yourself not joining up". Next day, in spite of being over age, he left for Aldershot and that was the last anybody saw of him'.

Mabel Whiffen, née Wooltorton, (1910-2004) lived at The Manse in Broad Lane.

'Our family moved from Norfolk to Newdigate in 1905 and I was born in the village. My father was a master thatcher and the weekly wage being offered by the Goldbergs was better.

Alfred was torpedoed and died of pneumonia and the family travelled to Edinburgh for the funeral. My brother Reginald John joined the Navy and another brother, George Edgar, joined the Navy but was transferred to the Air Force.

Mabel's memory appears to be incorrect with regards to Alfred as the official record shows that he died of scarlet fever and that the ship he was serving on, HMS Garth, was scrapped in 1923.

Mabel was the last person in the village to have a direct contact with World War One, they have now all gone. At every Remembrance Day Service all the names have been solemnly read out with due reverence but they had become just names. Hopefully this research will not only preserve the names but will also show that these honoured thirty-two people were real human beings with feelings, hopes and dreams. All of which were shattered, a century ago, during a period of history known as the Great War.

An unknown (Newdigate!) soldier of the Royal West Surrey Regiment
– He has two wound stripes and a good conduct stripe on his left arm.
Thus the picture is dated post 1916.

Where did they live?

Beadle family	Cider Mill Farm, Partridge Lane
Arthur Beck	The Lodge, Ockley Lodge, Dukes Drive (now The Haven)
Bedding family	Ash Farm, Cudworth (now Ash Cottage)
Bird family	The Rectory, Church Lane (now Medlar Court)
Tom Boult	Hillside, Parkgate Road
Bourne family	Bakershaw, Blanks Lane (now Blanks Cottage)
Bray family	The Greenings, Capel
Broadwood family	Lyne House on the Newdigate/Capel border
H. Brodie Rowe	Hatchetts, Cudworth (now Hatchetts, Hatchetts End and Hatchetts Cottage)
William Broughton	2 Kingsland (now Hawthorn Tree Cottage)
Miss M. Broughton	The Bungalow, Underhill Road
Sidney J. Burberry	Woods Hill Cottage, Village Street
Burrows family	Oak Tree Cottage, Broad Lane (demolished, site of Oak Tree and Dowces Cottage)
G.J. Butcher	Six Bells, Village Street
Capon family	Dean Cottage, Blanks Lane
Walter Carpenter	The Bakery at Dean's Stores (demolished 1988 and awaiting erection at the Weald & Downland Museum at Singleton) and Kingsland
Chatfield family	Oaklands Park, Partridge Lane
Frank A Clark	Omeo, Parkgate Road (now 1 Brook Cottages)
Clark Jones family	Bath House, Cudworth
Alfred Dean & family	Dean's Stores (now Zieglers), Village Street, and Crossways
Michael Dean	The Post Office, Village Street (now The Old Post Office)
Edwards family	Rakemakers Cottage (demolished), Trig Street
James F. Elliott	Brook Cottages, Parkgate Road
Nurse Elderson	Gosscroft, Henfold Lane
Farnell-Watson family	Henfold House, Henfold Lane
Beatrice Ferard	Ockley Lodge, Rusper Road (now Ockley House)
Mrs Gadd formerly Weller	Clarks Cottages, Church Road (now Church Cottages)
Luke Gadd	Lucy's Cottage, Kingsland (now rebuilt)
Capt. Alfred W Gibbs	Hillview (now Darragh House), Cudworth Lane Wood's Hill (now Atwoods), Village Street

Ghost story	Sturtwood Farm, Partridge Lane
Goldberg family	The Red House, Partridge Lane (original house demolished c. 1950 and rebuilt)
F.E. Green	Barings Field, Cudworth Lane
Henry Hackwood	The Cottage, Hogspudding Lane
Livingstone Haig	Beam Brook, Partridge Lane
Harber family	Myrtle Cottage, Village Street
G.C. Headland	Yew Tree Cottage, Village Street (whilst he was sexton as it was a tied house)
Hills family	High Trees Farm, Parkgate Road
Hopkins family	Gaterounds Farm, Parkgate Road Kingsland (now Bay Cottage)
Horley family	Rose Cottage, Broad Lane Rambler Cottage, Broad Lane
Howson family	New House Farm Cottages, Rusper Road
Hudson family	Home Farm, Dukes Drive
Innes family	The Greenings, Capel
Irwine family	Hallings Hatch, Parkgate Road
Janson/ Herron family	Newdigate Place (sold 1954 and subsequently demolished, now a bungalow of the same name)
Kempshall family	Six Bells Cottages, Rusper Road (now Old/White Cottage) North Barn Cottages, Lyne
Mrs Middleton	Fairholme, Church Lane (now Oakfield House)
Monk family	Brewery, Kingsland (now The Old Brewery)
Capt. & Mrs Palmer	Oaklands Park, Partridge Lane
Potter family	Brickyard Cottages, Trig Street (now Kettles Cottages)
Pratt, William	Duke's Cottages, Parkgate (now demolished)
Ada Roffey	Sot's Hole, Partridge Lane (now Partridge Cottage)
Rowland family	Yew Tree Cottage, Village Street Rowlands Drapery Store (now The Old Post Office), Village Street
Sanders family	Woodlands Cottages, Rusper Road
Miss L. Seward-Hill	Fairholme, Church Lane (now Oakfield House)
John Steeds	The Schoolhouse, Church Lane (demolished in 1965, now George Horley Place)
Trow family	3 Brook Cottages, Parkgate Road Rose Cottage (now Rose Villa), Parkgate Road
George & Margaret Trow	Reffolds, Parkgate Road
Tyler family	High Trees, Parkgate Road
Vine family	Village Club, Kingsland
Winfield family	Brook Farm, Cudworth Lane
Wooltorton family	Hatchetts Farm Cottage, Hogspudding Lane (demolished)
Wyatt family	Brendon Cottage, Kingsland (now Kingsland Cottage)

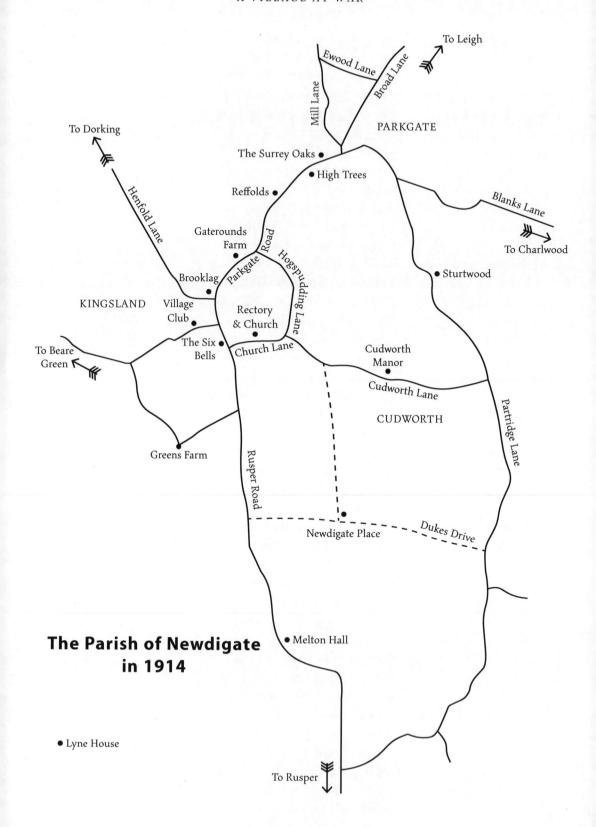

To Leigh

Ewood Lane

Broad Lane

Mill Lane

PARKGATE

To Dorking

The Surrey Oaks •

• High Trees

Reffolds •

Blanks Lane

To Charlwood

Henfold Lane

Gaterounds
Farm

Parkgate Road

Hogspudding Lane

• Sturtwood

Brooklag

KINGSLAND   Village
Club

Rectory
& Church

To Beare
Green

The Six
Bells

Church Lane

Cudworth
Manor

Cudworth Lane

CUDWORTH

Pattridge Lane

Greens Farm

Rusper Road

Newdigate Place

Dukes Drive

**The Parish of Newdigate
in 1914**

• Melton Hall

• Lyne House

To Rusper

Select Bibliography

A History of the 22nd (Service) Battalion Royal Fusiliers (Kensington) – Major Christopher Stone DSO, MC (London 1923)

The De Ruvignys Roll of Honour

Crockefords Clerical Directory

One Morning in Sarajevo – David James Smith (London 2008)

History of the Corps of Royal Engineers

Gallipoli – Alan Moorehead (London 1956)

English Life in the First World War – Christopher Martin (London 1974)

The Turkish Front – Field Marshall Lord Carver (London 2003)

A Scottish Tour – Edited by Lady Haig (Edinburgh 1935)

A Fiery Glow in the Darkness – Michael Grundy (Worcester 1997)

Khaki Vignettes – Padre Phil J. Fisher CF (London 1917)

Birmingham Pals – Terry Carter (Barnsley 1997)

History of the Queen's Royal (West Surrey) Regiment in the Great War – Colonel H.C. Wylly, CB

The Annals of the King's Royal Rifle Corps, Volume V – Major-General Sir Steuart Hare, KCMG, CB (London 1932)

Peacemakers – Margaret MacMillan (London 2001)

Diary of a Dead Officer – Arthur Graeme West (London 2007)

Seven Pillars of Wisdom – T.E. Lawrence (Privately and Middlesex 1935)

One Voice – Vera Brittain (London 2005)

Twenty Years After – Maj. Gen. Sir Ernest Swinton, KBE., CB (London c. 1938)

A Popular History of the Great War – Sir J.A. Hammerton

Index